MW00378516

Praise for
PAIN IS WEAKNESS LEAVING THE BODY

"This is not your ordinary military memoir. It is not often that one experiences a truly original mind, a way of thinking combined with literary skill and grounded in hard learned humility, but that is Lyle Jeremy Rubin on his path from acting as an instrument of empire to deconstructing it and understanding the true meaning of freedom, community, and ethics. Never has a takedown of militarism, capitalism, and empire been more powerful and persuasive."

—Roxanne Dunbar-Ortiz, author of
An Indigenous Peoples' History of the United States

"An instant classic of antiwar literature, Rubin's stunning coming-of-age story as a US Marine is an absorbing look at how imperial masculinity is made through personal experience and psychic transformation. But the book doubles as a political reflection on how to achieve a critical perspective on our times in a forgetful country. This is a must-read—especially for Americans who rely on the service of others without owning the damaging results."

—Samuel Moyn, author of *Humane*

"Few people have traced the connections between masculinity, American empire, and the ailments of our republic with as much unflinching grace as Rubin. Give this book to the angry young men in your life."

—Matthieu Aikins, Pulitzer Prize–winning journalist and
author of *The Naked Don't Fear the Water*

"Both a gut-wrenching portrait of the psychic, physical, sexual, and structural violence of American imperialism and a powerful conversion story of transformation from enthusiastic foot soldier to incisive internal critic of American empire. In a moment calling for reckoning with the ravages of America's wars at home and abroad, this is a worthwhile read."

—Adom Getachew, author of *Worldmaking after Empire*

"This is no equivocal or evasive military memoir, content to agonize over war's dehumanization but unwilling to name the exploitative, extractive, and racist forces that drive it. Rubin's experiences compel him to see his enemy as the socioeconomic system that rots America out and drives it to dominate the world."

—Spencer Ackerman, Pulitzer Prize–winning journalist
and author of *Reign of Terror*

"What's a nice neocon kid and AIPAC intern doing in a place like the US Marine Corps? Having his worldview shattered and coming to see American life in a new way, as it turns out. Rubin's memoir is more about his changing perception than his combat experience. Original, thoughtful, sometimes raw, and often provocative."

—Stephen Kinzer, author of *Poisoner in Chief*

"In recounting his own personal path into and out of the military, Rubin beautifully intertwines memoir, political analysis, and sweeping history. In the process, he offers a powerful articulation of the cycles of violence and discontent generated time and again, both at home and abroad, by the US security state. The result is essential reading for all concerned Americans."

—Aziz Rana, author of *Two Faces of American Freedom*

"Rubin has written much more than a riveting war story, which brings him from boot camp to Afghanistan's Helmand Province to kill or be killed. *Pain is Weakness Leaving the Body* is a distressing, humane, searching story of coming of age in 21st-century America—of joining the ranks of the angry privileged, of seeking to dominate but, in time, learning to listen. Engrossing to the last word."

—Stephen Wertheim, author of
Tomorrow the World: The Birth of U.S. Global Supremacy

"Weakness might or might not leave the body, but wisdom and empathy flow in upon reading Rubin's gripping account of his time as a post–9/11 soldier. Rubin's book is an intellectual and moral challenge, a war memoir that forces the reader to wrestle as much with ideas as with battle stories. Rubin's beautiful, Hemingway-esque clipped cadence is perfect for trying to make sense of our baroque, wounded world."

—Greg Grandin, Pulitzer Prize–winning author of *The End of the Myth*

"Like Orwell in 'Shooting an Elephant,' Rubin is disgusted by the work he did for a colonizing empire, and yet he remains fascinated by the thinking that brought him there. In shape-shifting prose both narrative and philosophical, Rubin shows the deep connections between masculinity and militarism as they play out in his own life and the larger world in which the American empire operates. This a book full of pain, weakness, and bodies, but it is wise enough to know that only the bodies are ever really gone."

—Baynard Woods, author of *Inheritance*

PAIN IS WEAKNESS LEAVING THE BODY

A MARINE'S UNBECOMING

LYLE JEREMY RUBIN

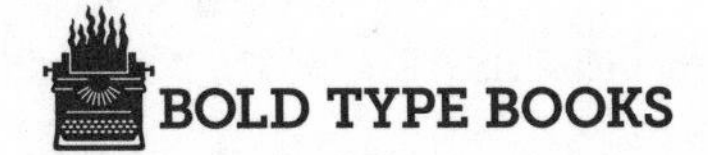

BOLD TYPE BOOKS

New York

Bold Type Books
30 Irving Place, 10th Floor New York, NY 10003
www.boldtypebooks.org
@BoldTypeBooks

Printed in the United States of America

First Edition: November 2022

Select portions of this book have been adapted from "Afghanistan Diary" in *CONSEQUENCE* (Spring 2012), "Modern Warfare's Secrets" in *Dissent* (June 6, 2019), "Base Culture" in *n+1* (Winter 2019), "The Long Arm of the Law" in *The Baffler* (January 27, 2020), "The Man Who Knew Too Much" in *Raritan* (Summer 2020), and "Intersections of Race, Racism and War" in *The Routledge Encyclopedia of Race and Racism* (forthcoming).

Published by Bold Type Books, an imprint of Perseus Books, LLC, a subsidiary of Hachette Book Group, Inc. Bold Type Books is a co-publishing venture of the Type Media Center and Perseus Books.

Print book interior design by Amy Quinn.

Library of Congress Control Number: 2022940706

ISBNs: 9781645037095 (hardcover), 9781645037071 (ebook)

LSC-C

Printing 1, 2022

To the fighters and the healers
And the healing fighters
And the fighting healers
On all sides
And for Colette—
For transporting me to a place where I could tell these truths

Reconciling empire and liberty—based on the violent taking of Indigenous lands—into a usable myth allowed for the emergence of an enduring populist imperialism. Wars of conquest and ethnic cleansing could be sold to "the people"—indeed could be fought for by the young men of those very people—by promising to expand economic opportunity, democracy, and freedom for all.

—Roxanne Dunbar-Ortiz

CONTENTS

A NOTE ON THE TEXT

What follows constitutes as honest a reckoning with my living past as I could muster. The names of family members and public figures have remained the same. All others have been changed, though I've tried my best to stay true to the spirit of their real ones. Identifying details have also, on occasion, been altered. And in cases of uncertainty, discrete events might be out of order in ways that don't detract from the underlying reality.

During the past two decades, it has become customary for officials, journalists, and others to capitalize "marine" when referring to individual members of the United States Marine Corps. I have chosen instead to adhere to the style standards more commonly in use prior to September 11, 2001, for reasons I hope will become apparent.

PROLOGUE

When talking to high school and college students across New York about my military odyssey, there is a story I often tell. It's about watching a half dozen marines level a corner of a remote desert hamlet near a small, platoon-sized outpost in the Helmand Province of Afghanistan in December 2010. I'm with one of my teams of four or five SIGINT guys, along with something like thirty to forty grunts, mostly young men on the tail end of their combat deployment. They're bored and bitter on most days, but at that moment they're excited to play with some powerful, underutilized toys before heading back to the United States. The exact pretext eludes me, but it has something to do with stray early-morning enemy rounds whizzing by our general vicinity. It's called harassing fire and it happens all the time, to us and by us. This time, if my memory isn't betraying me, it is happening to us. I do not feel threatened, but it is possible the grunts, who have been through much more than I have and are so close to making it home, do.

As I recount the tale to various audiences, I try to leave them with an indelible counterpoint to the usual heroics they've become so familiar with in the popular culture—or the standard pitch they've already heard from a local recruiter. This requires me to be nothing more or less than honest. I've nonetheless found, through years' worth of visits facilitated by an anti-war outfit in New York City, that there's no easy or obvious way to be honest. The shape of truth, as well as the meaning of it, tends to melt in the face of guilt-soaked recollections. There are so many reasons to forget or mitigate a past that haunts, to turn it into something digestible so that you can go on living, more or less, like everyone else. But if you're self-reflective, these retrospective corrections themselves will haunt you, until you come to doubt your memories altogether.

So, as a means to avoid outright lying, I've fallen into a strict routine of confession management. This means telling the same story over and over again, just as I told it the time before, and the time before that, going all the way back to the first time I told it, in an unsuspecting secondary school somewhere, impromptu and raw. And if, after being drawn back to buried photographs or dusty notes from the war, I discover an inaccuracy, I modify as required.

What I can say for certain is that the return fire on our part was disproportionate. The incoming rounds subsided within fifteen to twenty minutes after they started, yet the marines kept firing back with increasingly crippling firepower for what felt like (and still feels like) an eternity.

A piece I published years ago has the marines starting off with their M4 rifles, then an M249 small machine gun, then an M240 medium machine gun, then a Mk 19 grenade launcher, then an AT4 anti-tank weapon, then an FGM-148 Javelin anti-tank missile, and then the vehicle-mounted BGM-71 TOW anti-tank missile. And I've stuck with this combination ever since.

I've learned to add a few descriptors in the telling of this story. The M249 is the squad automatic weapon (SAW), the machine gun allotted to a single marine in each four-man fireteam of a thirteen-man infantry squad. The 240 is usually called a "240 GOLF" for the NATO phonetic *G* in its M240G specification, although I've never bothered to learn what the specification specifies. The Mk 19 is pronounced "MARK NINETEEN," and each rapid-fire round is a grenade; I ask the room to imagine the impact of such a machine. Marines rarely use the AT4 to immobilize tanks—the enemy isn't getting around in tanks—but they do use it often and at a cost: each unit goes for well over a grand and is made inoperable after a single use. Unlike the AT4, which is an unguided rocket that lands in the rough neighborhood of wherever you aim it, the Javelin and TOW are guided missiles, which means their aim is computerized and precise. How precise the weapon's user is in determining the target is another matter. As for pricing, the weapon systems themselves hover above and below one hundred thousand dollars, respectively, with each missile costing around the same.

Recently, I looked back at my relevant wartime scribbles and spotted an entry that cataloged the event in question, and I noted a discrepancy in the weaponry involved. Instead of having the AT4 listed as the fifth item, my notes had listed the M2 .50 caliber machine gun. The 50-cal is a tremendous force, and I'm baffled how I could have mistaken it for an AT4. Memory of this lacerating kind, I guess, speaks in a broken tongue.

There were other discrepancies with the story I tell. According to my notes, three locals approached the base sometime after we'd leveled their village to complain about the wounding of two women. My civilian linguist, a middle-aged Afghan American who had once fought as mujahideen against the Soviets not too far off from where we then stood, did the interpreting at the post's entry point, and I watched from a distance as the four conversed with a well-practiced ferocity. As my linguist reenacted the exchange for me later: "I told them, sir, 'You lie about not having control of who gets in and out of your town! I am a Pashtun—I know you have power over who is allowed and who is not allowed!'" In other words, it was the villagers' fault for letting the Talibs operate in their village.

I didn't remember the discussion until becoming reacquainted with it in my notes. And though I'd had some conception of my linguist interpreting at a distance, I had told myself one of the women was not injured but dead. This is also what I told the high school students during my initial confrontation with my war experience in a New York City classroom. I'd like to think I would have known, with all the marrow in my bones, whether I was an accessory to murder or just an accessory to attempted murder. But I did not.

The notebook contained other details, documented but forgotten: "The Texan" ragging on his friend, "the spic." An IED detector dog growling at "the spic." Others chortling at their presumed friend, "the spic." The ranking staff sergeant, someone who also would have been deemed a "spic" were it not for his authority, atop the vehicle turret where the TOW system was mounted, peering out through his binoculars and pointing into the unfortunate beyond of frenzied black, gray, and white dots, with nothing but a contagious electricity, his flak jacket and Kevlar helmet nowhere to be found. The 50-cal loosely attached to its tripod mount, the gunner or someone next to him shouting, "Some random hajji just got hit!" Everyone running away from the Javelin's back-blast area, fingers in ears. My Afghan American linguist running up to the berm to see the battle damage. "Missiles fired from infidel post! Village side!" says the enemy radio traffic. A marine with a glow-in-the-dark yo-yo, flinging it up and down, up and down. A cookie still baking in a makeshift kitchen corner. One of my marines looking like Groucho Marx but not knowing Groucho Marx. Another enemy radio transmission—"Nobody hit." Someone babbling about how Susan Boyle sells. Another marine humming to himself and anyone within earshot the old Vietnam War–era ditty "Napalm sticks to kids, napalm sticks to kids, napalm sticks to kids..." The TOW colliding against the faraway mud wall but failing to explode. "Let's send another downrange!" someone says. "If you hit any of the murder holes, there's a bad guy there," the staff sergeant says in reference to the holes that riddle the wall, holes used by those we've made the enemy, holes where they insert the barrels of their AK-47s and murder good men like us. "Go for any of the murder holes!" And at some juncture toward the TOW missile finale, all of us, me included, with our cameras or smartphones up in the air like mesmerized concertgoers, snapping and filming in awe.

PART ONE
THE GREAT GAME

Damn men . . . either want to hurt somebody or be hurt.

—John Updike

The baggage claim area of Reagan National Airport, a winter afternoon in 2006. The economical drop ceiling of the building's ground floor reminded me of grade school, and the rows of yellow stanchions stood firm like bored soldiers. After grabbing my hard-shell backpack and predictable duffel bag, I made my way over to the marine liaison team about half a football field away. They were instructing the Officer Candidate School recruits to arrange themselves into a model rectangle, which was taking up a significant portion of the walkway between the baggage carousels and the street-level exits. Civilians had to navigate around them, some taking a moment to stare. I stared, too—in fascination and trepidation.

In the preceding months, I'd worked with an Officer Selection Officer and joined other would-be marines at a Military Entrance Processing Station physical exam in New Orleans. I'd run a physical fitness test with these same aspirants in Atlanta. But, unlike a good number of them, I didn't come from a military family or town or school. I had never enrolled in Reserve Officers' Training Corps. I hadn't even played a team sport beyond freshman year of high school, when I took a shot at soccer, wrestling, and baseball. Military-style culture wasn't something I'd had much opportunity to breathe in, even secondhand.

That afternoon, there were many reasons to be embarrassed, but my decision to wear a fluorescent-orange polo shirt ranked highest. My conspicuousness was compounded by the fact that officer dress regulations required me to tuck the shirt into my belted slacks, like a college Republican. This shouldn't have been a problem since I *was* a college Republican, but I'd previously managed to resist the aesthetic. Now I was more than just a college Republican. I was headed to Marine OCS in Quantico, Virginia, for an initiation that would launch me on a winding five-year quest through the US military. I was about to become what college Republicans had been elevating to the level of sainthood for decades, especially since the attacks of September 11. I would soon be one of the troops.

When I joined the rectangle of young men also wearing tucked-in polo shirts, the stares from passersby felt overwhelming. The marines in charge ordered us to stand at attention an arm's length from one another's shoulders, in silence. Or had the silence been self-imposed? In any case, it was a silence fraught with apprehension. Most of the other candidates struck me as running backs, third basemen, a boxer or two. As I snuck glances to my left and right, I also got the impression that they had been here before. They were nervous, without a doubt. But they were accustomed to it. They knew how to stand straight without jittering. They had better eye control. As for me, I couldn't stop my gaze from darting in every direction. Eventually, I focused my eyes on the ground, toward my penny loafers.

Whenever I try to recount the bus ride from the airport to the OCS Marine Corps Base in Quantico, I mix it up with my later bus ride to boot camp at Parris Island, South Carolina. Both were quiet and lonely journeys, though the one to the notorious island was downright terrifying. The marines ushering us to either destination weren't friendly, but in the latter case, they were ferocious. They ordered us to fix our vision to the floor of the bus, if not for the entire trip, then for a sizable portion of it. I got it in my head that this was meant to prevent us, based on what we noted on the way, from planning an escape route. The thought sounds silly in hindsight, but it speaks to the presiding mood. The movement from the airport to Quantico involved a similar protocol of staring at our shoes, at least toward the end, as we off-ramped I-95. The mood was much the same.

After the bus ride came in-processing, a limitless fog. We were shepherded from one hallway, classroom, or warehouse to the next. Our squad bays were blocks of bed space, rows of symmetrical bunks jutting toward the center aisle at their feet ends. Gear or uniform supply here, medical or insurance paperwork there. If I said anything during the excruciating lulls in line, it wasn't memorable.

The whole bay, made of red brick on the outside and off-white-painted concrete within, was the shape of an elongated Tic Tac box resting on its side, with a narrow walkway dividing the starboard racks from those on the port side. It was upon that linoleum strip, almost tubular in its claustrophobic effect, that our sergeant instructors made their entrance.

Pandemonium defined the hour. And the hour after the hour. And the hour after that. That first week—hell week—never really came to a close. When, in the technical sense, it did, it was followed by another week just like it. And another after that. Had I been less out of my element, part of the majority who had experienced anything remotely like this before, I imagine the vertigo would have been less severe. But I wasn't, so everything ran into everything else like a continuous track of colliding trains.

The instructors commanded us to dump our belongings onto the parade deck (where we would practice close-order drill and one day, if we were lucky, graduate), then flung our items—hundreds of them—every which way, in a reckless ferment. We were then ordered to recoup, to make ourselves whole. And we did. Out in the wide-open wintry sun, we dashed and fumbled and barged through one another to retrieve what we could. We couldn't have had more than a minute. I was one of the few to fall, after running into someone, after someone ran into me. I retrieved very little. So much of what I had purchased in advance, after poring over past candidates' packing lists, was lost. The Lotrimin. The six-inch ruler. The premade name stencils. All four black erasable pens. All lost that day on the unforgiving blacktop of the deck. What flowed from that day was nothing but more fumbling, more loss. All of us men flailing about, and me coming up shorter each time.

To be made to feel so lost is to become small. To be made small is to see everything anew. The world became a jungle of bigger, more aggressive beasts, and steering my inappreciable frame through their marked territories became my only task. In high school, I had been one of the small ones, made to feel even smaller than my physique warranted. Once at officer school, though, my renewed smallness took on a different cast. Presentiments of danger, once familiar, returned with a vengeance. But in the intervening years, my perceptions had changed. Although I was surrounded again by beasts, they were at first caring and careful ones. As one day gave way to the next, they became more and less than that. They became clumsy beasts, scared beasts, and self-conscious beasts, unsure of how beastly to be and when. From the vantage of my smallness, I was able to spot movements or gestures no one else could see. Because I'd been made into something insignificant enough to be stepped on or discarded, I came alive to every motion or expression as a matter of survival, as a way of preventing the worst from happening. Or if the worst was going to happen regardless, there was still nothing left but to observe and wait. In that waiting, a stoic, almost religious waiting, a waiting divorced from spite, I came to empathize with the fragilities of those around me. Our uneasiness about ourselves varied from person to person, but we were all blundering in similar ways.

Admittedly, my blundering trended toward the exceptional. Perhaps it was for that reason I'd become a target of the command. The colonel, fond of chewing on literal straw while uttering things like "You don't belong in my gun club," wasn't having any of his superior's orders to lower the attrition rate, and so gave his instructors free rein. One of their favorite strategies for separating the wheat from the chaff became sleep deprivation, and their go-to tactic: assigning written essays.

At night, while my peers enjoyed their rest, I would sit solo in my rack with my headlamp on and pump out essays on "The Failure to Instantaneously Obey Orders" or "Lack of Discipline." These assignments spanned the gamut of violations, from improperly blousing my boots to improperly engaging in Marine customs and courtesies to improperly maintaining the standard of hygiene (I still hadn't figured out how to shave every hair follicle on my face in the allotted time). The essays were to total precisely three hundred words and fit within strict margins and other formatting constraints and be written in pen. No scratch marks or other mistakes, whether in spelling or grammar, were allowed. If a single error was found, or if an instructor located one where none existed, the essay was to be rewritten.

What I submitted each time is too long gone and suppressed to recover. I do know that I got into the habit of regurgitating the general utterances of my instructors, but in a rhyme and rhythm all my own. If we were told hesitation or disobedience would lead to combat casualties on our side, I would rhapsodize about "narcissistic refusals" and "needless blood." If we were told undisciplined behavior would result in mission failure, I would sing something to the tune of "incontinent conduct" or "bungled results." I was miserable then, half-conscious mostly, and not at all in a state to piece together the next great American novel—or even the next great American dos and don'ts list. But even in such a state of degradation, I clung to the whimsical possibilities of language as a means of provisional escape.

At that point, the grueling physical, academic, and leadership demands became too much for some, and targeted candidates either dropped out on request or failed out, short the minimum requirements to make it to the next week of training. I was too wedded to a Hollywood version of *Rudy*-like perseverance to quit, so I kept placing one foot in front of the other, expecting that failure would come soon enough. After all, there was so much I failed at.

Since no one had taught me any manual labor (and I had never bothered to teach myself), I was awful at playing the part of the breakneck weapons mechanic. My typing fingers may have been somewhat blessed, but my hands were weak. When it came time to disassemble and reassemble our M16A2 rifles, I was always the solitary contestant left lousing up the removal and insertion of the handguards. The steel or aluminum slip notched tight between the lower and upper receivers (the part of the gun with the trigger handle and, above that, the ejection port) and the handguards (the long section where your nontrigger hand lay during fire). This ring kept the bottom and upper halves of the plastic guards in place, and to disassemble them, we had to push it down far enough to loosen each guard. I could never, with the rifle in its most vertical position, press the slip ring hard enough to allow the bottom indents of the guards to slide in or out. It was like being asked to bear down on the total weight of the earth's surface using just your thumbs. Yet everyone else in the squad bay had somehow mastered this impossible craft.

During drill, I'd touch my face or yawn and sigh and let my eyes wander. I'd hold my rifle with the thumb a millimeter too far from the pointer or my elbows bent in a fifty-degree angle instead of a forty-five. I'd move an inch too much during the lectures or neglect to eat while sitting with a perfectly straight back. I drank with the cup in the wrong hand or poured my drink into the cup in the first place. I had trouble requesting my options at the mess hall within the allotted half seconds or eating what needed to be eaten within the allotted four minutes. I couldn't fold my uniforms properly within the few seconds allowed. I couldn't do anything within any of the times allotted.

The more I failed, the more intent the instructors became on making sure I failed some more. They'd flip my tray in the chow hall right before physical training or pull me out of formation to do another interminable round of diamond push-ups with my ALICE pack on my back. During our five-minute bathroom breaks, in a sleep-deprived daze, I'd misplace my razor and never have my fresh clothes prepped. I'd lose a precious minute rushing back to my rack for this or that correction, and gain another chewing out for malingering by our sergeant. Nervous after the scolding, I'd drop toothpaste or fumble a T-shirt; I then could do nothing but bend down amid a hyperactive squall of bare bodies to retrieve it. If the T-shirt happened to land in an unsanitary puddle, so much the worse. I struggled to slip on my socks within three seconds or to throw on my entire utility uniform, blouse and trousers and bootstraps included, within forty-five seconds. Sometimes I'd find myself on the line at the cutoff point standing side by side with perfectly groomed men who stood at perfect attention, while I was unshowered, unrelieved, uncropped, and unclothed.

"You privileged scum!" the instructors would hiss and spit. "You really think we're going to commission a lost little boy like yourself! You really think we're going to hand it to you like everything else handed to you in your easy life!"

Shitting might have been the only thing I wasn't worst at. All our shits were nonhuman, like unceremonious birds pelleting. There were no stalls; we shat in the open, so even our shits were chagrined.

From my attic in West Hartford, Connecticut, we could see the whole wide world. The thinned tree line guarding the grass lot. A squirrel chasing after her secret purpose. Patches of grass, some browned but still alive, enjoying the green weather.

In the distance, oceans of air away, the beige vinyl siding of a Colonial peeked from between the branches and the dark. Birds neither of us could name sang their songs as a breeze lifted a few threaded hairs on Ian's scalp.

"Grab me another of the brown sugars," I said.

"Nope," he said.

"C'mon, man. You know I never get 'em."

"Nope," he said.

"Fine, then... the strawberry."

"Nope," he said.

Ian had been cultivating a new sense of humor. It consisted of wielding power over those nearest to him while smirking.

Once the obligatory pause to play up the tension had passed, my friend handed me a Pop-Tart—one of the brown sugars. I broke off the first corner and let it melt in my mouth like a sacrament, then glanced over at the water balloons.

"I like the orange one," I said.

"You like everything orange," he said. Orange, for reasons I've since forgotten, was my favorite color.

"I like your mom," I said.

"My mom isn't orange."

We sat for a moment in silence.

"So you gonna drop one or what?" Ian said. He was growing impatient. It had been hours and the only life-forms we'd spotted were nonhuman. At this point he just wanted to see a splash. Some action. The measliest of destructions.

"You really want to waste one? It's not even noon. Brian and Dunn will come along. And then we make it rain." I liked the sound of that. MAKE IT RAIN.

Ian pointed his Super Soaker 200 at the latest squirrel: "Boom."

Dead space again.

"All right," he said, "let's drop one. I'm bored as fuck."

"Okay," I said, and reached for the orange balloon.

"I drop the first one," he said.

"Nah," I said.

Then I dropped it.

Splash.

It was all right. But I wanted more mayhem. More shrapnel. The bomb hadn't even made it to the stone wall abutting the driveway, my target.

"My turn," Ian said. He smiled like a poker joker as he strutted to the corner and snagged the blue one. The world was his.

"Watch this," he said.

I hung my head out, anticipating the havoc below. But before I could say, "Let's see what you got," my face and tee were splattered.

"Very funny," I said. "Good thing you're my best friend."

"Best friends forever," he said.

It was hot—still summer—so there was no problem drying off. Ian and I talked movies, *Lion King*, *Forrest Gump*, the second *Die Hard*, rumors about a third; computer games like *SimCity* and *Civilization*; and video games like *Sonic* and *Mortal Kombat*. Ian said he liked Tess now. I told him I didn't like Katy anymore, but Ashley was looking good. We were all going to be in class together in the Peterson team at King Philip Middle. We agreed we'd make our moves then.

I lay on my back, peering up at the pink fiberglass insulation. It reminded me of cotton candy, which in turn reminded me of Riverside. I pondered whether Ian's folks would plan another trip there for us.

"You know," I said, "I've been having those thoughts again." Ian was lying next to me, also on his back, humming Green Day's "Welcome to Paradise."

"What thoughts?" he asked.

"You know, the ones about asking who I am, who's doing the thinking for me. It's me, I know. But who's me? Like who's doing the thinking for me, you know?"

"Nah, man. I don't know."

"It gets really scary! I'm just lying in my bed, and then I start thinking about my thoughts and who's thinking them and I get all wigged out and start thinking I'm gonna be stuck like this forever. I had to run into my parents' room last night just to get them talking so I could snap out of it. Normally, I wake up Brett, but he's at camp."

"Sounds scary, Rubes." Ian's eyes were closed now, his hands folded atop his belly. Still humming, but softer.

That's when it happened. I was asking who was asking and then asked about the asking about the asking, in this terrible regression of confusion. My heart was grasping from the inside, like someone trapped, and I'd never felt such a terror.

"It's happening, Phelps," I said. "I don't know who I am or who's saying what. Snap me out of it. Say something. Anything."

I was rolled over now on my side, toward Ian. Crying like a fool.

"Umm... think about Ashley. Think about you and Ashley, you know, doing it."

That worked for a second or two, but then I flipped to thinking about who was doing the thinking about the doing. I said so to Ian.

"Okay. I don't know, man." He put on his thinking face for a moment and then said, "Pick your nose, Rubes. Pick your nose!"

"What?"

"Pick your nose! Just do it!"

Ian was on his side now, too, facing me.

"Okay." Nothing. "I'm still freaking, man. I'm still freaking!"

Another thoughtful pause from Ian, then with a eureka look, he said, "Eat it!"

"Eat it? That's gross, dude!"

"Just do it, Rubes. Do it!"

And so, I ate my own booger. And Ian started cracking up, and I started cracking up, and that was that.

Sometime later, Ian and I got bored and dropped the whole cache of unused water bombs. We descended the pull-down attic ladder with our water guns and trash, not bothering to pick up the balloon fragments outside, though we managed to toss our Pop-Tart wrappers in the built-in trash compactor in my parents' renovated kitchen. Then we headed out for more active hunting.

We hopped onto our Trek Single Tracks with our green Super Soakers on red shoulder straps and headed down Mountain View toward Blue Ridge. We cut left and then right on Asylum. Two cars passed us then, a sleek silver Beamer 5-Series and a red Ford Taurus, and I thought how badass we looked with our strapped Soakers and Treks.

We pushed up the last leg of Asylum but stayed off Fox Chase Lane since no one over there was taking part in our little water war. I hollered to Ian that I was bored and wanted some peanut M&Ms, so we decided to take a break at The Corner.

As we passed my neighbor Andy's house, I thought about how it was like yesterday that he and I had been writing and performing scripts on his backyard deck with swords and capes and pantyhose on our heads, building blanket forts in the basement and hitting each other with sticks in the mammoth yard, racing through the poison-ivied twenty-foot diagonal between our miniature kingdoms.

But all I said to Ian was "Yeah, we're not friends since he started at Kingswood Oxford."

At the top of Pioneer, we slow-biked left onto North Main Street and made our way through the crosswalk, away from the giant Caldor department store. As we crossed, we lifted our butts off our seats and perched upright on our pedals like kings.

Outside Ligget Pharmacy, I sat on a ledge near the pay phone with our bikes and gear while Ian made the run inside. About fifty yards out, near the bus stop, I spotted Martin. I couldn't remember the last time I'd spoken a word to Martin. He was standing there with a purple bouncy ball, bouncing it up and down, up and down. He looked lonely. I thought about yelling out his name but instead pretended I hadn't seen him at all. He probably did the same. Ian came out with the M&Ms, some Twizzlers, and Cokes.

"You want nuts," he said, tossing the pack to me, "here's your nuts."

That night at Ian's house, we stayed up late playing Monopoly and Risk. Around midnight, his older brother came home and slapped us around. He kept calling me Luis, which was a new thing, and Ian started doing it with him. I felt like I was being ganged up on, and since I didn't get the joke, and they were looking at each other like they did, I felt even worse. Fearful the veneer of geniality would crack if I said anything, I just grinned along with them.

Their dad came down to tell us to shut the fuck up—but in a playful way—and when I started losing all of Asia and went back to talking about the infinite regress of my ontological spiral, Ian took the opportunity to tell me to shut the fuck up, too.

Later that morning, as we fell asleep in our sleeping bags, we held each other's hands and said we were best friends for life.

The next night, I came home to Mom standing on the spiral staircase, screaming, apparently after another of Dad's outbursts, about how she did all the work in the fucking house holding everyone and everything together, and he didn't do jack shit except yell and make demands. How Dad got to come home from his doctor life to listen to jazz and read books while she did fucking everything, even though she was also a fucking doctor. How our ninth or tenth nanny wasn't doing her job or had been arrested, and now she had to find someone new. There might have even been a word or two about his infidelities, but I was too young and lost to catch it if there was.

I dropped my stuff inside the door and begged her to stop so that Dad wouldn't come get in her face like he always did, but she said he'd gone out for an angry stroll and it was just us. So I held on to her while we cried, and I thought of all the times the dad I loved was bad. The time he chucked the ceramic cereal bowl at her, and it had smashed into sharp, aggressive pieces. Close enough to frighten, but not to hit. Rarely ever to hit. All the pushes and shoves. All the spit and spatter. The time he'd hurled Mom's wardrobe almost right at us while I was sitting on her lap. When he'd told her to get the fuck out and, if I wanted, take me with her. All the times he'd told her to shut the fuck up, told me and Brett to shut the fuck up. I loved him, but I hated him. And then I loved him even more for hating him.

I was too young to know I had it good. That I was a rich kid in a rich family in a rich town in a rich state in the richest country the world had ever known. That I'd always have it good.

When I was in fifth grade, my mom enrolled me in a summer troupe, and I didn't exit the stage again until my freshman year of college. Between those two bookends, I occupied the imaginative worlds of dozens of characters, from the Tin Man in *The Wiz* to the Artful Dodger in *Oliver!* to Juliet in *Romeo and Juliet*. The esteem I commanded in costume, especially as a comedian and a showman, provided me with something I otherwise felt I was missing. To be in character was to be in another, lighter, more frolicsome universe. But it was also to step out of that universe and reenter my own as someone fearless, someone who had the power to pull hundreds of strangers, many of them adults, into my reveries.

For my role as Juliet, I stuffed balloons in my top and enunciated "O, Romeo, Romeo, wherefore art thou, Romeo?" in a farcical wig and even more farcical falsetto. I won state-level and New England–wide competitions for the bit, alongside two of my castmates, one of whom went on to make a living on Broadway. I might have done the same had I agreed, upon the request of a New York City agent, to drop out of high school and pursue acting full-time. The offer came around the time I had taken up jazz and ballet to improve my repertoire of bankable talents. I had already been tap-dancing since fourth grade—my single-footed double pullback was to die for—and, as the vernacular would have it, I could have been a star.

As the years went by, though, I came to see my stage skills as incompatible with the popular conceptions of Herculean manhood I had begun to entertain. Boys in the thick of adolescence were coarsening. Power struggles were playing out. Friends would hock loogies on my face, then strip me from the waist down to hock more below.

Despite growing up in one of the most liberal towns in one of the most permissive societies in history, I had learned to think that pretending to be someone else, at least when I wasn't already a movie star, would be seen by my fellow students as something done by fags, that putting on makeup and playing make-believe made me susceptible to attack.

The difficulty was that I was good at the make-believe, so for every jock who might give me grief for my well-practiced exuberance, there were two or three others who admired me for it. My instinctive (by no means conscious) answer, then, wasn't to quit—not yet, anyway—but to balance out this potential liability by cultivating a new facet of myself as a red-blooded American male.

I assumed a new persona, even more contrived than the last one, but also more aligned with the norms of the real or imagined men I feared the most. There was something in the Republican mindset of merciless hierarchy that made posing as a guardian of Western civilization and capitalist competition, in particular, seem serious and unsentimental. And I came to understand this hard-boiled posture toward the world as superior to the feminine self-indulgence of acting.

Because I'd been in so many plays, I was a well-known entity at my school, which helped me win class president three years running. Once I made my right-wing turn, I used my stage skills to raise money or arrange publicized student debates and guest visits from reactionaries. These included minor celebrity provocateurs like radio host Dennis Prager (whom I'd end up interning with in Los Angeles the summer before college; he even let me stay at his home in Calabasas). I became a Rush Limbaugh "ditto head." I brought one of our class's few other self-avowed Republicans to the prom, not because I was enthralled by her but because she seemed like a fitting addition to my new identity, as I probably was to hers. The emergent combo of stage flamboyance and retrograde opinion, in all likelihood, struck most of my classmates as an amusing curiosity, and I was too caught up in the thrill of it to brood over what it said about my private vulnerabilities.

All around me men, and aspiring men, were speaking a browbeating language and participating in a pervasive game of force: my father's wrath and the actions of putative friends, influenced by fathers like mine. The bullying I put up with as a boy wasn't at all uncommon. But even unremarkable doses of excess were brutal enough to convince me at such a crossroads that I needed an upgrade, and ultimately a ticket to war.

Sometime in a late spring or early summer during high school, at around seven or eight in the evening, I was studying in my bedroom on the third floor of my parents' red-brick Colonial, when I heard a squawk—part of the soundtrack to our homelife I was all too used to. This time, my father had come home to an empty cereal box, and realizing I was the only one within shouting range, he concluded that I must have been the culprit.

A screaming match ensued, and the argument soon moved to the far end of my bedroom, where in a rare act of brute physicality, my father hoisted me against the wall by my neck, my toes dangling a couple inches off the ground.

Upon his abrupt unhanding, I jetted as far from him as possible, out the back door and across our backyard. I must have shouted a reactive "fuck off" because the spirit of his chase intensified. I'd never seen the man sprint before. As I looked over my left shoulder, I saw the discomfort on his face, like someone in the early frames of a slow-motion video taking a cannonball to the gut. But if I hadn't scaled the fence of the adjacent condo complex, he may have still found it in him to catch me.

After moping about the adjoining streets, I reappeared at family headquarters within the hour. Still, during my escape, it felt as though something monumental had just happened.

During the same period, my buddy Adam's brother, a flabbier James Spader, flooded my earholes with wet willies and lined me up against their refrigerator and chucked sharp kitchen knives my way, most landing inches from my feet.

Adam recalls suffering far worse at his brother's hand.

When Adam was learning to walk, his brother would push him down. He'd shit on the floor and wipe his ass with Adam's favorite comic books. He'd piss on him and force Tabasco sauce down his gullet. He'd duct-tape his wrists around a tree and leave him there for the mosquitoes. He'd tie his arms behind his back and push him into walls. He'd batter him at school for numerous audiences. He once took a butcher knife and stroked it on Adam's face, drawing it across his teeth. He had a tendency to seize Adam by the throat.

My father never went as far as Adam's brother, and his temper was likely not all that far off from the masculine average. But, at the time, my dad's rage nibbled away at me. Eventually, it consumed me.

My thoughts would inevitably land on the worst-case scenario as the only possible outcome, to soften the blow when it inevitably arrived. I felt too untrained in the craft of physical negotiation or intimidation to protect my mom. I couldn't stop anticipating my dad doing my mom in, or my dad doing my older brother in, or my dad doing me in, or my dad doing himself in. Sometimes, I anticipated it would be my mom or older brother who would do themselves in.

Nothing like that ever happened, and physical violence usually remained preliminary. Invasion of space here. Pushing or nudging there. The occasional throwing of objects, almost always in a way to miss their targets. When I joined the Marines and heard the stories of those coming from families where targets were never missed, I was ashamed of my childhood terrors. But it was those terrors that had brought me to the Marines in the first place.

This is where the *he* and the *him* as the subject and the object of violence came to be elided for me, as if it were all just one infinite sweep of sanguinary gauze. Some lengths may have been more blood-soaked than others, but the red, in all its hues, bled across the whole. I was drawn to the extremes, the cutthroat splashes and the faintest seepings, and that allure had something to do with a counterintuitive promise of protection.

My thinking, if you could call it that, was that the more rendezvous I had with the cutthroat, the more capable I'd become at enduring the unendurable.

Though I remained a right-wing ideologue throughout undergrad, I fell in love during that time with a more liberal philosophy major. That warmer corner of my self, the one that had once drawn me toward theater and dance, still lived, and my attraction to Leah proved this.

Leah got me to read the Christian existentialist Paul Tillich's *The Courage to Be*, the philosopher Alvin Goldman's *Knowledge in a Social World*, and the feminist epistemology entry in the *Stanford Encyclopedia of Philosophy*. She pushed me to take courses in intellectual history, where I wrote papers on Martin Buber or Michel Foucault and pored over the essays of the theorist Luce Irigaray and postcolonial texts like Edward Said's *Orientalism*.

I found their most unsparing conclusions about prevailing structures of domination highfalutin, never mind isolated from hard-boiled professions where difficult decisions and trade-offs must be made. Writing in my school's newspaper and political magazine and in the *Atlanta Journal-Constitution*, I dismissed these scholars' alternative futures as impractical and even dangerous. In their rejection of all forms of authority, custom, and discipline, in my mind, they were leaving the door open for more authoritarian forms of the same. In the realm of international affairs, this meant figures like Osama bin Laden and Saddam Hussein.

When I wasn't indulging such dire hypotheticals, these thinkers began to destabilize my comfort with a status quo that had been good to me. But despite Leah's best efforts to reverse my ideological course and stop me from acting on it, I stepped off to OCS that winter of 2006 with many certainties intact, both about myself and about my society.

Leah and I nonetheless had covered a vast amount of ground back then, much of it brainy and grand, as it often is for young people first immersed in the deluge of undergraduate intellectual exchange. But for every seminar-besotted back-and-forth, there was a confession. She'd confide in me and I'd confide in her, and then we'd confide again at a higher plane. And again and again. We moved together like confessional ravens in aerobatic play. Somewhere along the sky dance, I told her about my childhood—my mom and dad, my brothers. I told her about my high school journey from theater to right-wing apologetics and about my friends who became enemies. I told all I could tell, and at the rawest of registers.

My confessions concerned my once fragile and untouched body, how others my age came to touch my body, and how their touch had touched me. Reclining in bed, our faces symmetrically aligned from eyes to mouth, I first murmured something to the effect that my original sensual encounters had been with boys.

I can't recollect with any precision what I said, but I told her it started in sixth grade at a sleepover party in a friend's basement. The concrete partitions gave off a mildewy stink. There were about eight of us, half on two couches that formed an L around the perimeter of the compressed bunker of a room. The other half, me included, lay with sleeping bags and pillows on the bare concrete floor. A modest television sat on the broad shoulders of a black TV stand opposite the couch behind me. The screen boomed Cinemax—this was the mid-nineties—and those who knew how to masturbate did so. I was among the uninitiated, left to observe and mimic my intimates.

The images on-screen weren't anything exceptional. A fit white couple performing heterosexual rites against a backdrop of drab solid-colored affluence and a wah-wah-pedal-heavy porn groove. The over-arching aesthetic wasn't far from the melodrama of *Days of Our Lives*. The very fact of their warm frames meshing into a single undulation, however, was enough to stimulate me, and any added stimulation on my part came naturally. When Adam, who by that point towered above me, recommended mutual contact, I wasn't in a state to object. "Hey, guys," he said, "I'm not queer or anything, but it really does feel better if you help each other."

I told Leah that he had been right. Despite being capable only, at first, of firing blanks, I kept firing with a couple of that night's participants for some time thereafter. Initially, I did it because others were doing it, and I was following along. Then, I realized I liked it. I would meet up infrequently with one liaison. Another relationship with a bigger friend named Jacob was more sustained. Provided we thought we could get away with it, we'd grope and press up against one another nearly anywhere—in household bathrooms spacious enough to allow for plausible deniability, on the back seats of Ford Tauruses, in the blackest nooks of moonlit inground swimming pools. There were occasions we surmised we hadn't gotten away with it, but by and large our secret remained ours.

Jacob continued to foist himself on me until eleventh grade. I guess many would consider Jacob the man of the relationship.

One evening during those early high school years, I got into a tussle with Adam's brother. Shoving me over a pool table, he held his hand on the back of my skull, squashing the left side of my face against the green billiard cloth. My torso made a right angle around the table's surface at its head rail, my legs perpendicular to the floor, my toes barely reaching the deck. Although he used the narrow end of a pool cue, my pants stayed between the thrusting stick and my ass.

The audience consisted of Adam, two of Adam's brother's friends, and a girl from my year. I don't remember the girl being there, but Adam assures me the act is ingrained in his memory, and he also insists the girl, one of the more desired by the boys in our class, then became obsessed with his brother after watching him perform the aggressor role with such carefree joy. It aroused or excited her, fulfilling some collective unconscious fantasy of the "sexually explosive, unpredictable, Marlon Brando–from-*Streetcar* type." It was, Adam said, "twisted."

Such activities were training for manhood. In this case, such training doubled as something not only macho but also sexual, and not only sexual but homoerotic. Whether the homoeroticism followed from homosexual preferences is beside the point, since sexual experimentation and experimentation with masculine violence get entangled during early adolescence. And this episode, in all its confusion, prefigured a world of sports, military life, and other gladiatorial arenas we would learn to harden ourselves in, largely by imitation, by alternating between offender and defender, victimizer and victim.

Reflecting now on my life then, I think about those caught up in or around my high school crowd. One died too young after ramming his car into a phone pole. Another took his life in his thirties. Another was convicted of drug and weapons possession charges, and then second-degree assault on a fellow prison inmate. Another was arrested for exposing himself to middle school girls. And still another marched to war like me. But the majority in this thirty-odd orbit seemed to do all right. They became, shall we say, "well-adjusted."

By the time I arrived at OCS, I hadn't touched or been touched by a member of the same sex since I was in my midteens, and I hadn't dwelled on the idea since my first heterosexual hookup in college—a hookup that heralded a somewhat less complicated sexuality. But the dual fear of being involuntarily touched and of wanting that touch, even though neither came to pass, returned within moments at Quantico.

To be a man in the Marines was to be like my father or Adam's brother. It was to channel life's difficulties into rage, store one's rage like a battery stores energy, and then apply such rage to whatever battle must be won. It was also to fail to contain that rage, like a corroded battery leaks acid.

But to be a man in the Marines was also more than that. There was a naturalization of the boyish violence I got to know as a child, a violence that conditioned everyone involved, from the perpetrator to the victim to the witness, to become not only accustomed to its blunt impact but also maybe even welcoming of it. And it was a special kind of violence that doubled as something sexual.

Reimagining that violence in recent years has meant placing it in its proper contexts. It has meant seeing it as of a piece with my decision to become a marine and recognizing how it played out in ways subtle and explicit once I did.

I often drift back to the collective humiliation, when we were all, the whole platoon, at our most exposed, at our most naked, literally. I think back to our headlong discarding of tops, trousers, and briefs in between our racks. I recall the tripping and wobbling as we barreled to the head all at once—its entryway halfway down the narrow building on the starboard side—to take our shits and pisses or scrub our bodies under the high-pressure showers. We had only five minutes to conduct the aforementioned, so we sprinted and elbowed as if future generations depended on it.

We were always aware of one another's bodies, bodies knocking into one another, moving in sync. Our sprints were expertly orchestrated, lest we slip on the wet deck. Our elbowing was subtle, just about invisible, lest we risk needless frictions or full-blown tussles with those we relied on. Our pisses were well-aimed and efficient, lest we frustrate the man to our immediate left or right at the trough urinal or the dozen men queued up behind us bursting to let one out before deadline.

Insecurities were everywhere.

I saw star lacrosse players bite their lower lips in humiliation after nicking themselves during a speed shave. I saw them jerk in all directions to make sure no one saw what I saw and dab the slit with toilet paper or resolve to let it dry in a manner least conducive to judgment. I saw former shortstops assess their own pecs, as they stood next to the more developed pecs of others. Then I saw them scour their breasts with a bar of soap in a self-conscious fit, as if peeking was a mere preparatory step to chest cleaning. I saw everyone sweat trying not to be caught stealing glimpses at other cocks, and I saw the childlike mortification of everyone involved when someone was.

The five weeks I spent disintegrating at OCS amounts to a haze. I was too beaten down to make much of it. But the one element that has always stayed with me, like a gelatinous burn, is the feeling of having been placed in an enclosed environment with men who were, despite their current attainments and skill sets, not all that different from my father or from me and Adam. That is to say, men who had once been made to feel weak or inadequate; men who, like most, were now figuring out roles passed down to them by patriarchs, whether from real life or from the big or small screen; men obsessed with protecting and enriching themselves and those they cherished; men who collected taxing experiences and challenges as if they were armor for battles ahead; men, in the ultimate instance, concerned with preserving and combining their gains, ordering and controlling anything or anyone on the outside who might get in their way; men, by gradations and in various phases, not so much in search of freedom and democracy as of their own manhood.

Over a half century ago, during the peak of the United States' war in Vietnam, a first lieutenant by the name of William J. Quigley was ordered to build a marsh-like training circuit at officer school, where, upon completion, "each candidate should look like they tangled with two constipated pit bulls, and lost."

The lieutenant was a mustang, a prior gunnery sergeant who had served numerous tours in Korea and Vietnam before transitioning to the commissioned officer brass, or as enlisted folks sometimes put it, the dark side. The good lieutenant, who ascended to the rank of lieutenant colonel before his retirement, never exhibited any signs of relapse to his lawless mustang ways. But the circuit he created, called "the Quigley" since its inception, bears the marks of lawlessness.

The circuit often hosts future executives and bankers from the business programs of schools like Johns Hopkins, Penn State, and the Wharton School, in what Wharton sells as a two-day "military simulation leadership venture." Its chief participants, however, are officer candidates looking to master a range of combat contingencies, from an ambush to a frontal assault, where mock fire or grenade eruptions determine the mandated formation. Along the way, each team negotiates hypothetically mine-triggered log barriers while maintaining concealed profiles. They low crawl in bog under barbed-wire obstacles and straddle ropes in tactical chicken-wing contortions. Before and after running Quigley's gauntlet, candidates pass through wooded terrain in various squad and fireteam formations with names like "the column," "the wedge," "the left echelon," or "the right skirmishers."

The Quigley more specifically refers to the swamp portion, where everyone slithers in the muck with their rifles held above the turbid waters. If it's winter, you are greeted with ice. If summer, snakes. A body-length culvert, overflowing with the bowels of the swamp, signals the climax. Candidates have to dunk through on their backs, weapons still held high, advancing far enough out the other side so that they can breathe again. If a body doesn't appear after an allotted number of seconds, an instructor standing above the culvert dips under to fetch it.

On the morning I did the Quigley, I was trending hypothermic by the time I reached the finish line. Within seconds, as my team and I turned toward the steaming showers about fifteen minutes out, a pack of sergeant instructors swarmed me. I was ordered to the mud-caked ground to conduct an indefinite series of push-ups. Their gibes were standard issue, though some were particular to my type. "You're so smart you're stupid, Rubin!" which, in my diminished condition, I received as a mild compliment. Then there was the cryptic: "Someone lied to you, Rubin!"—although the implication was clear enough, and it stung—and the ominous: "You're gonna get someone killed, Rubin!" or "Something's gonna happen to you, Rubin!" Even today I wonder whether there was wisdom in those warnings, especially considered alongside the perennial favorite: "You're weak, Rubin, you're weak!"

The greater part of the pain they inflicted that day, in any case, proved more immediate. Beyond the cold, I was exhausted, already existing on just two to three hours of sleep a night—if that. I made it to three or four push-ups before collapsing into the puddle of gunk.

For the first and last time in my adult life, I mewled in the open. Heads swiveled in my direction while seconds that felt like an age passed. But when my torturers resumed their invective, the onlookers went on their way. The hats had done what they set out to do, and I was dismissed to the showers shortly afterward.

The sense of their triumph stuck with me. But I felt a sense of relief ripple among my classmates, too, all of whom were thankful it wasn't them facedown in the sludge.

In the military, the weakest link receives both hatred and appreciation. They are hated because, on an hour-to-hour basis, they can make the workday more exasperating. If they're not reined in, they can even get someone hurt. Appreciation, on the other hand, stems from their hanging on to the lowest rung of the ladder, thus freeing others from occupying that position. Even the penultimate outcast could enjoy a sense of reprieve, because the person below would be scapegoated round the clock.

None of this departs much from the social norm, although the military does offer a heightened version. I had found myself last before, specifically as a strong-armed youngster, but I had been too young then to evaluate the logic of such a game. By finding myself last again almost a decade later, I was given another opportunity to see the problem. And once I began to see it, I never stopped.

During the first week of OCS, I commiserated with a candidate who had likewise been targeted for his bookworm habits. A fellow New Englander with Bobby Kennedy's grin, he'd run the fastest three-mile in the company. That, combined with his Ivy League pedigree, indicated advanced competence. I assumed I'd be the first to get drummed out of the program.

Each of us was slight, but whereas he looked like a hormone-supplemented stalk of hay, my body was more suburban, more in between. I'll never know what specific texts convinced my Dartmouth-educated counterpart to become a marine, but I suspect they were less wonky and more literary than mine. He was an English major steeped in the predictable canon, from Homer to Joyce. Probably, like me, he'd read the First World War poets wrong.

It turned out I would make it to the fifth week without volunteering my exit, whereas he hit the evacuation button sometime before the second. Maybe he was wiser.

The weeks that followed his departure brought further sleeplessness, horrendous paranoia and hallucinations, cerebral and bodily decay, and a platoon that had been made—partly by instructors who never let my smallest error pass without communal recognition—to despise me. Dartmouth had been the only person with whom I was able to pass a friendly word or two, and when he left, I was all alone.

Almost a month later, however, on the verge of my own exit, I did get to establish one other fleeting friendship. Reilly, another candidate, was all biceps and triceps, a college wrestler from a state school. He might have been prior enlisted, too. It was a frigid early morning around six, and the rising sun blasted the intense and foreboding red of Magritte's *The Banquet.* In the actual chow line, every candidate's sidestep from one menu requirement to the next was choreographed with mathematical rigor.

As the first to eat, Reilly and I were the first to be stationed outside the dining facility, holding down our platoon's turf before everyone would be called to attention for the post-chow formation. Most of the candidates were still inside the hall, so Reilly and I were free to talk for a few minutes.

We were fixating on the sun's dazzling imprints on the Potomac when he mentioned in passing the urban legends about despairing candidates who had tried to swim across the river in last-ditch breakaway attempts. Maybe not during the winter, he granted. But maybe so. I said something to the effect of "I guess I empathize with those sons of bitches, whether they existed or not."

He asked me how I was feeling. I told him not so well. He patted me on the back, a gesture as familiar as though we'd known each other since birth. "And why's that, buddy?" he asked, looking me directly in the eyes.

I told him he probably already knew the answer to that question. I'd likely be chopped at the fifth-week boards, and I was losing all faith in my ability to redeem myself. He told me not to give up, to keep persisting no matter how wretched it got or how much the other guys abhorred me. It wasn't me they abhorred anyway, but the part I was playing, and it was, as I myself had noticed, an abhorrence mixed with gratitude. The sun was almost all the way up, and most of the platoon was headed our way for the next formation.

At the end, when it was clear I would be leaving OCS, Reilly volunteered to see me out. He helped pack my gear at my rack, encouraging me to give it another go when I could. In the empty squad bay, while everyone else was off on a physical training exercise, he confided that he'd faced similar challenges, just as mortifying as those I'd endured. It turned out Reilly had flunked out of a military course, too. It had taken him years to tell anyone about it.

With the mask of self-command he'd worn placed to one side, a more flawed human underneath was revealed. As he told the story of his defeat, his pointer finger brushed under his eye. I now realize that, while he taught me the most effective way to fold and pack my wardrobe into a duffel bag, he wanted me to see him as something other than a coldhearted contender. Just as I wanted to be seen as something other than a fiasco.

Had I succeeded at OCS it is improbable such circumstances would ever have arisen between the two of us. But that day, they did. When he suggested my own failures would give rise to strength, it was not the strength of force he referred to. It was a deeper power.

It's shocking, the parts of ourselves we bury to become marines. Or the parts we hope to bury by becoming marines. Or the parts we find ourselves burying well after we've left the Marines. I'm still rediscovering those buried parts.

It's not that the Corps fertilizes those buried selves and allows them to grow into an organic whole. The human psyche is too stubborn and complex to take up such a contract. It's that such a revered institution draws from a pool of men aching to sacrifice their weaknesses on an altar of conventional masculinity.

The endeavor, I learned as a marine, is defined by a tragic tension: in lieu of the universal tenderness required of a true community, a brotherhood, each of us marines craved codes of masculinity—a virile individualism coupled with a self-denying solidarity. At the level of the person, the strain of this tension culminates, to an overwhelming measure, in misery or death. Raised to the level of a nation, especially a nation endlessly driven to expand its influence and power, it culminates in much more of the same.

This incongruity pervades America: in the corporate workplace, where laborers are expected to work together as a team while vying with one another to get ahead or even just to stay afloat; in rural or exurban towns, where communal esprit de corps goes hand in hand with little bourgeois fiefdoms or small business tyrannies; in cities, where infinite (and often bizarre) attempts to revive some approximation of trusting camaraderie coexist with an ever-intensifying anomie; in politics, where genuine efforts to forge religious, patriotic, or socialist bonds are poisoned by grifters, demagogues, and anyone else looking to make a buck or build a brand. Much of this can't be avoided. As the smart set has become accustomed to saying, it's the human predicament.

Freud provided the proof in *Civilization and Its Discontents*, published in 1930. He was reacting to the First World War while seemingly anticipating the Second. For all his blind spots and errors, he understood what happens when the strain between individualist and collectivist instincts goes untreated:

> If the evolution of civilization has such a far-reaching similarity with the development of an individual, and if the same methods are employed in both, would not the diagnosis be justified that many systems of civilization...have become *neurotic* under the pressure of the civilizing trends?...The fateful question of the human species seems to me to be whether and to what extent the cultural process developed in it will succeed in mastering the derangements of communal life caused by the human instinct of aggression and self-destruction.

The United States remains one of the most undertreated civilizations in modern times, suffering the highest suicide rate and lowest life expectancy among many of its high-income peers, despite the highest spending on health care. It has one of the highest poverty rates in the developed world despite being the richest nation. For a long while now, it has outranked other wealthy countries in homicide rate despite having one of the highest numbers of police officers—and despite those police being highly militarized. And despite repeated cycles of moral reckoning and attempts at police reform, the United States, according to the Council on Foreign Relations, "far surpasses most wealthy democracies in killing by police."

Many strategies could doubtless reverse these trends, even dramatically so. Universal health care, a revived labor movement, aggressive gun regulations and buybacks, abolishing the qualified immunity that protects cops from accountability, and redirection from carceral to social investments, for starters. But at some point Americans must ask themselves: Why has the country most successful at accumulating private wealth and power, in large part through the unmatched imposition of public violence at home and abroad, also proved one of the least successful at dispensing a baseline quality of life for its residents? What are the relationships among capitalist individualism, imperialist solidarity, and so much despair? And what are we as Americans prepared to do about it, beyond the usual fig leaf of symbolic action or patchwork refinements?

To move beyond the provisional fix requires facing these difficulties as integral parts of cultures and systems rather than as discrete problems to be solved. There is a reason, after all, the bipartisan congressional coalition most dedicated to maintaining the basic extant organization of a historically unequal society calls itself the "Problem Solvers Caucus."

This also entails understanding how behaviors interact with one another, and how extremes interact with norms. We may know that 37 percent of women and 33 percent of men have experienced rape, sexual or physical violence, or stalking in their lives, as of the most recent data. Or that every nine minutes Child Protective Services confirms or finds strong evidence for a child abuse claim, per the US Department of Health. Or that, according to a 2009 study, sexual assault victimization rates among high school peers is 26 percent for boys and 51 percent for girls. But statistics can never tell the whole story.

The gaps, especially the framing gaps, the lacunae that throw everything else into stark relief, can only be filled by art, literature, and other less quantitative means of communication. The fact that my father never beat me, my brothers, or my mom makes me in some people's eyes unqualified to speak about what he *did* do. The fact that I was not molested by adults but rather ensnared in everyday "boys will be boys" mischief renders me uninteresting to others. And these laws of intrigue or compassion don't just pertain to the patriarchal mainstream. They are found in inverted forms as well, including among those who loathe the patriarchy but who still feel a need to give each hardship a grade.

If these strictures did nothing more than discourage people from talking about their lives, it would be troubling, but not catastrophic. But what they also do, and are intended to do, is ensure an inertial discourse on violence that is resistant to investigating the vast continuities in which injustice develops, festers, and spreads.

My story is similar to others I've heard or overheard, particularly from disgruntled marines, however much it differs in intensity. When I gave my initial go at OCS, the outcome was not a commission but instead the smashing of both my person and my worldview into a thousand irreparable pieces; the unexamined life of my youth came to a close. It was then, by force of circumstance, that I began a process of interrogation—of myself and my nation. And it was then that I perceived the saga of pain-fueled masculinity, my own and others', and how this masculinity is cycled through a series of contests, as if we all were taking part in a unifying, lifelong tournament of pain.

PART TWO

DIVIDE AND CONQUER

Pain is weakness leaving the body.

—Any marine, ever

They say boot camp exists to break us down so they can build us up again. That's how you make marines. You have to start over, begin from some sort of Year Zero. We have to be purged of our sad, pathetic pasts. Or even, in some instances, our happy, enriched ones. To be purged of our incoherencies, both within ourselves and among ourselves. So then we can start to make sense, and we can begin to cohere. We can become something. As individuals. As a single organism.

I do not cohere. My past and present do not cohere. I never started over. The worst or weakest or most jumbled of my selves was never purged. I am still as broken-down as ever, without narrative, without integrity. All I have are these glimpses into something meaningful, something useful. Something I can offer to myself and to others that we can relate to and maybe, in some modest ways, rebuild from.

People join up for different reasons, often sympathetic reasons, like learning a craft, establishing a career, securing a job, getting free education or health care. I've known a handful who recited clichés about having either a life in the Corps or a life in prison. That or an overdose. Some, like my former self, believe in the mission, a mission they think is just. Or they believe in their country. And that is an innocence, a true and not entirely destructive innocence, that can and has been used for good. Some are escaping shitty families or towns, while others are following in the footsteps of families or communities they hold dear. Countless have been driven into the ranks by excoriating boredom, futility, or loneliness, but go on to conduct themselves nobly once they're in. They work interminable hours, make horrendous sacrifices, grow into authentic lionhearts. Others lead by example, day in, day out, in ways that make positive, lasting impressions on hundreds or thousands. Still others labor in high-responsibility professions like parachute rigger, or grueling and equally demanding billets like drill instructor. Many volunteer for the most racking and hazardous routines, like infantry, explosive ordnance disposal, or combat medic. The majority just do enough of what they're supposed to do, which is more than most would prefer. I often think about the handful of motor transport mechanics I got to know in Afghanistan when convoying from one outpost to the next. They were hit—specifically, their heads were hit—by multiple IEDs during their tours, but they kept hopping back behind the wheel or in the gun turret for more. What has been made of them?

And what has been made of everyone else? The children pursuing our vics, begging for water and chow as we rumbled through the desert. The men performing deference or disguising conspiracy and rage. Those glaring at us from a distance, or those aiming in on us and preparing our paths for blood. Those in the burkas—what else could I say besides those in the burkas?—those with postures of steel, as though forged in an arc furnace. Those with the incandescent, prismatic children. Those whose labor, whose very presence, was rendered more invisible than the gunpowdered air.

What has been made of those who'd lost more in a decade, year, week, day than I could lose in a lifetime? At the hands of men like me. Or rather, at the hands of those I revered, the trigger pullers. Who were encouraged and supported by men like me.

I wish I had an answer. But I was never trained to know such things or given much opportunity to know them.

I've arrayed materials from my youth in single file on my apartment floor, to discern what might have propelled me toward the service and better understand what I was thinking or feeling when I entered it.

There's a bag with photos of me in about a half dozen separate stage productions, plus several from my synagogue. A neglected yarmulke: small, knitted, green.

An orange sticky note has the name and phone number of Dennis Prager's assistant. A pink one records Prager's pager number, and a fluorescent green one the times and locations of each of his talks at Hall High, in a handwriting too composed to be my own. There are letters from two Jewish family foundations agreeing to match funds in the thousands for the event and a printout of an email exchange with an ophthalmologist, advising me on how to raise more money, as well as what to do if we ended up with too much. Give the extra funds to the Israel Emergency Fund, he writes. That or an organization combating teenage violence.

My two Hall High Warrior pins are blue with white lettering, each with an iteration of the caricatured American Indian at its center. "Just can't hide our warrior pride," reads one around the rim. "Warriors on the warpath," reads the other. Next to them a tiny, Jewish-starred American Israel Public Affairs Committee (AIPAC) pin and a Magic card.

A navy blue folder contains miscellanea: certificates of academic achievement from middle school; a finalist award and letter from Connecticut's secretary of state for an essay contest on "trust in government" (my mom wrote most of it); a school newspaper clipping with the headline RUBIN ORGANIZES STUDENT DEBATE ON CAMPAIGN 2000; a letter from the school principal and assistant principals congratulating me on putting the debate together; a picture of me at my bar mitzvah; a paper copy of an excerpt from the Pirkei Avot, a collection of Jewish ethical teachings:

The world is sustained by three things: By justice, by truth, and by peace.

—Rabban Shimon ben Gamliel

In my senior yearbook, *Hallmarks 2001,* friends composed long farewells and appreciations in whatever free space they could find. I'm surprised by how effusive they were. When I think of that period—most periods—I imagine that everyone held me in contempt. But despite their voting me most likely to lose my keys within the next five minutes (a hereditable maternal trait), there seems to be a sincere respect in their words. Considering the experimental cruelty characteristic of those years, I'm struck by how that viciousness coexisted with such pining innocence.

Then again were the remarks from Micah. My best friend had introduced me to the Atlanta Braves, *Star Trek: The Next Generation* (including the Prime Directive, with which we wrestled, however self-servingly), *Law & Order*, and right-wing politics. He'd gotten me to start eating kosher, as well as make every Shabbos minyan. In keeping with his brand, his comments were scathing:

"What can I say? You are an ex-pothead, absent-minded, and unreliable to the core. Your parents are living monuments to the profound moral decline this country has experienced over the last 35 years."

After graduation, we were headed to Emory together.

My student government confidante, Lindsay, had warned me in her sendoff not to live in other people's shadows, since I was a special person in my own right. She must have had Micah in mind.

I flip through the contents of the Parris Island graduation book. Note its blood-red cover, its golden-brown imprint of the iconic hoisting of the flag at Iwo Jima. Where my grandfather fought, where his friends were shot dead, where he was shot, and from which he has a metal plate in his head to show for it.

But when I glance at the faces of my fellow recruits, not much comes to mind. Even when I spot myself, I feel next to nothing. Like I'm staring through an empty glass, with nothing on the other side but a tolerable blur.

Boot camp for me was all blur.

I was there.

The OCS gods had invited me back for a second try once I recovered from an ankle injury incurred during a sleep-deprived joust in my last days in Quantico. I was tempted but uncertain I could endure it a second time. I wasn't ready. But I wasn't prepared to give up either. I had something to prove, and I still hadn't proved it.

The South Carolina peninsula known as Marine Corps Recruit Depot, Parris Island, juts out like a sandy thumb, bordered on all sides by palmetto and live oak trees, Spanish moss, and red-brick buildings, some of whose severe edifices are disrupted by the sudden curves of reverent white columns.

Years later I'd learn about the Port Royal Experiment, a Union government project during the Civil War that had established farmer-owned cooperatives for emancipated slaves along the local coast, with the hope it would serve as a prototype for other cooperatives across an emancipated South. But that history had long been erased from collective memory by the time I showed up on June 6, 2006. Few of us would have cared even if it hadn't, and the only topic of conversation I recall that first early morning concerned arriving as devil dog recruits on the auspicious 6-6-6.

From that recollection spring forth others.

The drill instructor from another platoon, the lengths of his arms and legs plastered with Satanist tats, displaying them to us like a diabolical diva. Whenever there was a lull, he'd advertise the Church of Satan, and I have a woozy memory of him encouraging us to join him in the Satanist section on Church Sundays.

There was Barrett Colson, the only other Jew in the squad bay. Somehow his name was Barrett Colson, and somehow he'd hailed from a small town in the Deep South and had worked at a local pizza franchise with his pops. I ran into him again at the School of Infantry in North Carolina. He had picked up a mammoth paint job by then, with the "Chesty" bulldog centered along his spine, encircled by the words KOSHER DEVIL DOG.

The term "devil dog" is said to have been coined by the German Imperial Army to describe their worthy marine opponents during the Great War (though this account has been challenged)—the war to end all wars. But before I could say anything to Colson about it, he had run off to be trained (unlike me) as a real marine, an infantryman, a grunt.

Why, after all us unformed, malformed men were placed into the H-shaped, red-brick monstrosities we called barracks and shaken around, did everything become so funny?

If you've never stood at attention in Receiving for hours on end, wondering if you'd ever be given the opportunity to shit or piss, stealing glances to see how those around you are handling the discomfort, you might not appreciate the humor in it. Same goes for the first issue of the uniforms, where a task as simple as being fitted in standard small, medium, or large morphs into an anxiety-charged obstacle course, where even after you've made it out of the warehouse with your blouses and trousers and brown socks, the fear of having ended up with a wrong-sized or missing accoutrement still pulsates through your shameful, puerile body. The gear and rifle issue is a similar scene, except there you stomach the additional collywobbles of mishandling objects of real consequence.

Us lining up for our one phone call at midnight or three a.m., or whenever it was that the buses first emptied and we stood rooted to those yellow footprints like they were narrow foot-shaped poles a thousand feet high, like if we misstepped, no matter how inappreciably, we'd fall to our decisive deaths—that was very funny.

The haircuts—watching all the mops or blocks get shaved off with so little care—were funny. Everyone standing at clumsy attention as they waited to have their own unprepossessing scalp revealed was even funnier.

Being scared shitless while reciting to our supposed loved ones the words printed on white paper taped to the inside covers of those ancient pink push-button phones affixed to the dismal concrete wall, prohibited from diverging from the script in the slightest, no matter what might be said on the other end of the line—that was very funny.

The "Aye aye, sirs!" and the "This recruit requests permission to go to the head, sirs!" are funny. The banging of the instructor's hatch three times is funny. The hours upon hours of close-order drill on the summer-heated blacktop, with never-ending port arms and left shoulder arms and inspection arms, are funny, especially when they come with puddles of piss at one's trembling, incontinent feet. And *especially* when they come with Smokey Bear hats hocking loogies on the wet, melting faces of us hapless recruits.

Basic training glasses, commonly referred to as BCGs back then—birth control glasses, given their appearance and effect—are funny.

As any marine would attest, running around in glow belts every morning and night, like Brobdingnagian fireflies with clipped wings and booted feet, amounts to the funniest shit on this sad, funny earth.

Comedy hinges on the quality or gravity of the reveal. What is revealed in entry-level training that drives at the heart of society's most protected concealments? No matter how chill or uncouth we looked with our fades, sideburns, twists, mullets, mohawks, high tops, Jewfros, no matter how much or little money went into those looks, no matter how popular or unpopular, how intimidating or suave or slick or kooky or unappealing we were once rendered by our peers, when every last hair follicle is removed from our heads, we are exposed as equally fragile bared skulls.

The obviousness of the surprise can't help but make us laugh.

Hilarities of standardized speech and movements on the Island contain parallel meanings. Our entire lives we learned to distinguish ourselves through conversational idiosyncrasies or signature gaits. We also learned to conform when toeing the conventional line brought similar rewards of attraction. And becoming a marine, as a completed process, does extend this latter rationale to just one of its many conclusions. But the forced everyday routine of the recruit comes with few to no wages of coolness. And again, it's this stripping of distinctions, of cliquish possibilities, and the simultaneously unexpected but self-evident result—unveiling our goofy, desperate, pathetic selves—that made us laugh.

Often what was funny wasn't funny at all. During pool training, the black recruits would end up on the remedial side while white recruits smirked with a look of "that's funny." Sometimes, if a pause allowed, someone would go ahead and say so. A history of segregated pools isn't funny, and neither is the failure to connect cause with effect. Denial of such historical continuity is far from funny. But I might have smirked with them. In any case, I didn't say anything.

What was so funny about what we were commanded to say during that early-morning phone call to our real or pretended loved ones?

DIALING
INSTRUCTIONS
DIAL THE AREA CODE THEN DIAL
THE PHONE NUMBER

YOU WILL SAY THE FOLLOWING
1. THIS IS RECRUIT (LAST NAME)
2. I HAVE ARRIVED SAFELY AT PARRIS ISLAND
3. PLEASE DO NOT SEND ANY FOOD
OR BULKY ITEMS TO ME IN THE MAIL
4. I WILL CONTACT YOU IN 7 TO 9 DAYS
BY LETTER WITH MY NEW ADDRESS
5. THANK YOU FOR YOUR SUPPORT
GOOD BYE FOR NOW

Whatever is said or unsaid on the other end, the script marches on. Its cold impersonality signals not just a scheduling constraint on the part of boot camp administrators but also an emphatic declaration from the society that wrote it: Your loved one is now ours. We will do with them as we please. We will send them where we like, when we like, how we like. We reserve the right to send them to their end. The contract has been signed and the verdict rendered. Even the conversations you share with them, from here on out, will be allowed or choreographed at our discretion.

And who is it that's speaking? It's the United States Marine Corps. Check. It is the Big Green Weenie. Check. But according to the mythology, it's more than that. It is Society. It is Us. We—the mythic collective—have chosen this way of life, one in which well over 150,000 of the nation's young people a year are wrested from their past associations in a similar manner. Tens of thousands, overwhelmingly aspiring men, are then sent off to wars that are almost never discussed or debated among the public. This despite mounting and searing evidence, inside and outside the United States government, that such wars have culminated and continue to culminate in destructions that have claimed the lives of millions, displaced and marred the lives of tens of millions more, and exacerbated the very violence they were supposed to contain.

What pains me now, though, beyond this abstract psychoanalytic take on the factory-like sausage making of a marine, was my own part in it.

Somewhere in the mix, phone in hand, was my own person. Born and raised by well-credentialed professionals, graduate of a fancy college, I dialed up the folks and read off that script (in my case, to an unmerciful answering service) like everyone else. And I did so with scarce conscious awareness of its lunacy, and little misgiving about the banality of its evil. From the perspective of someone who knew better, the irony of that mental snapshot of me, at that moment, pompously well-read but the dumbest of guns, might also call for a knowing chuckle.

We prove almost as opaque to ourselves as we do to others.

I still don't have a solid understanding of why I became a marine. The clues to be found in my yearbooks and miscellaneous memorabilia and what flickers of past consciousness remain are just that: clues and flickers.

A journal entry from January 4, 2006, written right before my first try at OCS, seems relevant:

> As a boy in the classroom, I would doodle near indestructible fortresses. Turrets reached outward from every mountaintop and well-fortified villages scattered the valleys and countryside. Battalions, regiments, whole divisions of armed force dotted what space remained. I would create these with the knowledge of their imperfections, which would become creative vulnerabilities, and if time allowed, sources of destruction. Invading tanks and jets and endless foot soldiers—mere squares or circles or specs of pen—would appear on the page.

Early in boot camp, I wrote home with the following:

> All in all, I love the Marine Corps. Watching all these young kids from broken homes building their own personal castles is a rare and beautiful sight, one that very few (if any) other major institutions succeed in doing. Most of all, my own castle ain't looking too bad.

Two stickers remain on the inside flap of my journal. The first, a crocodile with a pink umbrella, the second a yellow Post-it from Leah:

(This is a sticker)
(I wonder if you'll ever use it)
(love you)
(♥, Leah)

The friskiness of Leah's message brings me back to a moment months before college graduation. We'd been officially dating for about eight months and were sitting across from each other in a restaurant booth, at a taqueria we'd always ignored. She was clasping my hands in a way that put me on edge.

"Lyle," she said, looking directly at my sad dog eyes, "I think it's best we take a break."

Her hands still held mine, but I could sense the lassitude in her grip. Her face was devoid of all play or interest. I was somewhat relieved by this, since for weeks any playfulness and interest had felt forced.

"I was worried you were going to say that."

"You must have known it hasn't been working, right? Do you think it's a good idea for us to keep going like this? It's painful for both of us, isn't it?"

"I guess. I just don't understand what happened. Things were so good, and then suddenly—"

"C'mon, Lyle, it wasn't sudden."

She used the arrival of her water as an excuse to unclasp one hand. I took an awkward bite of what was left of my breakfast burrito, then carried on.

"Okay, fine. But why? Why did you end up so resentful of me? Like, I get that I've got a lot of growing up to do. And I'm absent-minded. And I'm not a great boyfriend sometimes. And I wasn't being respectful when it came to sex stuff. I should have been more considerate of what you wanted instead of always insisting on more..."

"We've talked about this." She was already planning her exit.

"But we were having a really good time, right? And then we weren't. And you didn't want me anymore. And I could feel it. And it sucks, and—"

"Lyle," she said, as she reclaimed her other hand. "I love you. I will always love you."

"Me too. I'm crazy about you!"

"It's because I love you so much that we have to do this. I want you to grow up. Get experience. Instead of just resenting you more and more in a long, drawn-out breakup that will suck for us both."

I thought about the last time she let me have sex with her, which must have been at least three weeks before. And I considered asking if we could still fuck every now and then because I loved fucking her. But I knew that would make her angry, especially since I'd just apologized for that sort of thing. And I knew if I did, I'd feel like shit afterward, too. Within ten minutes I'd paid the check and we'd conducted a polite but clumsy hug.

Every day after that I would spend handwringing over the certainty of her getting fucked by other guys, never mind the probability of her loving other guys. And the possibility of her forgetting me altogether. So if I'm talking about what was going through my head when I first became a marine—or when I was first trying to become a marine—I'd be remiss if I didn't mention that.

Leah was right. I was immature. I was unreliable. I didn't go out of my way to be romantic or helpful. I would have been happy if all we did was talk books and politics, go out for meals and movies, and have sex. I hadn't yet figured out that if you want to keep a partner, you have to put in extra effort. You have to surprise them with your efforts. I was a zero-effort, zero-surprise boyfriend, so of course I got dumped.

Yet Leah also came to find my preoccupations turnoffs. To her, they were signs of a fundamental lack of confidence on my part. And when I say preoccupations, what I'm talking about is my infatuation with great men. It's possible that, at first, she found this passion charming. But in time, I think, she saw it as off-kilter and even pitiful. Especially my infatuation with misogynist men, racist men, Nazi men—the frisson of the unkosher. I was still at that stage of the narcissistic young man's literary development when recording quotes and excerpts from the greats predominated as the chief task, as if were I to record enough of them, I, too, would become great.

I set down John Updike's cryptic observation in the Rabbit novels about "what we most protect is where we want to be invaded" and became preoccupied with Søren Kierkegaard's understanding of *hiin enkelte*, that singular individual who, as I took it, found integrity by submitting himself (*him*self) to an innermost tension.

I was reading anything approved by the usual suspects of the Jewish male or white male pantheons, which by the early 2000s had long since merged. Philip Roth had directed me to what he called the "great liberator," the antisemite Céline. My fixation with all things Franz Kafka, particularly his short story "A Hunger Artist," led me to the Nazi-supporting Knut Hamsun's *Hunger*, as well as the Yiddish fabulist Isaac Bashevis Singer's introduction, where he declared Hamsun "the father of the modern school of literature in his every aspect." The economist Milton Friedman had nudged me toward the political economist James Buchanan, a fierce opponent of school integration. When Saul Bellow died in 2005, I pored over the obits from neoconservative publications like the *Weekly Standard* or the *New Criterion*, more centrist or left-leaning venues like the *New York Times* or the *New Republic*, and whatever the high-culture aggregator *Arts & Letters Daily* happened to share on the subject.

Like many of Bellow's eulogists, I couldn't find much wrong with his oft-discussed remark from the early nineties, "Who is the Tolstoy of the Zulus? The Proust of the Papuans? I'd be glad to read him." The comment marked nothing more or less than common sense, or a general statement of fact. It didn't occur to me then to inquire as to the relationship between such a centuries-old mode of European dismissiveness and Bellow's own move to the right (I took the novelist's denial of any alleged dismissiveness at face value). Or to ponder why Bellow's gesticulation, and its army of defenders, cropped up amid the post–Cold War triumphalism of the United States and the so-called capitalist West. Or to question the ritualistic defenses of Bellow's quip over a decade later, on the heels of the invasions and occupations of Afghanistan and Iraq.

And I never asked, "Why must greatness always, first and foremost, prove manly?"

Instead, I dutifully read *Ravelstein*, Bellow's fictional encomium to his friend Allan Bloom, the great scourge of the campus Left, then cranky H. L. Mencken, a Bellow-inspired pick. It's not that these writers, from Mencken to Buchanan to Hamsun to Céline, shouldn't be read. Or those Jews who recommended them ought to be pilloried for having done so. I would be the last to say such a thing. I have learned so much about myself and my world from reading these brilliant, awful men.

The problem is that I never stopped to ask why I was so drawn to them and their Jewish votaries. What was it in their fortified self-conceits, their turreted condescensions or armored hatreds, that I loved? What were they doing for me? For those like me? For all those at the turn of the third millennium still being trained to be white? To be white men?

Leah had told me I lived my life as if I were a protagonist in one of my favorite novels. I yearned to be, at once, the great creator and the great created, and I seemed to be cognizant of, even embarrassed by, this hubris. I'd identify as a "blowhard" and seek recourse in a standard toolkit of self-deprecations, one I used to establish distance from my less appealing drives.

My fetishization of literary greatness functioned as a saving grace for shame, a buffer between continued class prerogatives and creeping doubts. All of literature, art, philosophy, all of creation was, for me, transmogrifying from a search for truth or progress to an experiment in restless confession. Friedrich Nietzsche had said so himself:

> Great philosophy has hitherto been: a confession on the part of its author and a kind of involuntary and unconscious memoir.

Late-twentieth-century Jewish intellectualism, neoconservatism, and Zionism were, for me, all intermingling in a byzantine dance. These traditions were whirling up a storm with more mainstream legacies. Jim Webb's Vietnam War novel *Fields of Fire*, and Steven Pinker's "philosophy for winners" *The Blank Slate*. To the degree I was still holding on to some hope for humanity, it was moving, however glacially, toward Anton Chekhov's formulation in one of his own notebooks (picked up from *Blank Slate*): "Man will only become better when you make him see what he is like." But if there was one multithreaded braid that ran through my thoughts at that juncture, it was of confusion, guilt, and pain.

The year between graduating from college and heading off to OCS for the first time, I was fired as an at-home physical therapy assistant to a man in his mid-twenties from a well-off family in an Atlanta suburb. He had suffered a pneumonia-induced collapse during a high school track meet, and subsequent complications at the hospital left him without command of his muscles, including his speech muscles. Every visit I'd repeat the same language and movement exercises, in the hope of reactivating his damaged nerve pathways and liberating him from the constraints of his own form. He put in his all, and he glistened in ways that both dumbfounded and disconcerted me. I could never be sure what he was thinking or feeling, and I was afraid to dwell on the question. And what I was dwelling on the day I forgot to lock one of the wheelchair wheels before guiding him into his seat I also do not know, but his mom spotted my mistake, and I was dismissed later that week.

It gnawed at me. My parents chipped in the remainder of my food and rent costs since I lost the job. I replayed that firing again and again, and then hated myself more for the self-pity that came of it.

On top of this were my derelictions as a student. Although I had become a political voice on campus, it had come at the expense of my studies. Or maybe my crap performance had nothing to do with my extracurricular zeal. Maybe I just felt like I didn't have to turn in papers, attend classes, or do the yeoman's work of learning conversational Hebrew. After all, like the protagonists in my favorite books, I did my own thing, marched to the beat of my own drum. And since I came from money, I hadn't yet learned that most people in the real world face consequences for such behavior.

Whatever the cause of my academic shortcomings, they played a role in my decision to become a marine. I didn't have the grades to follow my fellows to law school, medical school, business school, or graduate school, and my prospects in the job market weren't stellar either.

In a post from my short-lived blog titled *Thinking and Doing*, I connected what I saw as the twin mandates of thought and conquest, in which a thoughtful existence equates to one of dominating triumph. Thinking meant determining what was right and good, and doing meant making those things a reality. Both, I surmised, were what I was put on this earth to accomplish, and it was just a matter of negotiating the balance.

On reflection, though, I'm not sure it was a balance I was seeking. It was here where my odd sensibilities would find common ground with others who joined me at the yellow footprints of Parris Island. So many of us, in light of our defects, no matter how minor or major they may have been, sought a unifying strength.

I felt myself hurting from so much then—internal contradictions and pretensions, outward foundering, undeserved amenities, Leah. I'd flirted with the idea of military service since September 11, 2001, and had announced my commitment to serve in a school newspaper piece my senior year. But I'd be lying if I didn't admit these anxieties made sure I didn't back out.

Boot camp, like the Corps as a whole, identifies the "weakest links" both in ourselves and in our units and attempts to cull them, crush them, assimilate them, above all conquer them. And this process reproduces itself at all scales, up to the global wealth and power relations the United States military ultimately enforces.

We never stopped sounding off, shrieking, *Aye, aye! Aye aye!* like deranged songbirds. As the mad hats emptied our footlockers, we stood at post-shower attention for what felt like eternities. We dressed up by the numbers—those numberless numbers, those numbers that never seemed to end. The hats would count down from any number they preferred. They would skip or race by whatever numbers they felt like. And if a recruit didn't have the respective item properly affixed to their body by zero, there was trouble for the whole platoon.

On the most scorching rifle drill days, we were allowed four to six canteens' worth of water, despite being guaranteed a textbook ten to twelve. On other days we'd be forced, to everyone's dismay, to down entire canteens in a matter of seconds. Head breaks were few and far between. We pissed down our trousers, often during drill. When it stormed we'd drill inside the all-weather training facility and those who let rip wound up with puddles around their feet. Some wouldn't live it down. On the quarterdeck they pushed up and crunched to the untold woofs of the hats. The quarterdeck became their closest friend.

We scuzz-toweled the deck from dawn to dusk. After recruits doused the floor with their mop buckets, a handful assumed a push-up position, their asses extended upward toward the unseen skies. Rolled-up cloths in hand, they'd race from one end of the squad bay to the next, sometimes for five minutes, sometimes for twenty. Done in groups, fear of ending up last ensured a competitive race, thighs and glutes be damned.

Training began with five hours of shut-eye a night. That's when the most recruits broke. On one occasion, well after lights out, a poor soul got quarter-decked. One too many push-ups, crunches, or mountain climbers later, he cried, "Fuck this! Fuck the Marine Corps! I want out!" The DIs went berserk as the recruit squalled. He must have muttered something about taking his own life, because within seconds the hats had yanked his belt, his laced boots, and the strap from his BCG.

Afterward, I was awakened at 0300 for shadow watch for the suicide case. Had to shine my moonbeam on my shattered ward for two hours while he slept or pretended to sleep.

Eventually we were afforded eight hours of rest a night, along with four hours of square-away time on Sunday, some of which could be used for attending a religious service. Most did the religion thing whether they were religious or not, seeing it constituted one of few opportunities to elude the hats. When our senior drill instructor—SDI—informed us of our options, he offered the Christian menu first. Afterward, he moved on to the "other" specials: "Muslims, Buddhists, Judas, other shit like that."

I wrote home suggesting the Judas remark might have been a slip but I doubted it. As long as he didn't start targeting me, I didn't care. Wagner hated Jews, and I still listened to him.

I attended the Jewish services.

After appreciable heartache I finally learned how to carry out the drill movement that includes pulling back the charging handle with your right hand while holding the pistol grip with your left. It's called inspection arms, and it serves as the most onerous of drills for the novice.

When we made our way to the parade deck for the initial drill competition, all four minutes on the overcrowded bus convinced me this was what getting helicoptered to battle must be like. It was a ludicrous analogy, but one the SDI himself had used, with reference to a gamut of training exercises. The analogy answered everything on the Island.

Why did the hats regulate our every move when brushing our teeth, shaving our faces, and pissing out our waste? Why did they give us only forty-five seconds to shower? And order us to scrub each body part in tandem? In a space far too small for us, crammed into one another, nuts to butts?

To prepare us for the discomforts and uniformities of battle, of course. But not just battle at war. As I made clear in another letter home, parroting my instructors, they were also prepping us for "the battlefield of life."

All such antics were about hardening or perfecting us for a life of war, which is another way of saying for a life forever hurtling toward its own death and the deaths of others, like a meteor intent on nothing more than its capacity to destroy, break, splinter, crater, to disappear and be disappeared—the only life granted to most recruits, to most Americans, to most residents of an imperializing and imperialized world—and the only life worth building bonds around, worth romanticizing and worshipping, worth living.

We had all mastered inspection arms by then, anyway. Although my cover was knocked slightly to the side during one movement, the twenty-minute performance contained nary an error, on my part or anyone else's. As for the drill competition, we won.

The Marine Corps Martial Arts Program—MCMAP—proved tortuous but fulfilling. I earned myself the tan belt and felt, against all evidence to the contrary, that I was now capable of holding my own.

I was worried about reinjuring my ankle on the competitive pugil sticks but managed to win the first round. The second took place on a bridge about five feet off the ground, where each contestant sprinted at the other and met somewhere in the middle. I stayed low as instructed, with one end of the stick couched in my armpit and the other shooting out like a lance on horseback. I shot upward at my opponent's chest right before making contact, but because he managed to hit my head, which outranked the chest, he won.

I can't remember what happened the third round, though I suspect I lost that one, too.

I was happy with my performance on the strapless, unharnessed, thirty-foot Stairway to Heaven, as well as the Tough One portion of the Confidence Course, especially when I climbed up a twenty-foot rope with my feet in an S-grip, ascended another fifteen- to twenty-foot wooden A-frame, grasped a rope on the other side, swung off the tower with it, and descended with another S-grip.

We used old, very recently donned masks for the gas chamber, where we were shepherded into a concrete hovel and greeted by a few instructors with full MOPP suits burning CS gas in the center of the chamber. We did jumping jacks unmasked while holding our breath and closing our eyes, and then remasked. Releasing the captured gas from the insides of the device was a convoluted mess, and I breathed in and coughed it up like everyone else. I was also blazing like a fatal sunburn. I wrote home about it being nothing but good fun.

For Grass Week we lived in a different squad bay on the other side of the Island. That's when we learned how to fire the rifle without firing the rifle. Such firing would come the following week, on Firing Week. I didn't qualify my first pass but had a whole other week to remediate, when I scored a high marksman as early as Monday morning. I never made it to sharpshooter then, but years later I'd make expert.

On the week of Basic Warrior Training, we moved from accuracy shooting to combat shooting. This meant we got to shoot ten rounds in a matter of seconds, half standing and half kneeling. We got to shoot moving targets. We shot from simulated rooftops and windowsills.

I rappelled down a forty-seven-foot tower twice while an instructor kept ordering me to get the fuck down. It was the only time, up to that point, I had confronted a heights challenge like that without a blink.

During the Movement Course, we slithered through mud, under barb wire, and over walls and trenches in the blistering heat. During the Endurance Combat Course, we tiptoed through the woods while practicing combat formations and security positions. During the three-day Crucible, we found and settled on the most root- and rock-strewn surfaces one could find to settle upon. We strapped sharded backpacks across our waists. We assumed the prone position and made our way with our elbows and knees at the rapid rate. Every fifteen minutes we sprang to our feet, dashed five to ten feet, dropped back to our knees, and writhed some more. We dashed and writhed for three days straight, with three hours of sleep a night, on the merciless roots and rocks. We ate one meal a day. Every now and then we squirmed under more barb wire or clambered up and over obstacles the size of a large oak in under three minutes. We did all of the above with a rifle, a metal-studded cap called a Kevlar, and an ammo can, and with the meanest hounds on the Island haranguing us or striking us or expectorating on us every time we even gestured toward a break.

During the Night Movement Course, we did all the above in the pitchest dark, to a camouflaged loudspeaker symphony of machine-gun fire, exploding grenades, detonating mines, war cries, and yelps.

As I dragged myself through the sand a flare went off, the undivided topography lighting up a vibrant red. I closed my shooting eye to not lose my night vision. To keep some control of the situation, I hugged the ground as low as possible while homing my left eye—my nonshooting eye—to the immediate front.

We all felt so profoundly alone then, in the darkness, with sores and bruises and hopes of some variant of home. When I let my eye wander, I came upon the sight of over one hundred Kevlar helmets in the sand, protective atop countenances just as proud yet wanting as my own, all draped in the crimson-flared night.

Somewhere nearby, a CBS crew filmed our confusion for other far-off, hungering eyes. Perhaps the next generation of marines.

Military indoctrination disciplines initiates in the grinding arts of labor, mettle, sacrifice, loyalty, and machine-like precision, often in ways that can't help but be esteemed. But such indoctrination definitively undisciplines on a moral front. In the military one is conditioned to slowly indulge in (rather than restrain or check) wanton passions or acts of violence. This is the big secret of modern imperialist warfare and the training that goes into it. To be fashioned into an armed agent of empire is to be a frog being cooked in gradually warming water, and going to war represents just one pivotal stage of that process. Much of this training happens before and after one's formal uniformed service. Just as much of it happens without any service experience at all.

Woodstock '99 took place on the decommissioned Griffiss Air Force Base and Superfund site under the jurisdiction of Rome. The city of Rome is part of Oneida, which in turn is part of central New York. The festival's hundreds of thousands of concertgoers comprised a largely white cohort of working-class to upper-middle-class men who were coming of age during the triumphalist denouement of the Cold War. The three-day ordeal unfolded during one of the most suffocating summer heat waves of 1999, and water was either scarce or prohibitively priced. By the time the inflammatory Limp Bizkit made it to the stage, many were already primed to cause havoc.

An anti–gun violence nonprofit held a vigil for the victims of the Columbine mass shooting, handing out candles to honor the recent dead. The massacre had taken place only a few months prior, and Flea from Red Hot Chili Peppers urged his audience, once they made it back home, to throw all their guns or arsenals into the trash. But after some, in defiance, instead chose to use the candles to start bonfires and raze their surroundings, the lead singer, Anthony Kiedis, compared the scene to *Apocalypse Now* and the group played Jimi Hendrix's "Fire," a fitting tribute. This despite Rome's mayor imploring Kiedis to deescalate. Rapes and other forms of sexual and physical violence had already become commonplace, but now ATMs were being ripped apart as a Mercedes-Benz went up in smoke. Whole trailers burned, and a speaker tower collapsed. And boxes of bottled water were seized by force, amid mass riots.

The HBO documentary *Woodstock 1999* included one man at the festival who described the disaster as akin to *Lord of the Flies*. A security guard called the rapists "savages, straight-up savages." On the other hand, another attendee explained how the violence inculcated a "sense of purpose" and even a vague anti-capitalist solidarity against the price gougers and false advertisers, like those profiting from $4 waters and $150 to $180 tickets despite minimal hygiene amenities and safety protocols. Yet another participant in the violence declared, "We had all the power." The primary funder of the event, meanwhile, blamed the fiasco on a "bunch of knuckleheads." According to the wallet, it was a few bad apples who did it. A few bad eggs. Either way, Rome's police politely asked the white mob to please stop burning the whole place down.

Upon reaching the age of majority, Fred Durst, the future front man for Limp Bizkit, joined the Navy because he thought of himself as a "loser" who wanted to make his dad proud. After being medically discharged two years later following a skateboarding accident, he joined his father in landscaping and tattoo work. He first turned to a career in music to cope with his experiences of being bullied as a high schooler. As he put it, he was targeted for being "a nigger lover."

The high school in Gastonia, North Carolina, where Durst was bullied is situated six minutes south from the location of the legendary Loray Mill strike of 1929, a factory building now occupied by luxury loft apartments. As for Durst's provocative words at Woodstock '99—a gathering commemorating the more peace-loving original thirty years prior—they are worth documenting here:

> Take all that negative energy and let that shit out of your fucking system...if you got girl problems, if you got boy problems, parent problems, you got boss problems, you got job problems, you got a problem with me, you got a problem with yourself, time to take all that negative energy and let it the fuck out...You feel me, Woodstock?...I feel like shit, my suggestion is to keep your distance, cause right now I'm dangerous. We've all felt like shit and been treated like shit. All those motherfuckers who want to step up, I hope you know I pack a chain saw, I'll skin your ass raw.

My boot camp platoon started with eighty-nine recruits and ended with something close to that. Most of my peers weren't as fit or meritocratically practiced as my fellow candidates at OCS. They weren't as mature either, which makes sense given the age differential. Although many impressed me with their resourcefulness and know-how, it was disconcerting watching myself revert to schoolyard pettiness on an island packed to the brim with recent high school graduates. And despite the depot's physical and academic standards paling in comparison to those of Quantico, and the drop rate at the latter proving ten times as high, there was something even more menacing about the Island. Recruits, by and large, came from sectors of society more defenseless from abuse. Things could be done to them that couldn't be done to prospective officers, whose parents were more likely to be important. By the same token, recruits themselves were more inclined to become reckless with one another. In fact, our hats often encouraged it.

The class resentments didn't let up. I got ragged on, from hats and recruits alike, for being educated and coming from the sort of zip code that promised such an education. The regional resentments felt just as prominent. Most in my squad bay seemed to understand the South as their home and Yankees as objects of suspicion. Others, from rural or exurban areas, exhibited parallel wariness toward their city or suburban counterparts.

It was difficult to disentangle the overlapping antipathies. As I wrote in my letter home, I was certain most recruits came from broken families, many having been raised by their mothers. Those brought up by their moms, I suggested, were soft-spoken and insecure, and those by their dads combative. I had gotten into scuffles with both types. The former tended to back down. The latter upped the ante, at which point I'd back down. I told myself then it was because I didn't want to get kicked out for going too far, but I can say now it's because I didn't want to lose a fight.

I was intrigued by my new "Darwinian" and "animalistic" habitat regardless. Early on I identified about fifteen recruits who were struggling on the Island like I had struggled at Quantico. I felt for them, but I had also convinced myself the struggle was part of gaining a life-and-death fortitude. Only by suffering now would they suffer less later. I was self-aware enough to see this thinking as part of the brainwashing before me, as well as an instance of projection. But I was not self-aware enough to question it any further.

Unlike OCS, hygiene awareness at the depot was nonexistent. Thanks to our DI's penchant for dehydrating, underfeeding, and overworking us, nausea and dizziness rarely subsided, and everyone was always sick. I couldn't stop coughing. There was also a sprained wrist, a nasty foot blister, and incessant pangs in my lower back.

By the third phase we were banged up, angry, and despairing. Fights heated up, along with mindless mimicries. Recruits became fond of adopting DI stock phrases as their own: *Open your fraggin mouth. Louder. Lowwwder. I guess we don't blouse our boots now, right? I'm supposed to get out of my way for you, right? Riiight?*

For all the predictable frictions, I often returned to the contradictions or quirks that made up the Parris Island tableau. At a surface level, the cast of characters came from the big or small screen. When setting down their most obvious attributes, it's hard not to fall into stereotypical traps of one kind or another. Whether these are cases of life imitating art, art imitating life, or just me falling back on easy tropes remains unclear. There's no doubt much of Marine Corps life, like American life in general, reenacts the entertainment complex. But at a deeper register, what interests me are how each participant came to navigate through, between, or against prefabricated expectations, and how our physical or psychosocial hang-ups combined to steer us, sometimes in surprisingly wry or touching ways.

I remember Ricky Francois. We'd met at the recruiter's office in Hartford months earlier and took part in a few PT sweat sessions before getting shipped down together. In the beginning, he looked up to me because I was older and had some college and OCS time. It was the first taste I had of that unearned respect, but once he realized I was just as messy as everyone else, that respect dissipated.

Francois would always snigger like it was his job. It wasn't a mean snigger, even though some who didn't know the guy might have mistaken it for one. It was just how he communicated he was having a good enough time or something made him nervous or he didn't know what else to say or do. He'd get in trouble for that snigger. The hats didn't like it, and he'd be forced to push himself up a thousand times on the quarterdeck on account of it. But it never went away.

George Cortés was short and round, both his midsection and his head, like a two-balled snowman. He was a total dork of the trusting variety, and when we both got assigned the platoon scribe positions, where it was our responsibility to compose the fire watch and guard duty lists, we got along.

We were assigned the spots because I had four years of college and he had two. He used to say stuff like, "Emory, huh? I know Emory. That's a rich-kid school. Good for you." Or more frequently, "Hey, Rubin, you make sure to clean your asshole this morning? I'm not kidding, it's very important. I get really deep in there and I recommend it." And he really wasn't kidding when he said it. There were times in the showers I'd catch a glimpse of him making sure his asshole was the cleanest of the bunch.

There was Jeff Gambles and his lazy eye. Everyone was always commenting about his lazy eye, since it was the meanest thing you could say about him.

Daniel Shoemaker was tall, oval-shaped, and one of the only recruits older than me. He might have been a father, and most of the youngsters left him alone. If anyone gave him shit, he'd just roll his eyes.

Everyone liked Jonathan Grimes. He was quiet, competent, and tough, which was why everyone liked him, although I do wonder how many ever got to know him.

Brandon Rundle was my rack-mate, from some tiny niche in Mississippi. He told me he'd never once left his county before joining up and had never flown in a plane either. (Another recruit said he'd never been outside of Kentucky and had never heard of email.) Bull riding was Rundle's high school sport, and his father often sent him Bibles and other Christian paraphernalia in the mail. During the one-hour free time before lights out, we'd sit on our footlockers reading or writing letters and he'd tap me on the shoulder with something or other and say, "Look, Rubin, it's Mother Mary."

I kept telling him I was Jewish, but he wasn't sure what that meant, so eventually I just joined him in his appreciation.

Rundle was slow and would get the whole platoon in trouble for his slowness. I remember his face every time someone went after him. It wasn't so much blank as full of frustrated, divine love.

Patrick Vinson was a piece of work. A mean little Napoleon who used to speak openly about how his old man would beat him every which way. He also had a thing for cracking up about everyone and everything. This got him into at least as much trouble as Francois's snigger, but unlike Francois, he craved the trouble.

Along with Andrew Mattson, Vinson would torment anyone who'd let him. Vinson was white and Mattson was black, and I ended up perceiving them as a cross-racial tag team. They'd talk racist shit to each other and then racist shit to everyone else. They said something about me being a rich-kid Jew, and there was one time in the chow line it could have gotten physical if I'd known how to fight and they weren't always moving on to the next guy.

One very early morning, they, along with two or three others, poured baby powder all over Rundle's sleeping face while pounding him until he woke up. Once he did they held him tight to the rack by pulling down on the wool blankets and pounded him some more. He was screaming, but they had his mouth covered with their hands so the hats didn't show up. Still, it was loud enough to wake me on the top rack.

I started shouting at them to get the fuck off Rundle and so they poured powder on my face, too. When I kept shouting and swinging they tugged me off the rack and started pounding me just like Rundle. They were kind enough to tug me off in a way that didn't lead to a broken bone or a cracked skull, though. And they scurried away shortly thereafter, after others woke up and made sure they fucked off. So that was nice.

Oscar Hernandez wasn't all that different from Rundle. He had a talent for still finding himself naked on the line by the final count, even though most of the rest of us would have everything in place, to the very last button. If I recall correctly, Hernandez was a green card holder who spoke little English, which might have had something to do with it. He couldn't make out what the hats were saying.

Tyler Thompson got tons of shit from everyone. He was a lanky black kid with the cringey BCGs. He was from an inner city I've since forgotten, and I say "inner city" because that's what people like me called places like that. Like Rundle, Thompson was nothing but sweetness, but one time he flipped out and told everyone to rot in hell.

I had been one of the ones giving him shit because shit-giving is contagious. I felt terrible. Later I found a minute to pull him aside and apologize. I told him I'd been given the same shit at OCS, and I didn't even make it to the end, and he was going to make it to the end of boot camp no matter how much the shit-givers gave him. Later, he opened up to me, about how shit poor he was, and how shit poor his mom was, and how shit poor his entire life had been. I remember nodding and telling him he was tough as all hell and I had nothing but respect, which now sounds so scripted, cheap, and paternalistic.

Theo Alexopoulos was the BIG GREEK. He was big and Greek and the hats didn't even bother trying to pronounce his last name. The hats maybe called him "Big Greek" or "The Greek" or just "Greek." Maybe it was Alex. I doubt it was Theo, since first names were off-limits.

What I do remember for certain is that they used his body to hit other bodies. They weren't allowed to hit recruits themselves, although they did lots of pushing and shoving and spitting and any number of things that were not, technically speaking, hitting. They weren't allowed to order recruits to hit other recruits either, but they didn't seem to think that rule was all that serious since they gave that order plenty. And the Big Greek was their all-star hitter. Between him and Trevor Tiller, the latter being about two inches tall but twenty feet thick, nothing but grade A muscle between the two of them, they must have hit about a quarter of the platoon. Usually just a quick punch to the shoulder. Never hard enough to break anything or leave a visible bruise. Nothing near the face. Thing is, the two of them didn't even enjoy hitting the rest of us.

Colin Rogers was my three-month best friend on the Island. He slept a rack over, also on top. He'd tell me his life story, in alternating inflections, when the lights went out. About the caving of his shoulder that ended his all-American football career. About the years-long depression that followed his injury. About the breakup with his sweetheart, his girl back home, his Rosie Rottencrotch. I'd tell him about Leah, and how I planned to win her back.

As for the hats, Sergeant L. Butler, the kill hat or enforcer, returns to me as a more seasoned Vinson. He was short and compact like Vinson, white like Vinson, poor-born and beaten like Vinson. Although I wince at that last bit: what I mean is that he qualified, to my conditioned eyes, as a certain cinematic type that was poor-born and beaten.

What I do know is that Butler was mean like Vinson. He was a real hound, of the variety we were ostensibly being made into. And he loved quarter-decking Vinson. That and pitting Vinson, which was when the hats threw you in a summer sand pit full of mosquitoes, sand fleas, and fire ants to sweat you till you see God.

I think Butler quarter-decked and pitted Vinson so much because he saw himself in him, knew Vinson was lining up to be a grunt like him, and wanted to make sure he was being raised right.

Sergeant S. T. Franklin, the more-senior heavy hat, I believe (or had he also been a kill hat?), was tall, wiry, and black. I note his blackness because it's one of the most relevant facts about the Island. Military apologists love to talk up the fact that boot camp and the Corps in general encourage an environment where enlisted blacks and Latinos get to smoke poor, working-class, middle-income, and sometimes even upper-crust whites all day. And that's true.

What's rarely acknowledged, however, was that Franklin's boss, Staff Sergeant F. P. Slaughter, was white, and Slaughter's boss, Gunnery Sergeant M. J. Brackenbury, was white, and Brackenbury's boss, First Lieutenant A. R. Polk, was white, and Polk's boss, Major D. N. Norman, was white, and Norman's boss, Lieutenant Colonel H. E. Fisher, was white, and Fisher's boss, Colonel Paul B. O'Connor, was white, and O'Connor's boss, Brigadier General Ryan H. Archambault, was white, and so on all the way up to then Pentagon chief Donald Rumsfeld and then president George W. Bush. And it's been that way, more or less, for the entire history of the United States.

Condoleezza Rice may have headed up the State Department at that time, and before her Colin Powell. Barack Obama would soon become president, Joe Biden would later appoint the first black defense secretary, retired Army general Lloyd Austin, and blacks and Latinos are better represented among the senior enlisted ranks. But it isn't men like Sergeant S. T. Franklin (or Sergeant L. Butler, for that matter) who have been calling the big-bucks shots—or more to the point, profiting from them. That fact doesn't change no matter how many Vinsons or Rubins Sergeant S. T. Franklin has had the privilege to smoke.

Franklin's screech blasted windows miles away, and his long arms wended in ways that now reoccur to me as elegant. Most of the hats had a thing for the word *behoove*, but the way he said it was operatic. His "It would behoooooooove you to sound the fuck off" was all vibrato. Franklin didn't seem so much infuriated by me as bewildered. His rendition of "You're so smart you're stupid" came with a veritable sense of curiosity, and toward the end I almost felt like he liked me.

Staff Sergeant Slaughter was our SDI, and true to his name, he was as unhinged as they come. A rugged Michelin Man who would sometimes call himself "Mr. Miyagi" and us his "Daniel-sans," he was always reminding us that every time we scuzzed the squad bay or stood with our feet at a forty-five-degree angle while staying still or took a high knee on the concrete during a school circle that never seemed to end, we were waxing on and waxing off, learning how to endure warlike toils, negotiate the most treacherous terrain, and remain silent and undetectable to the enemy.

Sometimes Slaughter would appear in the squad bay frothing and maybe drunk. He'd rant about every person who had ever wronged him, especially his vampire bitch fiancée, who had left him, or who possibly was just on the verge of leaving him. It was, nevertheless, our fault. Everything wrong in his wrong life was our fault. He would flip over anything within spitting distance, propelling recruits from their racks before the whirlwind struck. The way he spat in our faces had a special gallantry to it, like we'd just offended his entire lineage, leaving him no choice but to flood our eyeballs or nostrils as recompense.

Slaughter rigged every major company-wide competition so we won them all. Mostly this was accomplished by sending the worst performers off to the infirmary on a given tournament day: the worst drillers on initial and final drill days, those in the worst shape on PFT day, the worst students on knowledge day, and the worst shooters on rifle day. By the end, the five trophies stood tall on a table on the quarterdeck.

Staff Sergeant L. Burke, the SDI for the adjacent platoon, wasn't happy about this and let us know it. He slipped into our squad bay one day while none of our hats were around and berated us at length about our chief hat being a crook and a liar and how we didn't deserve any of those doggone trophies on that doggone table on the doggone quarterdeck.

Series Gunnery Sergeant Brackenbury didn't like Slaughter either, and the two of them almost went to blows once on the blacktop during close-order drill. It was sweltering and everything solid was melting into hot air and it looked like they were going to rip out each other's Adam's apple with their bare hands. But nothing happened.

All the hats croaked from the diaphragm like frogs. We called this "frog voice," but later I learned that their doctrinal scream was called "command voice" and frog voice was the permanent affliction instructors risked if they didn't properly execute their command voice. DIs have developed numerous methods to prevent short-term voice loss or long-term damage to their vocal cords. They treat their throats with mixtures of hot water, honey, and lemon, or pickle or lime juice with salt, but nonetheless continue to spit blood and many suffer long-term dysphonia. Given the strenuousness and aggression of their daily routine, they are also overrepresented, both within the Corps and in society at large, when it comes to divorce, addiction, mental illness, and suicide attempts and deaths.

Somewhat early in the boot camp cycle, when I was still writing letters to friends and family about how well I was doing, and how much I loved the Corps, I retold a revealing incident. Franklin and Butler had swarmed a recruit designated as night firewatch. They pulled his ear, speckled him with spittle, and thrust him into a corner when he snapped and started blubbering. It ended with the sudden replacement of both hats by Slaughter. Slaughter pulled the recruit aside and asked him if he was hit, adding in a voice loud enough for all to hear, "No one hits my recruits under my watch."

The recruit said he'd been slapped, and the SDI asked if any of us had seen. By this point we were muttering words like *pussy* or *wuss*, and that's all you could hear from one end of the squad bay to the other. I justified this response in my note, saying I'd been subjected to far worse and hadn't once made such a scene, never mind accused one of my hats of wrongdoing. I made another obligatory nod to the possible brainwashing at work but invoked Slaughter's next words with approval.

"Son, I was just reading the most recent internal wire story from Iraq. Three people were beheaded in response to Zarqawi's death. That's the kind of shit we're training you for."

The SDI was right, I wrote. At the end of the day we were being trained to kill or be killed, and in a world full of mad killers there's a need for just killers. Sure there were some bad apples in the Corps, and I cited the Haditha atrocity, where marines murdered twenty-four unarmed civilians. But we had all signed on the dotted line. We had a job to do, and we weren't in a position to cry about a slap in the face.

Putting aside that I had signed up to be a tactical data systems administrator in the air wing, and that most marines never experience combat, and that even many who do receive combat action ribbons haven't engaged in the sort of combat I had in mind, which was increasingly reserved for special operators, my bravado still rings false. Clearly my derision amounted to an overcompensation on my part, and it was that very overcompensation my SDI, the Corps, and the empire itself were counting on.

In 2014, the American Medical Association's *Journal of Ethics* published an academic literature review claiming the US military has been moving away from hazing-like rituals and that the evidence suggests such abuse does more harm than good. If true, it would be a welcome shift, though I'm not all that interested in reforming the military. My concern, rather, lies with how the boot camp experience acts as a mirror for the society that inspired it, and so I have my doubts.

When I talk to high school and college students about boot camp with my anti-war outfit, I emphasize two keywords, *depersonalization* and *dehumanization*. Like a good schoolteacher, I walk them through the definitions nice and easy.

Depersonalization is when you first arrive on the Island and you're no longer allowed to say "I" or "me." It's when you're allowed to refer to yourself only as "this recruit." And, if you're speaking at all, you're usually not speaking as an individual anyway. You're likely sounding off with everyone else. "Aye aye, sir!" or "Yes, sir," "No, sir!" If they say, "Five Navy Crosses," you say, "Chesty Puller, sir!" If they say, "Two marines, two medals!" you say, "Dan Daly, Smedley Butler!"

Except you never learn that Butler, after becoming the most decorated marine of his time, would go on to expose what he alleged was a far-right plot to overthrow the Franklin Roosevelt administration in 1934, pen an explosive pamphlet titled *War Is a Racket* in 1935, and support the socialist Norman Thomas for president in 1936.

You never learn that on October 11, 1968, a booby-trapped howitzer round claimed both legs and most of the fingers of Chesty's son, Lieutenant Lewis Puller Jr. Or that from April 19 to April 23 of 1971, Lewis Puller Jr. pondered joining disillusioned veterans at Operation Dewey Canyon III on the steps of the Capitol, where they chucked their medals at the feet of Chief Justice John Marshall's effigy. Or that his Pulitzer Prize–winning memoir, despite expressing a deep affection for his father, military service, and the United States, was nonetheless titled *Fortunate Son*, an allusion to Creedence Clearwater Revival's anti-war song of the same name. Or that the song included the lyrics "Some folks inherit star-spangled eyes / They send you down to war / And when you ask 'em, 'How much should we give?' / They only answer, 'More, more, more.'"

Or that on May 11, 1994, a few years after publishing his uplifting memoir, Lewis Puller Jr. blew his brains out.

(I did learn, some years later, that my uncle on my dad's side had been a friend of Puller at William & Mary in the sixties. According to my uncle, he had never been enthused about Vietnam or going to war.)

To dehumanize anyone is to dehumanize everyone.

So much of entry-level training is about hardening distinctions between friend and enemy. But the result proves too savage to be narrowly administered or kept in check. To be groomed to kill is to be groomed to see all of humanity as expendable. This includes one's sisters and brothers. This includes oneself.

We are judged by how well we play the part of pure functional instrument, and how well we foist that part on others.

During the Revolutionary War, Albigence Waldo, a medic at Valley Forge, wrote in his journal about a fallen Indian soldier he served with who "fought for those very people who disinherited his forefathers."

His "memory ought to be respected," Waldo continued, "more than those rich ones who supply the world with nothing better than Money and Vice."

In the War of 1812, soldiers joined forces against their own command on account of miserable pay and rations, and Andrew Jackson replied by pointing his cannon in the direction of his hungry, sick, and underclothed troops.

You don't honor any of that at boot camp either.

Dehumanization is when you're taught to refer to one of the rifle drill positions as the "fag wrist." It's when you bayonet a stack of tires in the Island's backwoods for hours on end, each time crying in unison, "Kill kill kill hajji!"

You never learn the last official bayonet charge on the part of the United States was during the Korean War in 1951. You do learn about the Battle of Chosin Reservoir, when marines fought with fortitude in the extreme cold during the war in Korea. You do scream "frozen Chosin" at the top of your lungs hundreds of times over, even though it was Lake Changjin for the Koreans who lived there—we call it by their Japanese occupiers' name. If you scream "Frozen Chosin!" enough, and enough time passes, and you're still there, you do become a marine. As the slogan goes—the one that stretched across all four decades of the Cold War—the Marine Corps *does* build men. You do become a man.

In Afghanistan I'd come across an "Afghanapoly" board left by the British: Kandahar (400 pounds); Bagram (200 pounds).

You do pass Go.

At my graduation, Gramps was still together enough to hold a conversation before getting overwhelmed. He wore his Purple Heart cap. The sleeve of his white dress shirt was rolled up just enough for the seaweed-green eagle, globe, and anchor on his forearm to peep out. He used to tell us about the origins of the tat, how it was imposed on him some soaked night in the barracks. But as its contours faded through his final years, he told the story less and less.

Gramps said he was proud of me. I'd set out to earn my own "EGA" and I'd done it. That was something. Surely he harbored misgivings about how a precious soul like me might fare in the service, even if he never voiced them. He did express concern about what I would be doing and how the journey would end. I assured him I had a comms job in the air wing. I'd be all right.

My maternal grandmother sat next to him in her black sundress and black straw hat. She held a plastic water bottle for herself and Gramps and kept making sure he drank up. She wasn't finishing his sentences yet, or not to the extent she would later on. But she was already practiced in curating his every move. If his stories went on too long, or he ventured off into territory she found unwelcome or uncouth, she redirected him.

My cousins Sherry and Benny had driven up from Georgia. To me, Benny had always been *Beany*. That's what it sounded like when Sherry called him by his name, and it had a soothing air to it. Beany was a lieutenant colonel in the Army National Guard at the time, and he'd worn his green service uniform. It was a quiet, stolid getup, and it suited him well, though the flamboyant black beret struck me as too Gallic. I'd absorbed the Republican dismissal of Iraq War critic President Jacques Chirac and the French in general as—in *Simpsons* parlance—cheese-eating surrender monkeys. I felt the same about most Europeans. I hadn't considered my wool gabardine cover, a peaked cap just as European (its puffed-up majesty had originated with the Germans and Russians). Nor did I consider that so much of the military lexicon in the United States had derived from the French: *admiral*, *aide-de-camp*, *army*, *artillery*, *battalion*, *bivouac*, *brigade*, *camouflage*, *captain*, *cavalry*, *colonel*, *cordon*, *corporal*, *corvette*, *espionage*, *general*, *guard*, *infantry*, *latrine*, *lieutenant*, *logistics*, *major*, *morale*, *officer*, *pistol*, *platoon*, *reconnaissance*, *regiment*, *rendezvous*, *sergeant*, *siege*, *soldier*, *sortie*, *squad*, *squadron*, *surrender*, *surveillance*, *terrain*, *troops*, *volley*.

Up to and including *Marine Corps*.

My little brother, Ethan, was a teenager then, with all the typical try-hard coolness. Sweating in his purplish polo, he congratulated me with a look of bewildered respect, as if I'd just taken an extended beating but come back to my feet to stare down my assailant. The austerity of the Island seemed to fascinate him, as if he were participating in a field trip to another side, where hardship reigned supreme.

Then there were Rick and Carrie, close friends of my cousins who had accompanied them on their drive up. Rick had served as a grunt decades earlier and brought along his own graduate book to show me what it was like in the Old Corps. Like Beanie, he was a taciturn and humble man, so it was his wife who made clear Rick had earned the highest rifle score in his class.

Despite the presence of such men in my entourage, fear and trembling had overtaken me. My white tee, spotless; my short-sleeve "Charlies," beige type, faultlessly ironed. The rifle badge suspended against my left chest pocket was made up of concentric circles and a bull's-eye in the center, meaning I'd barely made marksman. But it, too, carried a quality of achievement. As for my frame itself, an excess kilogram of fat couldn't be found. I must have lost thirty pounds, just a sprig of brawn. Inside my head, though, I'd come undone.

Those I loved, and who loved me, had reentered my life as liabilities. They were too degreed, too familiar with the *New York Times* and the *New Yorker*. They were obviously too moneyed, even if no one happened to be wearing anything all that steep or showy. Maybe that's what made them too obvious, the way they walked and talked, like vacationing tourists.

There was also the problem of their Jewishness. I'd become a red cell for my people, reactive to any hint of unchristian conviction, any whiff of the Pale of Settlement or, closer to home, my father's childhood Pelham Parkway in the Bronx. This was for our safety. I spent those interminable remaining hours on the Island corralling them as far away from everyone else as I could manage, lest someone catch a stray remark in a syntax reserved for experts and snobs. Now that I was back with my originators, those who had raised me with too many cushions and crutches, I feared the reversion of my own verbiage.

It didn't matter Sherry and Beany were devout churchgoers or that, as Southerners wrapped up in lives of uniformed service, they evinced enough signifiers of the fabled white working class to pass as friendlies. It didn't matter that my grandfather sauntered along the walkways with tantalum in his skull from his post-Iwo cranioplasty or that he'd survived the Great Depression by boxing and running odd jobs. Or that my grandma, at age eight or nine, even before the Wall Street Crash, was whisked off from the Lower East to a foster home every time her mother had another breakdown, to a family in Queens, whose meals always proved inedible. The dressmaker neighbors above her and her sister's guardians were often too busy to cook at all, subsisting on outsized cans of peanut butter, which they allowed the girls whenever they liked. Thus peanut butter became their means of survival, and thereafter, they never ate it again.

I would come to admire my family for their tenacities, yet upon earning my Eagle, Globe, and Anchor, all of this had been consigned to irrelevance.

In truth, though, it was probably a desire to be cut off from my past, more than a fear that my family's advantages would be apparent to my peers, that drove my neuroses that day. As I watched my father exit the Parris Island Museum gift shop, his bumblebee-yellow US Marine Corps baseball cap in hand, a goofy ebullience coruscating across his face, all I could see was my prior luck. All I wanted was out. Away from all of it. I belonged to the red brick now. The drab rectangular signage reading PARRIS ISLAND MUSEUM. The severe lettering arrayed against the concrete facade reading PEATROSS PARADE DECK. The standard guidons and bleak canteen cups and omnipresent pull-up bars. I belonged to the log walls and splinters and fetor and stink, the anonymity of obedience.

That weekend we visited Charleston, the town named after the clandestine Catholic king Charles the Second, in South Carolina, one of the two states named after King Charles's beheaded father, Charles (Carolus) the First. We passed by the Greek Revival of Congregation Beth Elohim (House of God), the original synagogue having been founded in 1749 by expelled Spanish and Portuguese Sephardim from

London. Many of their fellow exiles had first fled to places like Croatia, Holland, London, or the West Indies as extended waystations. Some other Sephardim may have come over with the conquistadors Juan Pardo and Hernando de Soto. Others may have descended from the Roanoke colonists who merged with the Croatans and then the Lumbees. Still others could have set sail with Columbus, someone numerous scholars suspect was himself a Sephardic Jew.

In the nineteenth century, Beth Elohim would lead American Jewry in a nascent Reform Judaism, just as Charleston came to house the most substantial Jewish community in the nation. The temple counted among its members future United States senator from Louisiana and Confederate cabinet officer Judah Benjamin, along with the reputable Cardozo family. Jacob Cardozo made his living as a pro-slavery economist and newspaperman. The son of his brother Isaac and Isaac's common-law wife, the free black woman Lydia Weston, became the first statewide black officeholder in the United States, Francis Lewis Cardozo.

Francis would distinguish himself as secretary of state for Reconstruction-era South Carolina, and his granddaughter, Eslanda Cardozo Goode, would achieve comparable distinction as an anthropologist, performer, activist, and business manager and wife of the eminent singer and communist Paul Robeson. Justice Benjamin Cardozo, one of the liberal "three musketeers" of the US Supreme Court during the New Deal and namesake for Yeshiva University's law school, descended from the same line.

These crashing whirlpools of past and present, near and far—all so suggestive yet ambiguous, incriminating yet spiraling with contingencies—carried us like a subliminal undercurrent to Marion Square. We stared up at the pink fortress crowned with turrets and parapets. It was the old Citadel, the Arsenal, built to defend the white ruling class against their slaves in the wake of the Denmark Vesey uprising of 1822. A bronze statue of John C. Calhoun, the great slaver-intellectual, stood on the other side of the green, atop an eighty-foot Doric column, surveilling outward toward a conquered beyond. It was built by black wage workers about three decades after their hard-fought liberation.

I must have said then, "It's all so fucked but beautiful." Whatever I said shouldn't have been said. Nothing could be said. The whole scene, from the buildings to the monuments to the people circulating in and around them, defied any possibility of redemptive speech.

Next to Calhoun, behind a consolidated squad of magnolia trees, stood a Holocaust memorial.

PART THREE
HARSH TERRAIN

We should have learned from our frontier forebears that there is little use planting corn outside the stockade if there are still Indians around in the woods outside.

—Maxwell Taylor

Before combat training in a remote, wooded part of North Carolina just west of Croatan Forest, I was awarded the standard ten days of leave. The first few of those days were spent in one of the second-floor guestrooms at my parents' downgraded two-story in one of the cheaper municipalities abutting my hometown, where I'd spent my childhood in two consecutive houses much larger. The Regency at Bloomfield, its planned community, sat upon denuded rolling hills now replanted with youngish beech, oak, maple, and evergreens. Azalea bushes, along with professional mowing, shoveling, plowing, and blowing and a monthly book club, were included.

The Neocolonial's facade alternated between vinyl siding and a near-white brick veneer. Inside were hardwood floors, cherrywood cabinets, granite counters, downlights and cornices, bar seating, and a capacious island. The master bedroom had an equally roomy bathroom, and the bathroom had a spa tub. The common area spanned nineteen feet and took up most of the residence.

In the fall of 1992, Democratic presidential candidate Bill Clinton chose West Hartford for a speech in which he distanced himself from the Left while claiming a "Third Way." Clinton and his new Democratic Party would go on to implement their vision on numerous battlegrounds, undermining public housing, expanding policing and incarceration, chipping away at what was left of social services and public investments, reregulating Wall Street in favor of financial kingpins, and championing corporate-friendly domestic policies like subsidies, tax loopholes, and privatization and plutocratic trade policies like NAFTA.

Most of all, according to his national security team, Clinton was intent on renewing America's project of post–Cold War "global leadership." Or as Secretary of State Madeleine Albright put it in 1998 when threatening another major military intervention into Iraq (after years of crippling sanctions):

> If we have to use force, it is because we are America; we are the indispensable nation. We stand tall and we see further than other countries into the future, and we see the danger here to all of us. I know that the American men and women in uniform are always prepared to sacrifice for freedom, democracy and the American way of life.

Such a polite vernacular of "freedom" and "democracy" obscures a reality that the history of towns like West Hartford and Bloomfield can elucidate.

When the Roosevelt administration began building public housing for laborers during World War II, West Hartford residents protested the inclusion of black workers in one of the new developments, worried their presence would hurt property values.

This dynamic intensified in the coming decades. Locals introduced restrictive covenants to ban housing for those deemed nonwhite (an exception did allow for lodging of owners' and tenants' servants). Residents increasingly relied on "redlining," a practice historians have long thought arose from the Home Owners Loan Corporation recommending areas where banks should and shouldn't lend, with the bad investment areas color-coded red and, as one would expect, disproportionately black or brown. More recent scholarship has suggested that the Federal Housing Administration's racist lending policies are arguably more to blame for this discrimination. Either way, whites in towns like West Hartford were able to avail themselves of affordable mortgage loans and build wealth while these options remained unattainable for the most exploited Americans.

Real estate agents in the sixties and seventies found ways to make money off this arrangement, namely by steering black and brown people to some housing markets while steering whites to others. In one maneuver called "block-busting," agents sold homes to nonwhite residents, using these sales to encourage scared whites to sell their properties at low rates. Agents would then resell those same properties at much higher prices to further nonwhite aspirants who had no other means of achieving the American dream.

Lather, rinse, repeat.

Despite these operations being challenged during and after the civil rights movement, exclusionary zoning has persisted. Laws originating in the 1920s criminalizing the construction or maintenance of multifamily homes ensured those white and wealthy enough to live in single-family houses in the most prosperous suburbs could continue to do so without fear of integration.

When asked to comment on this chronicle of injustice in 2021, West Hartford's mayor, Shari Cantor, said she was committed to making her town more inclusive but was skeptical of anything that might harm real estate values, which clearly included affordable housing. Cantor's plan for "increased housing choice" amounted to no real plan at all, or nothing that would mean much of anything to the vast numbers most in need of one.

My middle school, King Philip Middle, was named after Metacom, the seventeenth-century Wampanoag leader who lost his life fighting settlers who reneged on their treaties in Connecticut, Rhode Island, and Massachusetts. The settlers wanted indigenous land and the prosperity it promised, so they took it by force. When Metacom, the Wampanoag, and others rebelled, the settlers vanquished them in one of the most destructive wars of the colonial era. Historian Jill Lepore has argued that it was this act of pillage that forged an American colonial identity distinct from diverse European ancestries.

A through line runs from the crushing of the Wampanoag and their indigenous allies in the 1670s to West Hartford's history of racial segregation to its current residents' prioritization of property values above all else. A direct line runs from that prioritization and the bipartisan consensus in Washington to prize national primacy and conflict above all else.

For all its attempts at reining in the worst manifestations of the American ethos (which has always been an imperialist ethos, even before it became a capitalist one), mainstream liberalism in the twenty-first century remains entranced by that ethos's most basic siren call.

Bill Clinton knew to whom he spoke in the fall of 1992. This was the same town that would later vote for Hillary in the 2016 Democratic Party primary (the sizable Republican minority would side with John Kasich). In the contested 2006 Senate race between Democrat Ned Lamont and newly independent Joe Lieberman, a majority would line up behind Lieberman.

By that time, Lieberman had made a name for himself as a "centrist" renegade. In the most immediate sense for Lieberman and his supporters, this meant continuing to underwrite George W. Bush's wars in Iraq and the Greater Middle East. It also meant the continued and nigh unconditional support for the Israeli government, an appealing promise for a town with so many older Jews still looking to the Jewish homeland as a necessary refuge. Most fundamentally, though, Lieberman's agenda was the same agenda well-to-do communities like West Hartford had been buttressing for generations—that of US-led global capital.

Regardless of racial identity, the more capital one accrues, the more likely one is to oppose any significant redistributions in wealth and power. Along with that comes an increasing sympathy for police and a heightened acceptance of (or enthusiasm for) military interventionism, corporate trade agreements, and what, among genteel company, has been referred to as "US primacy" or the "liberal international order."

Meanwhile, towns like West Hartford are vastly underrepresented in the frontline military ranks their "middle of the road" elected officials so eagerly expand and deploy. Just 17 percent of enlisted recruits come from neighborhoods with a median household income of $87,851 or more (West Hartford's is $105,230, according to the latest US Census). Sixty-two percent come from neighborhoods with a median household income of less than $66,597.

Boosters are quick to tout these numbers as proof that the military represents a healthy cross section of the American middle class, but this only makes sense if you ignore the drastic differences in quality of life among the supposed "middle class." Upward of 60 percent of Americans live paycheck to paycheck, at least half are struggling to build up a sustainable retirement, and around half are defaulted on medical debt. These are the people most likely to fight America's wars, even as they remain the least likely to support those wars and the elite institutions that demand them.

Those towns with the highest military casualties, in fact, seemed to have been most attracted to Donald Trump's anti-war messaging in 2016 (putting aside its insincerity). The decision of wealthy voters and their favored politicians to wage war at the expense of America's poor and working-class warfighters has repeatedly come to haunt the body politic, to say nothing of the greater costs others have been forced to endure abroad.

As a child, I watched Bloomfield High's football team (the Warhawks) pummel, more than once, Hall High's football team (the Warriors). From the sidelines to the finish lines, the game always remained a segregated affair. The same could be said for the elevated Regency and its encircling perimeter a decade later. When I jogged outside the bounds of the upscale community, the contrast was clear.

Growing up, I was told Bloomfield prided itself on its black middle class. I hadn't yet read up on how discriminatory practices and the overarching criminalization of black and brown America ensured a non-white middle class would never flourish in West Hartford, or anywhere else in the greater Hartford area. Today West Hartford is estimated to be almost 80 percent white and 7 percent black. Bloomfield, majority white just a few decades ago, is now estimated to be 35 percent white and almost 60 percent black. The median value of owner-occupied housing units in the latter is around $110,000 lower than the former.

I found these spatial fractals extended beyond Bloomfield. They were everywhere. If I wasn't jogging or sleeping or masturbating, I was gobbling up half the inventory at the IHOP on the more affordable side of West Hartford. I was drawn to it. And not just for the pancakes. It was the relative bargain-basement liveliness and color I craved: the volume and sartorial pandemonium; the enthusiasm for oversized platters and sugar-high drinks; the collective suspicions of snobs and deep pockets.

The more I wallowed in my class estrangement, the more ridiculous I became. But self-loathing scarcely took up my whole headspace. Back in the guestroom I scrolled through old emails on my laptop, tracking down a note from my father sent two years earlier, pleading with me not to join up. A military contract was too dangerous, he told me. I'd be putting my talent and intelligence at risk. I was "too much of a free spirit," he said, and he "couldn't bear the thought of losing" me.

At first I almost cried. As his work hours became more reasonable, and as he settled into a slower life as an empty nester, my father had started relating to the rest of us—the kids anyway—with fewer eruptions. He'd also done so right when I decided to flirt with the prospect of departing as a glorified cipher.

My mom told me the same things in person or on the phone. Over and over. She squeezed me and teared up and told me I'd always be her moosh.

It was preposterous how good I had it. More preposterous was how much I hated myself for having it. My confusion had been rushing to the surface for years, and would continue to surge: my father, who had thrown me into a state of regular alarm, now, despite relapses (often at Mom's expense), becoming an emotional ballast; my mother, always away with her career, in both body and mind, carrying on with that saccharine word: *moosh*; an extended family that sustained me while unnerving me with their (our) riches. The only thing that surpassed my gratitude was my aching need to flee—to surrender, to pass on to those more deserving—all of it.

That morning, before breakfast, I plodded down to the gargantuan walkout basement to find a book to read from a dozen boxes in storage. A paperback of José Ortega y Gasset's interwar classic *The Revolt of the Masses* caught my attention:

> The most radical division that is possible to make of humanity is that which splits it into two classes of creatures: those who make great demands on themselves, piling up difficulties and duties; and those who demand nothing special of themselves, but for whom to live is to be every moment what they already are, without imposing on themselves any effort towards perfection.... Man, whether he like it or no, is a being forced by his nature to seek some higher authority. If he succeeds in finding it of himself, he is a superior man; if not, he is a mass-man and must receive it from his superiors.... The man with the clear head is the man who frees himself from those fantastic "ideas" [of clarity] and looks life in the face, realizes that everything in it is problematic, and feels himself lost. As this is the simple truth—that to live is to feel oneself lost—he who accepts it has already begun to find himself, to be on firm ground.

Ortega y Gasset's liberalism belonged to the old European bourgeoisie, an upper middle class even more detached than the postwar American iteration that was still reproducing peculiar, lethal men like me. I was torn between the romance and the callousness of the book's hierarchies, between the desire to earn a spot among the noble few and the revulsion of such an outdated want. I ached for a future where I could stop worrying about my advantages because I had, at long last, attained them by my own effort. By tried experience, yes, but also by accrued wisdom.

Holding a now ancient handout with guidelines for the medical physical portion at the Military Entrance Processing Station, I thought back to my own MEPS excursion. It was a drawn-out, demeaning affair, punctuated by awkward half-naked duck walks and rectal exams. A few aspiring recruits had Confederate flags, German crosses, and, in one case, a swastika inked into their skin, and I never knew what became of them. Others had questionable family crests or likely gang tattoos. Later I'd hear certain tats were waivable and others not permanently disqualifying provided the offender removed them and demonstrated adequate remorse. Even at the Island I saw some suspect tats whose owners would explain them as "tribal." We were fighting a two-front war at the time. Demand was high.

Before my initial misadventure in Quantico, I had dutifully recorded the Marine Corps basics on loose-leaf paper. Flicking through my notes that late Monday morning, I was struck by such a faith in studious preparation.

I had listed the eleven General Orders for guard duty and the four safety rules; written out the textbook definition of the M16A2 service rifle, its caliber, weight, and length, its firing characteristics and max effective ranges; and drawn a perfect sketch, including labeled nomenclature for every component, from the forward assist assembly to the bolt catch to the bayonet stud. I had recorded the eight cycles of operation, the five types of ammunition, the three weapons conditions, the six weapons commands, the three weapons carries, and the four weapons transports.

I explained the difference between "on deck" and "on hand" and traced out the rank structure and insignias for enlisted and officer. I copied the sacrosanct terms and sayings from "First to fight" to "Retreat, hell! We just got here!" I regurgitated the mission and organization of the Marine Corps as delineated by the National Security Act of 1947; defined the infantry units from division to platoon and the air wing units from the MAW (Marine Air Wing) to the MASS (Marine Air Support Squadron); marked the differences among the MAGTF (Marine Air-Ground Task Force), SPMAGTF (Special Purpose Marine Air-Ground Task Force), MEF (Marine Expeditionary Force), and MEB (Marine Expeditionary Brigade); put down the six articles of the Code of Conduct, from "Prepared to give life" to "Never forget I'm an American fighting for freedom with faith in God," and when to apply deadly force, from "self-defense" to "in defense of property involving national security" to "in defense of property not involving national security but inherently dangerous to others."

The phrases already, at such an undeveloped stage in my disaffection, came across as unworldly. Fight only enemy combatants. Do not harm enemies who surrender. Do not kill or torture prisoners. Collect or care for the wounded, whether friend or foe. Destroy no more than the mission requires. Treat all civilians humanely. Do not steal; respect private property and possessions. Do your best to prevent violations of laws of war. Report all violations to superiors.

There were hip-pocket lessons in Marine Corps history. The Barbary Pirates War (1801), when the ruler of Tripoli declared war on the United States. The Mexican War (1846), when the Marines fought in California and Vera Cruz. The Civil War, when a supposed (and doubtful) 40 percent of officers resigned their commissions to fight for the South. This wasn't true for the enlisted, however, because most came from the Northeast.

On and on it went, a collage of truths, half-truths, mistruths, untruths, ellipses, obfuscations, provisional facts, appropriate facts, motivating facts, telling facts, aimless facts, mystifying inclusions and exclusions. A disjointed, postmodern summoning of past and present.

On the sixth, I snagged an evening Peter Pan to New York to see some friends and family. Ortega y Gasset's *Revolt of the Masses* accompanied me, and I spent half the ride whiplashed between two opposing suspicions: one, I'd be serving in the Corps on behalf of the masses; two, I'd be serving against them. The other half was spent stealing a few minutes of sleep, a tattered hoodie to pillow my head against the window and spare foam earplugs from the Island.

As the bus crawled down Ninth Avenue toward Port Authority, I thumbed through a GChat with Micah, whom I'd recently reconnected with after an early falling-out at Emory. His grandfather, a marine who'd trained under Chesty Puller at Camp Lejeune in North Carolina, had told him that as troops dropped their rifles during runs, Chesty had a habit of picking them up one by one while he kept running. Sometimes he carried up to six rifles.

When I told Micah about my next order to Camp Geiger, he asked me when I'd be going back to OCS, and I replied that it was looking likely I'd have to first attend my military occupational specialty school in California. He said I should call whoever was in charge and do whatever paperwork needed to be done to make sure I didn't have to take the MOS detour. I told him the person in charge was a general and I couldn't just call him. He said I had nothing to lose by trying.

Right before entering Port Authority, I texted Liz to let her know I'd arrived. She was a friend from back home I sometimes messed around with, and someone I figured I might end up marrying if Leah didn't work out. I was planning to crash at her skyrise apartment in Hell's Kitchen.

I cringe now at how entitled I was to assume she'd always play the part of my runner-up. Or that she was even down to play the part then. For all I know I was her runner-up. Or I wasn't really anything. Still, my entitlement came with a sincere affection. She had always treated me well, with such respect and warmth. And though I'd never felt the same heat with her that I had with Leah, there was something liberating in that. Heat inevitably cools. It can be dangerous and, while it lasts, disorienting. I sensed that warmth with Liz was more sustainable, and though I was too oblivious to know it then, it was sustainability I craved.

Looking out Liz's giant window that night, at that giant town, I felt so small. And that, too, was humbling. Like I didn't matter. That no matter what I did, it wouldn't matter. So I might as well embrace my smallness and be happy.

Another thought comes to mind via that night I surveyed Pax Americana's great metropolis, one that doesn't necessarily deny the truth of the last one but does complicate it. It's a favorite passage from the Welsh writer Raymond Williams's *The Country and the City*:

> H. G. Wells once said, coming out of a political meeting where they had been discussing social change, that this great towering city was a measure of the obstacle, of how much must be moved if there was to be any change. I have known this feeling, looking up at great buildings that are the centres of power, but I find I do not say, "There is your city, your great bourgeois monument, your towering structure of this still precarious civilization" or I do not only say that; I say also, "This is what men have built, so often magnificently, and is not everything then possible?"

The next day I met with my brother Brett and my college buddy Luntz at a pub near Luntz's apartment. Luntz had been part of my inner circle at Emory and was now matriculated at NYU Law. He was involved in student government, and when I first met him, he considered himself a Democrat. But it didn't take long for him to concede to me and the rest of our right-wing cohort that the Democrats hated everything that made the United States great: our capitalist dynamism, our eagerness to lead the world toward a freer and more democratic horizon, our freedom fries.

I would like to think if we did talk about freedom fries, it was with a sardonic accent. Regardless, we were some of the post-9/11 generation's truest believers, and it was those beliefs that had shaped our shared identity in Atlanta. Luntz and I were also the two Jews in our squad, which strengthened the bond. There were our Zionist commitments, something I suspect played a crucial role in Luntz's rightward shift. But there was also our added tolerance for intellectuals and academics, a trait related to growing up in similarly liberal, cerebral, and (most of all) Jewish households.

One of our first conversations involved a debate over the "third way," Clintonite-Blairite ideas of the British sociologist Anthony Giddens. When it came to what mattered—freedom, free markets, small government, individualism—I thought Giddens was too wishy-washy and Luntz thought he was just right. Within a year of our friendship I had won that argument and my friend had become just as dogmatic as I was, but those were the kinds of arguments we tended to have.

As for Brett, my grandparents and uncle had pulled strings in the industry to find him a job at a paint shop on the Upper East Side. He'd been working the floor there for a couple years while taking night courses at Hunter. He'd also been getting up at five in the morning from his place in Spanish Harlem to hit the gym or go running. I was impressed and said so.

I told the usual war stories of someone who'd not yet been to war. How we started prepping the rack and uniform and morning chores at 0330 every morning, all in the dark, before the bullhorn reverie or "Lights! Lights! Lights!" About the forelimbs that would shoot up in the middle of the night replaying rifle drill positions, often attended by commands like "Present, Arms!" or "Order, Arms!" Sometimes the sleep talkers seemed to converse among themselves, in reflexive calls and responses. Sometimes their wrists would bend or curl just as instructed.

I mentioned the recruit with cellulitis that ate up his hand and almost made a corpse of him. How he hid it for days for fear of being held back while recovering in the infirmary, and how revolting it looked when he finally announced its presence on the line. He got held back a week, and I saw him postsurgery, but never again after that. At the time I found his refusal to get help when he needed it misguided, but not altogether irrational. The goal wasn't just to make it through boot camp as quickly as possible but also to speed through one's contract with the same single-mindedness. Today, I'm shocked by the madness that this kid put his life on the line just so he could make it to the fleet a little sooner. Then again, we were all putting our lives on the line, and most of us were doing it for mad reasons of our own.

I told Brett and Luntz about the boot camp crud, how all us marines have it, how we'll always have it. How it will burrow into our throats and lungs until the day we die.

Luntz said it didn't sound too bad and he could have done it, and Brett scoffed at him for that. Brett scoffed at the two of us for many things. Like the time a friend and I had taken over the political magazine on campus and published pieces titled "Empire Without Imperialism," "Hizbollah: The 'A-Team' of Terrorism," and "In Defense of Torture." He wasn't all that political, but he was basically a good liberal.

Brett changed the subject and asked about Rosen, another Emory chum who had enlisted in the IDF infantry about a year earlier and was fighting in Lebanon when I was stumbling about Parris Island.

Luntz was already tipsy and blurted out "To Rosen!" and we all drank to Rosen.

My glass was empty and I was eyeing another draft at the bar. When I came back, Brett said, "We were just talking about how long you've been helping Jonah," referring to Jonah Goldberg, a conservative I'd been doing research for on a book about liberal fascism. "It's been years, right?"

"Yeah, a couple," I said.

I told them about the book's premise and how it wasn't all that different from what leftists had been saying about liberalism the past century and a half. I knew this not only because I'd read radicals for Jonah's book but also because I'd read some in my European intellectual history classes.

"Jonah's been real good to me. Paid me way more than I deserve, and he's always inviting me to big-time events. I mean, the guy got me into both major party conventions in 2004."

"You're big-time, Rubin," said Luntz.

We started talking about our recent conquests, and something in Brett's face when Luntz asked about his (nonexistent) sex life got me thinking about Mark Schell. It was a bizarre association, but Brett had the look of someone who could very well have disappeared, out of attrition or a sense of insufficiency. Whenever Schell had looked like that at the libertarian club meetings or the few get-togethers in one of our dorm rooms, I'd chalk it up to him being a strange cat.

But then, early one Friday morning, as the rest of us slept, Schell had parked his car along the turnaround in front of our residence hall. Walmart gun in hand, purchased the prior evening.

Muzzle to muzzle.

As the opinions editor for the school newspaper, I wrote the anonymous staff editorial a week later. My repeated use of the word *surrender* in the context of a suicide couldn't have been more insensitive, and I'm surprised, in hindsight, that it didn't get edited out. But even now I think what I was trying to say had less to do with scolding Schell or others for considering a similar path and more to do with shaming the rest of us for our thoughtlessness. How grim events remind us of our responsibilities to one another, but only temporarily before we return to a hard-hearted norm and surrender to mass forgetfulness.

That said, it was the same language I had deployed, again and again, in relation to the attacks of September 11. And the underlying assumptions of the piece fit nicely with my militarism: life wasn't just a struggle but a war, and those who refused to surrender had yet to be defeated. As if having not yet been defeated translated into a win.

Although I no doubt worried about Brett, I was also worrying about myself.

I hadn't yet come to terms with how my failure at Quantico, and my experiences on the Island, were affecting me, perhaps even humbling me, but in ways that were disorienting and scary. I was beginning to see myself as a product of my class. And I wasn't liking what I saw. It struck me as unfair that others didn't have to know the violence I was now having to know. And I was ashamed I'd gone so many years without knowing it. But even so, I was also calling for more.

The day I met with Brett and Luntz was my birthday. The next day, on a whim, I purchased a flight to Atlanta, where Luntz already had plans to visit our friend Bill and asked if I'd tag along. It helped that the airline rewarded me a $300 military discount.

At Ruth's Chris Steak House we rehashed our conquests. I shared a picture of Liz on my phone but then felt bad for how I was talking about her, so moved on to Leah. I said I wanted to hatefuck her. I felt bad about that, too, so added that I also wanted to lovefuck her.

Bill sent back a red wine bottle in high dudgeon. He said it was foul. He liked to order wines from South Africa just as much as he liked talking shit about the country's African National Congress. He tended to indulge in both activities at the same time.

Once I had a couple drinks in me, I launched into a disquisition about those propagandizing the wars and those fighting them.

"The pro-war punditocracy is composed of sexless dweebs," I said. "The guys with the guns, meanwhile, are sex-soaked. The gap between the bloodless elites and the lusty front-liners couldn't be wider."

We returned to more comfortable shibboleths.

"So the idea is," said Luntz, "the world can only be constituted by four types—unipolar, bipolar, multipolar, or anarchic. Unipolar or bipolar orders had proven the most stable, but since the Cold War wasn't ideal, a US-led unipolar order proved the worst option except for all the others."

I quoted Churchill on democracy.

Luntz and I, with Bill's addition, resumed the litany of triumphs we'd begun the day before. We saluted our roles in smearing the reputation of Mary Robinson, a former president of Ireland and United Nations high commissioner for human rights. She'd been invited to Emory as a commencement speaker, and I led an effort to paint her as either antisemitic or too close with antisemites to bother making a distinction. I boasted about serving as an AIPAC summer intern and one of four student members on AIPAC's Executive Committee, and about appearing on the front page of the *Washington Post* dancing the hora next to the Capitol during a rally in solidarity with Israel. I'd introduced the columnist Charles Krauthammer at an AIPAC conference and written press releases in the AIPAC comms shop about America and Israel sharing intelligence, technology, and military techniques to combat terror.

For all my bluster, inconvenient memories bubbled up. Like the time an older AIPAC hand corrected me for dismissing Noam Chomsky: "Chomsky is very smart and very informed. You should read him."

Or the time I had a crush on a fellow intern and sobbed for my unrequited love in a lonesome hotel bathtub. I mentioned neither incident, but even if I'd wished to, the conversation had already moved on.

I asked Bill and Luntz if they'd stayed in touch with Robb Fischer.

"A little," said Bill. "But not really."

"The guy's pretty much a coked-up playboy, right?" I asked. "Like, didn't he carry on an extended affair with a Lebanese American male prostitute?"

"He likes the boys just as much as the girls," said Bill matter-of-factly.

"It's wild," I said, "because he'd show up at parties with hot Latinas on each side. One time he told me—in front of the same girls!—that they'd talk about me in the bedroom. I might have accepted that unsubtle invitation had I been drunker."

So many of our conversations vacillated between standard homophobia and racist innuendo, and uninhibited debauchery and ideological twaddle.

Luntz and Bill paid for my meal and drinks. A belated birthday.

We drank more at the Brick Store Pub, our old haunt in Decatur.

We clinked glasses and drank to our absent friends Phil and Rick.

We maundered across frat row like the happiest of lemmings.

I didn't make it back to Bloomfield until late on the tenth and spent all of the eleventh—September 11—packing for Marine Combat Training. I didn't have enough time to visit Micah and his family, even though I said I would, and I shipped out to North Carolina on the twelfth.

Upon our arrival at Geiger, we were drug tested, and the last names of all the positives were called out during a chow break. They were lined up amid a clearing in the woods, next to a carport-looking beast stocked with Meals Ready-to-Eat and other provisions. Some of them—all men—were on edge or giggly. Others cried. All were too young. An instructor yawped a drug for every private and private first class he passed.

As we stood near aligned folding tables and chairs, we murmured about each culprit's crime. I wondered how much they knew about the legal consequences awaiting them. Since they had volunteered to serve what they believed to be their country, they now risked the scarlet letter of the Other Than Honorable discharge. The OTH would make it difficult for them to find gainful employment. Many would be automatically discarded during hiring inquiries. Many others would be locked out of acquiring professional licenses and stigmatized in their communities. All would forgo the veteran benefits that had led them to the Corps in the first place.

The signage at Geiger was familiar. The same signage as at the Island but, somehow now, reaching further back into my past. The rusted frames securing the location markers reminded me of elementary school swing sets. The capitalized text of the markers, uniform in their yellow block lettering and red backgrounds, reminding me of grade school stencils. The coarse, twisted ropes sent me back to trust games and tugs-of-war. The wooden planked obstacles to summer camp. The faces war painted and glazed in sweat and innocence and fear. Most of all the women's faces, the girls' faces, the most boyish faces of the bunch.

Women made up only about 6 percent of the Corps in 2006, and it was at Geiger I first trained with them. At the Island we had marched by female platoons, after which our hats would order us to ignore their stinky cunts or pussy squeals. But at Geiger we ate with them, marched and ran alongside them, teamed up with them during educational huddles or field exercises, and showered or slept in the same general vicinity at night. It was also at Geiger that I became familiar with what would later become, at MOS school and beyond, continual claims of sexual harassment, abuse, and rape. Phrases like *barracks slut* or *carpet-muncher* would naturally follow these accusations.

The three weeks at MCT were nothing compared with the curriculum at the infantry training battalion, but they were still intense. We learned how to assemble, disassemble, and use the M203 grenade launcher, AT4 anti-tank weapon, M249 squad automatic weapon (SAW), M240G machine gun, .50 caliber machine gun, and Mk 19 grenade launcher. We memorized the max ranges, effective ranges, rounds per minute (RPMs), and velocities. We shot a tracer out of the AT4, training rounds out of the 203, and simulated fire for the 50-cal and Mark 19. We threw grenades.

Much of our time was spent patrolling—sometimes just standing—in single-file lines. We took knees during instruction and gathered in sitting circles during chow. We were bordered by pond pines, towering longleaf pines, oaks, American sweetgums, and waterlogged cypresses. I'd breathe in the open savanna one hour and the stink of the swamps the next. When conducting close-quarter combat and urbanized terrain training, our boundaries shifted from mucked-up treelife to dirt-filled Hesco barriers, pebbled floors, and cinder block walls. We turned corners of the concrete, formed stacks as we breached and entered hardened or plywood doors. We ducked below or around windowlike openings in the cement and pointed our rifles upward toward roofs, downward toward stairs or floors below, diagonally around every bend. During enemy prisoner-of-war schooling, we crooked the forearms of our comrades into agonizing, reversed right angles. We lined our foreheads and cheeks with stripes of brown, black, and green and convoyed in low-ceilinged Humvees whose ancient, unarmored doors neither opened nor closed. When bivouacked, we slept in moss, shamrock, and fern that must have looked like moldy pimples from above. For land nav we paced in tight straight lines, heel to toe, heel to toe, and practiced the compass-to-cheek method when determining azimuths. Looking through the lens like a rifle sight, we extended our index finger along the compass's side, aiming as if fastened to a pistol grip.

We maneuvered defensively and offensively, screeching numbers and commands down the line as we squad rushed. We ran downrange, first as thirteen-marine squads, then as three- to four-marine fireteams, while others laid down suppressive fire. We rushed as individuals, live rounds whizzing by both sides.

By early October I had been dispatched to Marine Corps Communication-Electronics School (MCCES) in a somewhat deserted edge of Southern California called Twentynine Palms. Most marines called it "the stumps," probably because there weren't so much lively palm trees there as echoes of past life, protruding from the ground like episodic, vandalized trunks. But I became accustomed to calling it by its less poetic diminutive, "the Palms."

A US Geological Survey from 1968 describes the Palms' "wind-blown sand," "alluvium," "clay," and "older gravel." Judging by the lyrics and mood of Robert Plant's "29 Palms," the legendary front man must have identified with the place's sultriness. Others have inferred something more sinister. Deanne Stillman's *Twentynine Palms: A True Story of Murder, Marines, and the Mojave* narrates the killing of two teenage girls by a disturbed marine, situating the event in the larger context of US violence. And in his film *Twentynine Palms*, the French auteur Bruce Dumont conjures a portrait of the American wasteland even more unsettling.

When I first set foot there, though, I couldn't help but hark back to something more demotic: namely, Jabba's Palace on Tatooine, shot four hours up the road at Death Valley National Park.

Lodging within the military installation was indistinguishable from any multistory motor lodge with exterior corridors. Off-base lodging resembled a series of disheveled single-story motels or flats encircled by chain-link fencing. Materials ranged from adobe to stucco with Spanish roof tiles, and the colors from pink to salmon to beige. Were your typical Vermont or Colorado ski resort to be denuded of its fertile treescapes, wildlife, snowcapped mountains, and wealth, it might look something like Twentynine Palms. Never once did I catch a whiff of the higher-end amenities afforded to tourists just twenty minutes down the road.

A great number of palm trees—queen palms, foxtail palms, California fan palms—hovered over the main thoroughfares. Joshua trees held watch like sentries in the distance, while yucca and an undazzling array of scrub brush surrounded the Quonset huts or city mockups where the simulated death making took place. The galactic skies ranged from alabaster to parchment to crimson to fuchsia to indigo to lime. In a matter of a few hours, the temperatures would soar from the twenties to the nineties. Marines marched to their early-morning schoolhouses with winter gear and marched back for midday chow with rolled-up sleeves and unmanageable perspiration. When it rained, the earth gave off a sulfuric stink, and effluvium from the Combat Center's Waste Water Treatment Plant, which marines passed during their jogs, flew around the clock. Everyone called the irrigation-conducive cesspool "Lake Bandini" in honor of the area business Bandini Fertilizer.

Despite these distinctions, there was a placelessness to the Palms that made it easy to talk about it by talking around it. Like many desert settlements, it exuded a nomadic quality, as if its official purpose was to serve as a waystation for wayward lives. The presence of the largest marine base in the United States contributed to this feeling. It was the largest by area, though its day-to-day density varied drastically depending on how many marines were in town for pre-deployment training, this being its primary mission.

That last fact added another layer to the community's elusiveness. So much of its character was derived from the personalities of those inhabiting it at any moment, from its hippie remnants to a wild mélange of uniformed servicemembers.

Even when the place itself, along with its permanent residents, became the subject, it still lent itself to microcosmic musings. During my stay, there were the meth addicts risking their lives scrounging about impact areas for shell casings, unexploded ordnance, and other scrap metal they could cash in at recycling centers or hawk on the black market. Some, during the summer, would expire from thirst, while others would freeze to death during the winter. Some would self-detonate with what they had found. I remember briefs that indicated some had met their end in the thick of live fire itself. Some were chased down, cuffed, and sent to prison. Some were deported.

The fact that so many of the scrappers joining the addicts in their scrounging were immigrants from south of the border lay bare another dimension. It was one that suggested parallels between the empire's outer wars and the wars within its most hopeless communities.

I didn't think much of any of this at the time. This was how it was, how it had been for a while, and I had yet to allow myself to explore the realities hiding behind such a thin layer of bureaucratic instruction. Others had taken on a superior posture toward the region's *Lumpenproletariat*, much like they did toward most civilians. They were lazy, undisciplined, the sort that warranted whatever came their way. In a word made popular on the Island, they were *nasty*. That they had managed to find themselves in such a helpless state made them all the nastier.

I'd like to think the cause of my indifference lay elsewhere. In retrospect, I wasn't so much contemptuous as I was afraid, afraid of what their bare existence said about me and my place in the world. The thought that I had been living at the expense of others had crossed my mind more than once, but to see that cost in the flesh was too much to bear, and so I didn't think about it.

Occasionally I'd hear stories about marines who were assaulted by resentful townies or desperate transients. The "town," as a unified organism, was presented as hostile. The station or unit commands issued warnings and advisories of their own. Perhaps the superciliousness of my peers was related to this underlying fear. We were all eager to prove our toughness, yet anxious about having had it easier than the people we considered ourselves superior to in strength, courage, and integrity. That is to say, we were soft, and those we saw as losers were hard.

This self-emasculation, along with a pervasive bias toward the status quo and propensity to follow orders, made us uninterested in their plight. At one level this was to be expected. We didn't sign up to help the stray or downtrodden. But according to the agitprop—and many of our own rationalizations—this was precisely what we had volunteered for: we were supposed to be nation builders, culturally sensitive agents of humanitarian intervention, winners of hearts and minds. That we were nothing of the sort, even in relation to our compatriots, did not bode well.

Meanwhile, marines were being discharged dishonorably or on bad conduct for adultery. They were divorcing after walking in on partners committing adultery. Being punished for pummeling the people they walked in on (or the people they walked in on were punished for pummeling them). Marines were marrying locals either because they were young and in love or because they were milking the system through contract marriages. They were caught in threesomes or foursomes or some other *n*thsomes. Sometimes these tales were told with a lightheartedness they may have deserved. Sometimes they came loaded with hints of something worse.

New arrivals each week contained a trickle of female marines, who promptly became the quarry of at least half the battalion, and their faces tended to undergo a jaded metamorphosis as the weeks progressed. In short, we (predominantly the men) acted like a higher caste. Surrounded by a desert of suffering, we nourished our emotional lives by inflicting suffering on those we cherished or said we cherished. If we weren't doing the inflicting, we took our entertainment from the spectacle of other people's affliction.

Pain is weakness leaving the body.

Most had internalized the boot camp mantra.

Although few marines I served with at the Palms hailed from the upper reaches of society, in relation to the area's addicts and immigrants, we enjoyed our status and whatever happiness or gratification it afforded. Often that enjoyment came at the expense of fellow marines and was of a survivalist character, a kind of necessary Keynesian stimulus at the level of the individual. Compulsive, cruel banter to keep the self-esteem inflated. But at least we weren't torturing ourselves for a fix, like those tweaking and scrapping on the outskirts.

The political economy of the Palms treated us better than it treated them.

I waited a month before my first class in basic electronics commenced, during which time I was paid to show up in a lusterless room at 0715 every morning. On occasion I'd join a working party and rake, mop, sweep, or take out trash or have a blast riding the industrial floor buffer like a scooter. The workday ended at 1630, weekends off. Except we had to stay on base until late November.

Girls were sparse, and the ones I liked were already married or taken. It wasn't worth the effort or risks regardless. I reached out to Liz one day on GChat. She had gotten back with her hometown boyfriend. She said he was a psycho the last time but this time it might work out. The news left me unmoored.

That opening month at the Palms lent itself to idle pursuits. Thanks to another curious marine, a Guatemalan American film geek, I discovered the Criterion Collection and related fare and was particularly enthralled by Italian cinema: Fellini, Antonioni, Pasolini, Bertolucci, Marco Tullio Giordana's *The Best of Youth.* Anything approaching—like Icarus approaching the sun—the wonders and horrors of sex, the agonies of love, the ubiquities of violence and domination and death, the stubbornness of joy captured me.

If I wasn't gallivanting across male movieland, I was writing bad poetry. And because I knew my poetry was crap, I sometimes featured this fact in my poems: "Broken lazy language / But it will do for now."

When weeks went by without sex, and still no word from Leah, I groaned that "Truth is a woman . . . playing that impossible game of hide and seek / With that part of me / that hopes."

Or this, which had the added benefit of nearing real craftsmanship:

Is there a grasp
Of shredded, grained earth
That will not slip
Through the soft cracks
Of these strong, trained hands?

If Quantico and Parris Island had split me in half, it was in the Palms that I became obsessed with the rupture. A chasm was opening between my softer and harder parts. The two directions seemed to be baiting one another, like antagonistic voices calling from opposite cliffs. Sometimes that meant progress. Oftentimes it meant a strident regress. So much of that interval was characterized by a doubling down on the arrogance, impulsiveness, and rage within and around me.

When I wasn't flirting with a more skeptical politics, I was retreating to the cold comforts of misanthropy (misogyny's final refuge—or maybe it's the other way around) and lapping up the parallel chauvinisms of my Emory gang. Many of our conversations online or over the phone involved lashing out against one subaltern or another. Anyone who wasn't a reactionary was fair game. And even then, one was at risk of being subject to debasements provided they belonged to any of the out-groups: fairies, cunts, wetbacks, towelheads, injuns...we were cultured enough to steer clear of the most piercing anti-black slurs, although the anti-black memes or presumptions still flowed. We might have used "darky" and we certainly used "mutt."

And who knew what the others were saying about our kike asses behind my and Luntz's backs. It sounds petty when put that way, but that's how it was. And though it's hard to explain the bond now, even if I had caught them saying something untoward about my people, I would have still stuck with them. I would have still felt treasured by them. And I suspect I wouldn't have been wrong about that either.

To the extent I was becoming critical of the war in Iraq, it wasn't with the aid of the Chomskyite Left but with that of Henry Kissinger and company. I was exploring the possibility with my friends that perhaps the United States had to either go full fascist or get out.

My neoconservative idealism appeared at times to be souring into an authoritarian pulp. I mourned the passing of Milton Friedman and extolled the economist's defense of the dictator Augusto Pinochet's "Miracle in Chile." I loathed Jimmy Carter's book critical of the Israeli government and recommended regime change in Tehran. I maintained correspondence with one of Jonah's most racist colleagues, despite finding his racism disconcerting, which may have been what attracted me. That might have been the reason I kept up a friendly acquaintance with the *Ramparts* editor turned far-right firebrand David Horowitz, too, someone I first met at Emory during one of his madcap campus tours.

Such a trendline was complicated by more promising interests. I read Melville's *Moby-Dick* as an indictment of the worst aspects of myself and my society and the cultural critic Clive James's *Cultural Amnesia* with an eye to its egalitarianism, despite the author's late-life retrogressions. I read William James, specifically his pragmatism lectures and his essay "The Moral Equivalent of War" as a retort to everything I had ever known or thought.

I read James during firewatch patrols. Whenever I was about to pass by a security camera or a marine, I'd wedge the paperback into my upper trousers, right behind my lower blouse. I performed the same routine, under my orange reflective vest, when reporting each hour to the duty officer at the front desk.

Sometimes the duty officer was Sergeant Sergeant.

"Good morning, Sergeant [Sergeant]. Lance Corporal Rubin reporting firewatch for building 2200. There is nothing unusual to report at this time."

"Very well. Carry on."

"Aye, Sergeant [Sergeant]. Good morning, Sergeant [Sergeant]."

A salute had to be made, meaning Sergeant Sergeant (or whoever the NCO was) had to stop watching *Jarhead* (marines loved to hate *Jarhead* but watched it anyway) or playing *Halo*, stand up, get in the position of attention, and return the salute. I could never actually say "Sergeant Sergeant." It had to be the less screwball "Sergeant." But I always wanted to.

If it was the weekend or a holiday, I'd read some after watch. If others were up for it, I'd go bowling.

In any case, Yossarian lives.

The Palms was where I met Morgan, an observant Jew who had suspended an offer to Cornell so he could serve. He was adopted at an early age by two devout Protestants in Ithaca, New York, but had always been fascinated by the Hebrew Bible and, while in high school, found out his biological parents were Jewish. One was Moroccan and the other Algerian. Upon this discovery he started attending Jewish services and by the time I met him he'd become a full-fledged, yarmulke-bearing, tallit-wielding Jew. His Christian parents called him up every Shabbos and wished him well, although it had taken them a long time to get there.

Morgan reminded me of Micah, and when I told Micah about Morgan, he was thrilled. When I told him we were davening together, he was overjoyed. When I told him how much I thought the two resembled one another, and how I'd always thought Micah was a closeted Sephardi, he was incandescent. Micah wished he could claim the Sephardic mantle. He worshipped the Sephardim.

When I told Micah that Morgan had been dropped from consecutive boot camp platoons and had to put up with a boatload of shit not only because he couldn't shoot the rifle but also because he was an Arab Jew (emphasis on the Arab), Micah was quick to reply that Sephardim aren't Arab.

"He is African. But at least he's not an Arab and Muslim. I would hope he would have gotten an even harder time for that."

I'd like to think I was repulsed when Micah said that, but I just said, "Right." I said marines were more philosemitic than anything else, and Morgan maintained he'd received nice comments since he started wearing his kippah. Micah said he was so warmed by all the young *baalei teshuva*—all those Jews who were born secular but later chose an observant life.

Alongside my poetry I enjoyed putting to the page the idiosyncrasies of my classmates, particularly the ragtag six I wound up with, after a few months of basic electronics, in the Tactical Data Systems Administrator Course.

Lance Corporal Grubbs was the short, famished one. His diet consisted of two packs of cigarettes and one meal a day. He hailed from

Mississippi, his bald head always gleaming from the heat. He'd signed the dotted line before the rest of us (and like me, had enough college to skip the rank of private), so he got tapped as our dear leader. Whenever he reprimanded someone, he looked like a pimple about to pop.

"This is the United States Marine Corps, Rubin! If you wanted to read books all day, you should have joined the staff of your local library!"

Grubbs liked to pretend we weren't both lance corporals and the dear leader thing was anything other than a formality. He was having fun. The moment the uniform came off he was as jolly as a rancher. The rounds ceased at dusk.

Timothy Patrick's parents were drunks. He was twelve when his mom left his dad for his dad's best friend. Pat, being the eldest of three sons, was the one his mom scooped up and swept away. A note left on the kitchen counter read: "Timothy is the only one who is on my side. James, Oscar: I love you but you have made it clear where you stand."

At the time James was eight and Oscar was five. His mother's romance proved short-lived, and by the eve of Pat's fourteenth birthday, she was brooding in her kitchen, intoxicated. That's when she started drinking with Pat and his pals, who had been in the apartment that night playing videogames in another room. It went on like that until the day he landed on the Island.

Pat told the story constantly, and the man never missed an opportunity for a deflection or blocking foul. The meaner the better. Like the time he informed PFC Mason, the lone female (that was the respectful term for her: *female*), that it should have been expected her husband would cheat on her given her "monstrous lack of looks and smarts."

Pat got ragged on for being a fat, drunken, bigoted mick.

Peach, our colonel, our "Captain Cripple," got ragged on for being a fogie with back problems.

Mason got ragged on for being the female, the girl, the cunt.

Bax, my roommate, got ragged on for being incorrigibly dense. He was our "Captain Retardo."

Pearson got it for being black. Although after he knocked out Anthony, a good ole boy in another class who went too far with the black thing—the two of them became buds afterward—everyone eased up on the black thing.

Grubbs got ragged on for being a redneck, though this characterization was complicated when he showed up to class with *On the Origin of Species*, just days after he'd ragged on me for *Moby-Dick*.

I got it for being the Jew with the Jew gold.

It was all in good fun, nothing a thick skin and a day at the gym couldn't solve. Besides, whining was for losers.

I have not re-created the speech of my prior selves, friends, and peers because I find such language tolerable. Nor do I aspire to a role as word cop. As a writer, I'm sensitive to the words one uses. I prize kindness and consideration. I also recognize norms are fluid.

I would say the same about gender and sexuality. A world in which there is only one proper set of behaviors for this or that gender, one set of rules for being romantic or sexual, is not a world I would like to live in. There are infinite ways to explore one's needs or desires without superfluous pain. Some more conventional, some less so. Some gravitate toward softness, others something harder. Sublimated brutalities can prove healing—and fun.

The problem is when these things *become* problems, not just for those most enwrapped in them but also (and of more relevance) for the world. Machines of exploitation and violence leverage these problematic means of relating to one another through language or touch—the line here can blur.

Research has shown that those who exhibit the personality trait of "fearless dominance" gravitate more toward professions of domination, whether in the armed services, the policing panopticon, the carceral archipelago, or perhaps the upper reaches of corresponding domains of finance, real estate, fossil fuels, corporate law and politics, media, or lobbying. Likewise, those who display this trait are often those who have experienced prior trauma. This is not to say those who have been hurt are bound to hurt others (although we all are, to some degree). It is that those who hold the grimmest whips tend to be those who have themselves been scarred.

I'd also submit that it is those who have become convinced that the only way to survive and thrive is to be on the more comfortable end of the whipping. And that the empire makes use of this drive and those prone to it. And in a very literal sense, the empire *weaponizes* such people and their drives. It manufactures them. Through the exacerbation of machine-like cruelties, it reproduces and disseminates them, from one place to another, from one time to the next.

It might have been Pat who started "Captain Retardo" and "Captain Cripple," but most of us used them at some point. Putting aside the intent of such turns of phrase, they tell us something about those who use them and the communities in which we learn to use them. These are communities where the ability to protect or enrich oneself, in the most practical or macho of ways, is held in highest esteem, and where those incapable of doing so are seen as defective. Their primary worth for others becomes that of punching bag. Or maybe, for training purposes, a stack of bayoneted tires.

Communities like this have existed across cultures and eras. The earth is made of bitter, barren stuff. But empire—the maximal achievement of unjustifiable, organized force—not only guarantees these communities but also cements them as our only fathomable possibility.

We'd headed out to Pasadena. Grubbs was on his sixth Bud. I'd downed three Coronas and now I was working a Bohemia. It was my first, and I liked it. Or maybe I just liked the stocky bottle. I'd always been a sucker for aesthetics.

Bax was at the bar sipping water. He'd turned twenty-one a few months earlier, but I'm not sure it had hit him yet. He was a real mama's boy. We caught him calling his mama during smoke breaks, sometimes because one of us had called him retarded.

Not long before, he'd asked if I supported the state of Israel because I'm Jewish. I told him I didn't know how to answer that. He told me I shouldn't because real Jews, the ones who are religious, take the Quran seriously. And the Quran says the state of Israel shouldn't exist. I told him Jews don't follow the Quran—that's Muslims. We follow the Torah. He said whatever, that's what he meant. I explained that he was thinking about a fringe view among Jewish theologians and scholars, and it wasn't as clear-cut as he was making it out to be. He asked me what "fringe" meant and I said "extreme minority." He said I was wrong and asked for my email address; he wanted to send me a website his mom had shown him about why Jews shouldn't support Israel. I said no thank you. He called me ignorant. That got to me.

Between sips of water, Bax was playing with his straw. He kept bending it every which way and then attaching one end to the other end to make a loop. He'd stare at the loop from different angles, then start all over. Was I sober, it would have been entertaining. But since I had some beer in me, it was hilarious.

A blonde was doing a shot two seats to Bax's left. I considered taking the empty stool and using Bax as my pickup line. *Hey, what's up? Is my little brother bothering you? He's retarded.* But I held off on the idea. It wasn't a good pickup line.

"Hey, man," I said to Grubbs, "look at Bax with his straw."

"Captain Retardo strikes again." We laughed.

"Hey, Bax," Grubbs shouted across the bar. "What's the one continent that's also a country?"

Bax looked over his shoulder with irritation. "What?"

"You heard me, Bax. What's the one continent that's also a country?"

"Why are you asking me this?"

"We're just curious what the answer is, that's all."

"Oh," he said. "It's Asia."

We laughed again, but louder.

"What's so funny?"

"It ain't Asia," Grubbs said. "Want to try again?"

"Oh, that's not what I meant. It's Africa. I thought you said something else."

We laughed some more. Bax was at his funniest when he started digging a hole. I was hoping the blonde would hear and look over.

"One more chance, Bax," I said. "Concentrate, buddy." I could be real condescending when I was drunk. I could be real condescending even when I wasn't drunk.

"China?"

We exhausted whatever laughs we had left.

"Was it a trick question? What was it?"

"Australia, Bax. Australia."

I took a final swig and leapt up to the pool table, where Pearson and Miller, my two favorite marines on base, were shooting pool. Later an older Chicano-looking couple asked if I wanted to go home with them. That was after the man had flicked my dog tags and said they were shit. I said he didn't look too great either. After a tense second he back patted me with a touché twinkle and we spent the rest of the night sweeping the table as a team.

Anyway, they weren't my type. Even if they were I would have been too chickenshit to roll with them.

Regarding the important things, I knew as little as Bax. During another desert excursion, he had taught me how to change a flat. So, in a way he knew more than I did.

Back in Pasadena neither of us knew much of anything. We were conditioned to not know what we'd rather not know. To choose not to know it. And since I was the one with the fancy education, I had less of an excuse.

To remember the worst of living pasts is hard.

When the Nazis—and before them, German administrators in the country's African colonies—searched for precedents for their program, they looked to South Africa. More fruitfully, they looked to indigenous genocide and eugenics in the United States, as well as the country's anti-miscegenation, nationality, and anti-immigrant laws.

To remember the most promising living pasts can prove even harder.

Despite my disdain for Bax's questioning, I had no idea how sizable Jewish opposition to a Jewish state was in 1950s America, or how it wasn't until the late sixties, in the wake of the 1967 Six-Day War, that Zionism, rendered as a key component of Judaism and Jewishness by Jewish leadership, became broadly popular. Or that it was 1976, in San Francisco, when the Reform Jewish establishment in which I would be raised made Israeli-state worship official policy. Or even that, for most of modern Jewish history, many Jewish rabbis, from Reform to Conservative to Orthodox, declared state Zionism a secular nationalist ideology in conflict with the precepts of Jewish theology or Jewish universalism.

I'd read Martin Buber but wasn't familiar with his advocacy of a binational government in Palestine for both Arabs and Jews. I'd never heard of Brit Shalom, the most prominent Jewish organization in favor of such a democratic solution. I knew about Henrietta Szold and her founding of Hadassah, the Women's Zionist Organization of America, but I didn't know she'd called for a binational answer too. I'd yet to come across Hannah Arendt's writings on the subject, or her warning about Jews becoming clients or enforcers of the very powers that had lodged their boots on Jewish necks for centuries. Same went for the hundreds of thousands of communists, socialists, and other working-class Jews in the Pale of Settlement who opposed the colonization of Palestine altogether, and the Bundists who proposed autonomy within the Russian (later Soviet) empire instead.

My dad had told me about his socialist summer camp near the Catskills, Camp Kinder Ring, but I didn't know it was founded by the Workmen's Circle, a Jewish labor organization that many Bundists joined. And if I had, I wouldn't have bothered to know who they were. And if by some quirk I had bothered, I would have dismissed them as a minor curiosity.

I would have done the same for the Black Panthers of Israel, a coalition of Sephardi and Mizrahi leftists in the seventies. They connected dots between their own iron-fisted treatment at the hands of Ashkenazi Israeli elites and the more horrendous management of the Palestinians.

They also saw imperfect parallels with the oppression of blacks and indigenous people in the United States and the exploitation of the disproportionately nonwhite poor across the globe. For them, the Israeli state had become a crucial exploiter, and not just in Israel or Palestine.

I hadn't read Du Bois and Davis and Dunbar-Ortiz. I had yet to take in the discernments of postcolonial leaders like Kwame Nkrumah and Aimé Césaire on how the global capitalist economy perpetuated (rather than broke with) what Du Bois called "the color line—the relation of the darker to the lighter races of men in Asia and Africa, in America and the islands of the sea." I thought the genocide of the American Indians, the enslavement of Africans, and the Jim Crow South were things of the past and refused to entertain the possibility such ghosts were still living. Not only that but, as a certain kind of man, a certain kind of marine, a certain kind of American, and (yes) a certain kind of Jew—a certain kind of white masculine Jew, a Jew whose Judaism and Jewishness had become defined by a longing to think and behave like our historic tormenters—what I was doing was giving those ghosts of death ever more life.

On the off chance I had found myself in a shul again for a dutiful Rosh Hashanah or Yom Kippur, I would have recited the prayer for the state of Israel without qualm. I would have done the same for the prayer right beside it, the prayer for the United States.

I could go on drawing lines from one era of domination to the next, as long as the annals of empire, all the way up to Pax Americana—and not just among those ruling classes who chose to be white men. The history of humanity is, to a paralyzing extent, a history of conquest. But it is the oppressive systems of self-anointed white men that have taken over the world in which we now live.

Understanding that world means understanding the imperialisms of "the West," that delicate but prickly flower that has always stood in as a euphemism for the superior world, the reigning world: White Mankind.

Who: Ximena. Latasian. Half Bolivian. Half Asian. Filipina? Indonesian? Thai? You would think I'd have known the difference, but I didn't.

What: Fuck.

Where: Chicken Ranch. A brothel in Pahrump, Nevada. An hour out from Vegas.

When: Some long holiday weekend.

Why: Why the fuck not?

I'd been drinking the entire weekend with Miller, Grubbs, and the recovering heroin addict, Harrison, who was from the area. We'd swung by his hometown, neighborhood made up of anonymous cubes, bordered by nothing but sand, on the way to Sin City. It seemed poor, although coming from wealth made everything look poor. Harrison's family appeared wary of him. He might have passed the drug test, but he was still using before he made it to the yellow footprints in San Diego (the depot for the West Coasters) and had left home on bad terms.

We'd pooled our resources and crashed at the Bellagio the first night. The next night we hit the casino and club circuit while Harrison, who was underage, went off on his own. When we returned around 0100, Harrison was missing, and by 0300 we were awakened by a biblical knock and two security guards. Harrison sat in the wheelchair between them, his bloodshot eyeballs veering backward, speaking incoherently. The muscles had found him on a balcony, threatening to jump. A crowd had coalesced below. The duo talked him down and found a chow hall card from the Palms base in his pocket. One of them had served in the Corps, and were it not for that discovery, they would have called the cops. Instead, with help from the front desk, they tracked down the room with the marines and delivered our prodigal son free of charge. They even threw in a hearty *oorah.*

The next day the man of the hour reassured us he wasn't suicidal and it was all a blackout joke, courtesy of Jack Daniels. We believed him enough to scorn him for his irresponsibility—we didn't scorn ourselves for ours—and were off to Pahrump in the crap rental to celebrate the near miss. Once we made it to the Ranch, Harrison, still underage, waited outside.

The Ranch evoked a nineteenth-century frontier holdout, a Twilight Zone inhabitance thronged with spirits. A dodo dressed up as sheriff guarded the gates, and after much ado about all three of us joining in the approach, Grubbs stayed back with Harrison. He was out of cash.

It was me and Miller.

Draped with ornate wallpaper and outback society portraiture, the interior reeked of gun-toting musk. Two Mexicans sat beside us on a velvety couch, waiting for the fifteen options to arrive. The Madam intervened every five minutes to assure us they were coming. I nibbled at my fingernails. At one point I turned to Miller and told him I couldn't do it. He told me I was doing it.

When the lineup arrived, we both eyed the same prize.

"Okay, go ahead, pick one," said the Madam.

"Should I go first, ma'am?" said Miller.

"You best be," said the Madam.

Miller pointed at Ximena, the twenty-something one. She strolled up and reached out. That was it. They were gone.

"Your turn, hon," said the Madam.

"I'll pass for now, ma'am," I said.

She turned to the man on my left.

"Okay, your turn, chief."

"I pass, too," he said.

"And you?" she asked the final patron. He pointed to one of the older women. They made their exit.

For a few minutes I wallowed in my guilt. I'd been to strip joints, some that played fast and loose with the rules. I'd felt guilty then, too. It's not that I believed sex work was immoral or beneath me. It was that I sensed, even then, such scenes—sex work aside—spoke to larger cruelties I was still too self-interested to name.

For a moment I considered the possibility I shouldn't feel guilty at all since all I was doing was availing myself of a velvety couch.

"Hey, darling."

It was Ximena. I was clenching my fingers, my eyes to the deck. I looked up.

"Hey…what's up?"

"What's up is your friend over there doesn't have enough cash."

I peeked at a blushing Miller.

Ximena eyed my cock. "Can I sit on your lap?"

"Sure." She sat on it.

"Your friend says *you* have cash."

"I do."

"What do you want, sweetie?"

"Umm…what can you give me?"

"Everything but the sex, four hundred. Eight hundred for everything." She wiggled.

"Wow, that's steep."

"It'll be worth it, I promise." She wiggled again.

Usually this step in a relationship is marked by some sense of accomplishment. But when you fork over hundreds to make it happen, there's no win. At best, it's a draw.

The bedroom continued the theme of anachronism. The lamp fixtures were ancient and the lighting medieval. Nevertheless, atop the secretary sat a CD player.

"What kind of music you like?"

"Oh, almost everything.…Should I take off my clothes? How does this work?"

"R&B it is."

She bent over to put it in.

"You can start taking off your clothes now, honey. We need to do the dick check."

"Dick check?"

She laughed. "Yeah, regulations."

I disclosed it, worried she might find something she didn't like.

"Looks clean."

She pushed me down on the mattress so she could climb on top. She undressed me, button by button, piece by piece. I remember her waxing me over with a spermicide, but that doesn't make sense. I remember the gel smelling sweet. I remember the half-hour massage and the wrapping of my prick. I remember the hand job and the blow job and her insistence on the whole job.

Somehow I resisted.

She cajoled me. Milked me with compliments.

We talked New York. We inquired, however gingerly, how we both got here. It was complicated, but she needed the money and I wanted the sex.

She said she had to stay on the property for months at a time. Per regulations, only way to make sure no one picks up STDs along the way. It was all right, she said, plus, the money was good.

When I made it back to the parking lot Grubbs was smoking a cig out the passenger window. Miller was perched on the front of the car with his legs hanging free. Harrison was asleep in the back seat.

Ximena told me she'd once appeared in *Hustler.* I wanted to confirm this on my LG Chocolate, but no longer had my LG Chocolate. Harrison had removed it from its charger during his blackout, never to be seen again. I did verify Ximena's appearance when I made it back to base. And I boasted about it for months, for years.

I bought a new LG Chocolate.

I'd often switch up the details when I bragged about Ximena. One day she was Bolivian. The next Filipina, Indonesian, or Thai. All places marked by American imperialism. I didn't know her ethnicity, nor was I all that interested in knowing. For me she was an exotic object that I could bandy about for shits and giggles. Most of us availed ourselves of these objects at one point or another. Sometimes they were a prostitute or a stripper. Other times they were a one-night stand, a crazy but wild girlfriend, a freaky ex-wife. In time I came to spot resemblances between how marines talked about these sexual experiences and how they talked about their deployments. I even came to see the latter as just a scaled-up version of the former. Instead of a single person, we'd objectify entire peoples and places.

A direct line runs from US involvement in the slaughter of at least five hundred thousand civilians in Indonesia in 1965 to 1966 (all suspected leftists) to kindred US-backed extermination campaigns, coups, and other harmful interventions across the planet. This includes operations in Bolivia and the Philippines, as well as in Argentina, Brazil, Chile, Colombia, East Timor, El Salvador, Guatemala, Honduras, Iraq, Mexico, Nicaragua, Paraguay, South Korea, Sudan, Taiwan, Thailand, Uruguay, Venezuela, Vietnam, Cambodia, and Afghanistan.

Vegas became a repeated destination spot. Sometimes I'd stop by with marines. Sometimes with other friends from my past. It is said to have become America's Sin City in 1906, ever since it became a city of gambling, prostitution, and booze. But starting in the 1950s, for the next decade or so, it went by another name: Atomic City.

By 1951, six years after the United States claimed the lives of tens of thousands in Hiroshima and Nagasaki—becoming the first and only government to deploy nuclear weapons against fellow human beings—the US Atomic Energy Commission began testing such weapons sixty-five miles out from the gambling, the prostitution, and the booze. The Las Vegas Chamber of Commerce lobbied for the nickname of Atomic City. Miss Atomic pageants sprung up. The Sky Room restaurant advertised its Atomic Cocktails and the best aerial view of the mushroom clouds. The municipal government embraced the tests as a veritable tourist attraction.

In 1963, the Partial Nuclear Test Ban Treaty mandated the tests be moved underground. Untold numbers had already been exposed to the fallout.

A bipartisan Senate resolution in 1994, on a 99–1 vote, declared "the role of the *Enola Gay* during World War II was momentous in helping to bring World War II to a merciful end, which resulted in saving the lives of Americans and Japanese."

The resolution was used by those in power to suppress scholarship arguing the bombs had far more devastating effects than a potential invasion of Japan would have had, and that the United States wasn't considering an invasion either way. Some historians argued Japan was defeated and prepared to surrender as early as July, and it was the Soviet entry in the Pacific war on August 9 that played the decisive role in Japan's unconditional surrender. These findings, which made their way into a script for the National Air and Space Museum's *Enola Gay* exhibit, are what prompted the Senate to call them "revisionist and offensive to many World War II veterans."

Neither Truman nor his advisers, it seems, ever gave much thought to *not* using the bomb. They appeared to welcome the prospect, above all else as a striking gambit in their expectant cold war with the Soviets. According to the historian Gar Alperovitz, they figured the bomb's devastating impact would discourage their imminent adversary from aggressions in Europe and Asia. In fact, Truman had rejected a proposal to gather the UN's representatives for a "demonstration" of the bomb on an isolated island or in a far-off desert. He rejected this far more humane option in a matter of ten minutes during lunch.

Air Force general Curtis LeMay was the architect of the "strategic bombing" doctrine—the mass targeting of noncombatants, specifically industrial workers, designed to decimate enemy logistics and morale. The doctrine had come straight from Mussolini's air commissioner, Giulio Douhet. As late as 1943, plenty of US air officers still considered Britain's indiscriminate air raids of German cities barbaric, echoing President Roosevelt's words four years before about the savagery of targeting urban areas. But by 1945, General George Marshall was itching to "set the paper cities of Japan on fire."

This was the same time LeMay was asking his weather officer how strong the wind had to be "so that people can't get away from the flames." He followed up, "Will the wind be strong enough for that?" LeMay continued to lead from the highest reaches of the US government under Presidents Truman, Eisenhower, Kennedy, and Johnson, all of whom had faith that such a man would carry out his responsibilities with utmost integrity as commander of the Strategic Air Command and then as chief of staff of the US Air Force.

Humans have been normalizing such violence for centuries, at least since mass killing and policing machines first came on the scene. Americans, however, have forged a proud identity around it.

A decade and a half ago, during my ten months stationed at the Palms, I had yet to read or write or even think about such things.

But I was feeling them.

In 1848, toward the end of the US war in Mexico, Sam Houston, the former president of the Republic of Texas, riled up a crowd in New York City by claiming all of Mexico as an American "birthright." It was the job of the US government to "take it," as the *New York Herald* had written the year before, on the assumption Mexico would "learn to love her ravishers."

Tom Friedman, in an interview with Charlie Rose in 2003, at the onset of the Iraq War, echoed these sentiments. Iraq was begging for Americans to "take out a very big stick...and burst [its] bubble." Iraq claimed to care for a "balance of power" and claimed all we cared about were our "stock options and hummers."

"That, Charlie, was what this war was about. We could have hit Saudi Arabia. It was part of that bubble. We could have hit Pakistan. We hit Iraq because we could. That's the real truth."

For every passionate opponent of the American intervention in Mexico like Frederick Douglass or Henry David Thoreau, there were tenfold more Sam Houstons. For every dissenter against the post-9/11 wars, there were a hundredfold more Tom Friedmans.

In the Tactical Data Systems Administration course, we worked through a stack of stapled tracts, of various thickness, each with its own cover color with the same lame air wing graphics of a jet or chopper

I couldn't name and titles like "Unix Essentials I Lab Workbook" or "Theater Battle Management Core System—Annex H."

The quizzes included prompts and questions like "Describe a dumb terminal" and "What is a shell?"

Once I wrote a damn good paper titled "Network Research Paper 2."

> Imagine a postapocalyptic world rife with anarchy. All great cities have been burned to the ground, all great books burned to oblivion, and a good portion of the earth's human population burned out of existence.... You have managed to find a safe haven in the woods, seemingly isolated.... Except from one man, a middle man, a man of great courage, but most of all a man you can trust.... And what name does this man go by? Firewall.

We did PT as a class on Mondays, Wednesdays, and Fridays from 1530 to 1630 (winter hours) or from 0530 to 0630 (summer hours). We were given "Liberty out of bounds" handouts to make sure we knew where we weren't allowed to go on weekends or more extended liberty periods. It looked like one of those earthquake epicenter maps emanating outward in concentric circles.

Whenever we took long liberties or leave, we completed Operational Risk Assessment worksheets that went something like this:

Major Steps: Drive to San Diego

Sub-Steps: Eat dinner with family, prepare barbecue

List Hazards: Fall asleep at the wheel...food poisoning

Develop Controls: Stop every hour and a half of driving... thoroughly cook meat

How to Implement: Pull over at rest stops...eat well-done meat

When the seven of us graduated in the late summer of 2007, most were lance coolies, proud members of the lance corporal underground. We posed for photographs on top of a rusted M1 Abrams tank, not too far off from where we had wilted in the schoolhouse.

A schoolhouse instructor took the shots above the tank. At the end everyone but Mason withdrew their blouses and olive drab tees. We flexed and sparkled, yet no one seemed at ease. Bax and Pearson emerged as the two with the strapping chests, although their shoulders slouched inward as if ashamed. Peach stood on the turret with an expression suggesting he'd plopped on hot coals. Pat was leaning so far back it looked like he was about to fall. Grubbs and I were also slouching. Mason came off as the most relaxed of the bunch, smoking a cig in the center like James Dean. Even she betrayed a nervous grin.

In Afghanistan a fellow officer informed me of the derogatory origins of the word "coolie." Europeans in the nineteenth century shipped in Asian and Indian "coolies" to plantations previously worked by slaves. They were the peons, the post–Civil War sharecroppers of the South, those paid just enough to keep working and nothing more. No benefits. No protections. No futures.

The M1 Abrams tank was named after Creighton Abrams, the golden-boy general of Indochina. He was a trailblazer in the implementation of counterinsurgency theory and led the troop drawdown during the Nixon years. One of the great prosecutors of a new kind of war all about "winning hearts and minds" had a tank named after him.

Abrams reviled war profiteers just as he did pointy-headed advisers. He rounded out his life and career as the Army's chief of staff all the same. And his downsizing in Vietnam was no innocent affair. He played a leading part in expanding the war into Laos and Cambodia, and the blood of Operation Menu belonged on his hands.

Leah reached out to me a couple months after I settled in the Mojave Desert for MCCES. She was living in Washington, DC, at the time, working as a production assistant for a television news show. A few texts followed a brief email exchange, and then I got a ring. I waited three vibrations before picking up.

"So hey," she said.

"Hey."

I don't think I'd heard her voice since we'd run into each other jogging around a reservoir in Atlanta, months after our breakup. There was one email from her after boot camp, but it had been over a year and a half since I'd heard her voice.

"You still there?" I asked.

"I'm here."

She had been planning a trip to Los Angeles to see a couple people, and I made clear I'd find a way to be there the same holiday weekend she was. We arranged it so I could also see my parents and extended family on my father's side, who would be in town for unrelated reasons.

I wanted to say I was ready now. I'd grown up. I loved her. But to avoid scaring her away before even getting to see her, I kept it businesslike. I presumed she was strategizing along similar lines, but neither of us said so.

Instead I said, "All righty then, so you got the flight?"

It was a surreal series of reunions. So much complicated history wrapped into a brisk interval. I rented a Ford F-150 at the base Enterprise. It was the cheapest vehicle on offer. It might have been the only vehicle on offer. Either way it made a dent in my $1,500 of monthly pay. I drove the three hours to LA and had dinner with my mom, who was attending a healthcare conference. The next day our big happy extended family dashed up and down the California coast, from LA to San Luis Obispo and back.

On occasions like that, when everything felt so far from threatening, I doubted whether it had ever been any different. There ought to be a word not so much for unconditional love, which implies a preordained contract, but for the perennial state of confusion that befalls someone when they attempt to make sense of their relationships with those who have done so much to shape them.

Leah and I met up for an afternoon coffee. I had yet to learn how to clean up nice. My jeans were baggy, my Under Armour hoodie too shiny, too purple. I realized I should have asked the base barber for the low fade instead of the medium. I had made sure I'd not shaved since leaving the Palms so I had more than a little five o'clock shadow, which was one of the only things going for me.

As for Leah, she hadn't changed in the slightest. She wore a simple navy blue top with her usual variety of skirt, nonflashy and cute, and her droopy handbag rested on her shoulder. It stretched the full length of her torso and then some, and its winsomeness charmed me.

We embraced for a fleeting second and I offered to order for the two of us. When I came back with our cups, she was smiling.

"What's up? Are you not entertained?" I said, throwing out a clumsy *Gladiator* reference, though she didn't seem to mind.

"I'm enjoying your walk."

"Different than my old walk?"

"Sorta. It's hard to explain. I think it's a Marine thing."

She had tucked her bag in the booth. She'd had something similar back in college, and I loved it then, too. I don't know why.

We passed stories about our coworkers. She gave me updates on her Emory friends and I gave her updates on mine. She poked fun at my Neanderthal politics and I promised her I wasn't so bad anymore.

"I'm just not as confident as I once was. I guess that's it. I've moved from overconfidence to something else."

"Plain, underserving confidence?"

"Touché," I said. "More like confusion. And I'm finding that confusion both welcoming and not welcoming."

"Confused about what?"

"Everything. But mostly I'd say about what I'm doing as a marine. And what marines like me are doing in Iraq and Afghanistan and wherever else we are. Everything just seems like more of a mess than it used to."

Leah told me about her stint teaching English in Hong Kong and her solo travels in the Pacific. She'd always known the United States had its problems, but seeing how other governments ran things really opened her eyes to how bad we have it. And how Americans, along with maybe Australians, are the worst tourists.

I told her about OCS and boot camp. I toned it down, but I still wanted her to know I was hurting in ways I hadn't been back in college. That OCS had fucked me up but also in a way humbled me and forced me to start seeing things about myself and others I hadn't seen before.

"Like what?" she asked.

"Like the way I talk with my friends and they talk with me. We can be assholes, and in ways that I think speak to broader stuff going on."

"Such as?"

"I don't know. Like society and shit."

"Brilliant insight, Lyle."

We read the *Times* together in our radiant alcove, and we both wished that it could be that way till the day we died, though we didn't say it at the time. That day in LA, the closest I got was by way of a farewell kiss on the forehead.

I was at a crossroads that had me moving in opposing directions. In one direction I was approaching my mid-twenties, out of college, and growing up. The Marines, for all its harms, was sucking the charmed life out of me, pressing me to come to grips with the unequal society that had afforded me that life, and on whose backs it had done so. It was humbling me. This was the beginning of a protracted transformation, and Leah picked it out and figured it was enough to give us a second try.

In the weeks ahead we talked on the phone for hours a night. We had our first post-LA rendezvous in Scottsdale and Sedona, courtesy of another F-150. We visited the Palatki cliff dwellings. Snapped photographs of the ancient homes of the Sinagua from a distance. We ate at El Rincon, the best Arizona-style Mexican joint in the northern Verde Valley. We spent a night and early morning on a hotel room carpet, drinking a bottle of Malbec and stripping off our garments one by one.

The next morning we took selfies of Leah sitting on my lap at the foot of the bed, each of us making faces. That same morning we had our first major fight since getting back together. Earlier I had ditched the condoms and pulled out instead. I told Leah what I wanted to do, and she didn't object. But since she hadn't been on birth control because it made her sick, we both got anxious afterward and went searching for Plan B. I thought what I had done was fine, that we had both agreed to it. She said that if I was responsible I would have never suggested the idea in the first place. I raised my voice, and it went on from there.

In the weeks and months ahead, a further fury was unleashed. I went from hugs and kisses and comforting words to something like my worst, least generous reconstructions of Dad. I was playing out the classic, intergenerational repetition compulsion between father and son. I wasn't physical like my old man could be, and not only because Leah and I were in a long-distance relationship. I just didn't have that side of him. But I could still be mean.

I told Leah she was too weak and docile to excel in her journalism career. I told her she moped and whined too much. That she was holding me back. From what, I didn't say, but I suspect it was my right as a man to be a man as defined by men like me. If you were to ask me now, I'd say it was my unregulated right to regulate. That I had assured myself of this right while conforming to one of the most regulated institutions on the planet did not occur to me.

My misogyny kept accumulating with the momentum along with my gentleness. I'd swing from one extreme to the other. And in some deep way, it was the gentleness I feared most. I had been running away from it for so long. The empathy in me, the part that could descry even the subtlest doubts in others, was being remolded into a dagger. And whenever I felt Leah was asking too much of me, asking me to relinquish too much of the protective antagonism I had done so much to acquire, I wielded that inverted empathy against her.

It was only a matter of time before even my fantasies took on a sharper edge.

Me fucking her with another marine in the room watching.

The other marine fucking her with me watching.

Two marines fucking her.

Three and four and five...

Every marine everywhere fucking her while I watched.

Once we lost control, she'd start shrieking and I'd sob with her. I'd never push like that again, I'd say. We'd agree to controlled parameters. We'd violate the controlled parameters. After the next fight, I'd bitch to my college posse about how Leah was inciting me to hate women. I'd yowl about her irrational, contradictory demands and her cunning, rail against the feminization of politics.

The desert, the desolation, the Corps—the same environment that was awakening me to so many of my society's ills was also inuring me to them. The double pull would eventually lead to a creative tension, but in the Palms it just led to scraps with roommates and heartache for the person I loved.

Before the Corps I could tell myself whatever I liked about the United States and believe it, in large part because I had never seen it. I had passed through it or nearby it or over it, by way of roads and highways and rail tracks and jet streams. The Corps obliged me to lift my standard-issue blinders and really see it, even though it had always been around me, beside or below me, even affixed to me and everyone I knew, a squadron of swirling phantoms.

PART FOUR

BEST AND BRIGHTEST

It is a beautiful country because you are still breathing.

—Ocean Vuong

You can toss a George Washington quarter, Thomas Jefferson nickel, Abraham Lincoln penny, Franklin Roosevelt dime—a fleck of dust—at a map of the United States and be certain it lands somewhere visited by a grave crime. It doesn't matter the size of the map or how one defines a crime that is grave. Few would dispute that any of its definitions include mass bondage, exploitation, desecration, starvation, pillage, rape, torture, murder, ethnic cleansing, and genocide. And these injustices have been committed on every inch of the United States, spanning centuries, chugging along to the present.

Surely this can be said about any territory on any map, disparagers might say. Much of that crime was committed by the British, French, Dutch, Spanish, Mexican, and indigenous themselves, they might add. Learned critics, perhaps, will insist that even the Marxist Walter Benjamin conceded there "is no document of civilization which is not at the same time a document of barbarism." What they would be leaving out is Benjamin's upshot:

> A historical materialist therefore dissociates himself from [barbarism] as far as possible. He regards it as his task to brush history against the grain.

What one discovers when they brush the history of the United States against the grain is that its ruling classes, with the help of too many of its less charmed admirers, have proven themselves exceptionally adept at the barbarism. Which is why, to a large but by no means complete degree, the United States has managed to achieve such reputed heights of civilized greatness.

Upon completing my final comms course in the Palms in the summer of 2007, I returned to Bloomfield as a reservist and set to work regaining a fall spot at OCS. I mustered for a single reservist drill weekend at Westover Air Base, outside Springfield, Massachusetts. The base had been built in preparation of World War II, in a town called Chicopee—translated from its original Nipmuc as either "of cedar" or "violent waters."

Twenty minutes down the road from the air base resided the Springfield Armory National Historic Site. Founded as a settler bastion during King Philip's War, the armory played a pivotal role in arming the revolutionaries during their war of independence, arming the Americans against the revanchist British during the War of 1812, and arming the Unionists during the Civil War.

The armory also marks the spot of the decisive 1787 battle that defeated Shays' Rebellion, when over a thousand disgruntled farmers in western Massachusetts attempted to capture the arsenal and overturn the new national government. Many were exploited soldiers who had been paid little for their battle-hardened service. All were being forced to defray war debts that ought to have been covered by a rising, urban bourgeoisie poised to profit amid the financing and building of the new state.

Thomas Jefferson, to the dismay of many of his fellow founders, famously remarked of the revolt, "The tree of liberty must be refreshed from time to time with the blood of patriots & tyrants." He spoke similarly about the French Revolution, when he wrote in 1793 that the "liberty of the whole earth was depending on the issue of the contest, and was ever such a prize won with so little innocent blood?" And when an uprising against a regressive whiskey tax blazed across western Pennsylvania from 1791 to 1794, Jefferson again sympathized with the downtrodden rebels, who in this instance also doubled as proud but aggrieved Indian hunters. The Virginia patriarch, boss of slave-driving lash hands—a plantation slaveowner of great wealth who refused to emancipate the bulk of the enslaved people under his charge—and rapist,* seemed to have retained a soft spot for a certain kind of radical to the very end. As late as July 11, 1816, the then former president, in a letter to the lawyer Samuel Kercheval, composed an eloquent if baffling ode to progress:

> Some men look at constitutions with sanctimonious reverence, and deem them like the ark of the covenant, too sacred to be touched.... I am certainly not an advocate for frequent and untried changes in laws and constitutions.... But I know also, that laws and institutions must go hand in hand with the progress of the human mind.... We might as well require a man to wear still the coat which fitted him when a boy, as civilized society to remain ever under the regimen of their barbarous ancestors.

If I'm going to expound on the evils of the empire, I should also make the concomitant claim: one can tell a different story about where that coin lands, about what the United States and the world could have been, at times almost seemed in the process of becoming, and still might become. This story is more ambiguous and fraught with contradictions. Most patriots have told something like it, time and again, to better obscure or rationalize evils than to overcome them. But if told in

*It's impossible to know what affections existed between Jefferson and Sally Hemings, but sexual relations between an owner and his property cannot reasonably be conceived as anything other than rape.

a way that still runs against the grain, still demands a thorough reckoning, it, too, should be told.

In 1843 the celebrity poet Henry Wadsworth Longfellow penned "The Arsenal at Springfield." When prefiguring a world beyond armories and war, he wrote:

The warrior's name would be a name abhorred!
And every nation, that should lift again
Its hand against a brother, on its forehead
Would wear forevermore the curse of Cain!

Longfellow was a confidant of future senator Charles Sumner, and both became critics of America's war in Mexico. Longfellow likely also agreed with his friend's assessment that the war was just as much about expanding slavery as it was about conquering the West.

Although each would celebrate the day the dream of abolition became a reality, neither could have departed with much faith concerning their nation's ongoing militarism. According to the arsenal's former commanding officer Colonel MacFarland, by the time Longfellow set his anti-war verse to paper, the Springfield Armory had already supplied US troops with Model 1795 muskets during the Indian wars in the Ohio country and the Indiana territory throughout the early republican era, the war in Tripoli, the antebellum Seminole Wars, and the Black Hawk War of 1832. In the coming years it would do the same for the war in Mexico, while the Springfield Model 1873 rifle was unleashed against the Apache and Sioux (among others) throughout the latter decades of the century. During the century's turn, the armory's Krag rifles would cause further havoc for outmatched Indians and, during the Spanish-American War, many unlucky inhabitants of Cuba and the Philippines as well.

Springfield Armory's manufacturing might—a model for industrial organization across America's emergent high-efficiency economy—became responsible for the mass use of the M1903 rifle during the First World War, the M1 rifle during Second World War and the war in Korea, the M1903 again in Korea (this time as a sniper rifle), and the M14 rifle in Vietnam. In 1964 the military released the M16, thus replacing the M14 as the nation's standard-issue rifle and Springfield Amory as the country's indispensable arms producer.

Colt's Manufacturing Company produced the new weapon, and Secretary of Defense Robert McNamara, one of John F. Kennedy's original "Best and Brightest" advisers and, before then, the top "whiz kid" executive at Ford Motor Company, quietly shuttered the famous federal armory during the worldwide revolutionary spring of 1968. As young people demanded a more just and equal world, McNamara took a significant leap toward a future of privatized, subcontracted war.

Samuel Colt had staked a name for himself as the inventor of the six-shooter, the "gun that won the West." The revolver had helped the Texas Rangers triumph in their war with Mexico and, after that, assisted settlers across the western territories in their related conquests. He raised enough capital from the sales to start an arms company in his hometown of Hartford in 1855, and from then on, Colt made its slow and unsteady climb to glory, culminating in its government contracting coup in the sixties.

By 1994, however, the same summer I was getting ready for King Philip Middle, the company had fallen on hard times. The end of the Cold War hadn't treated its profit margins kindly, and in 1990 its laborers won a four-year strike that resulted in them gaining partial ownership of the corporation. To cut costs while still maintaining decent wages and protections for its workforce, Colt consolidated its operations in its West Hartford location, a five-minute drive from my family's new home on the other side of town.

As an eleven-year-old, I wasn't keeping tabs on any of this. If any thought crossed my mind when I heard the word "Colt," it was of the giant blue and gold-starred Hershey Kiss dome crowning the original factory building off I-95. Maybe the mysterious golden horse atop it, rearing up.

By 1998 Colt was suffering yet another spell of financial hardship, this time because gun owners across America were boycotting the company after its CEO supported a permit policy for national gun ownership that required training and testing. Business roared back in the early 2000s, though, thanks to the auspicious start of the War on Terror. Vietnam War hero and Marine general William Morgan Keys took charge and returned Colt to the center of the global arms industry.

Even then, though, a more competitive market would challenge Colt's primacy, and in 2021 it would be acquired by a Czech company for $220 million. Around the same period, the standard-issue rifle for infantry marines switched from Colt's M4 carbine to the M27 infantry automatic rifle (IAR) produced by Heckler & Koch, a defense company based in Germany.

I served two drill weekends with my Chicopee reserve unit. We conducted annual quals for the gas chamber and combat marksmanship training, and I got lost during a night land-nav exercise. When not twiddling my thumbs as an accidental reservist, I was making sure all loose knots were tied for OCS. A government employee named Mr. Asman (whom I called MISTER ACE-MAN to avoid calling him MISTER ASS-MAN) helped me put my application together.

Mr. Asman was a former combat engineer and what marines like to call a real hard charger. He spoke with regular splashes of "Err!" and "Good to go!" or "Semper Fidelis!" and his email signature went as follows:

> "Before God, I swear this creed, my rifle and myself are the defenders of my country, the master's [*sic*] of my enemy, the saviour [*sic*] of my life. So be it! Until victory is America's and there is no enemy but peace."
>
> Marine Corps Rifleman's Creed 3rd verse
>
> GOD COUNTRY CORPS

A week and a half before shipping off to OCS, I flew down to South Florida to visit my dad's side of the family. I went to Rosh Hashanah services with my aunt, uncle, and cousin and schmoozed with their friends when not at the shul. The last time I had done anything Jewish was with Morgan the previous fall, but I'd lost touch with the born-again Sephardi thereafter. The closest thing to Jewishness then became chatting with Micah. It was nice to be back in a house of worship, if only because it made me feel like I had God back on my side.

My cousin was beginning college at University of Florida. He, like his older sister, had gotten a free ride there on account of the Bright Futures Scholarship Program. The scholarship was merit-based, meaning it favored white students from wealthy school districts. It was also funded by the Florida lottery, meaning it was funded by the poor.

I felt older than him, so much more practiced, even though I wasn't. I was cocky and self-assured, even though, at a deeper register, I wasn't. But my cousin looked at me like I was. Years later I asked him if my becoming a marine had any impact on him deciding to become a cop. He said it did, probably.

Scuzz brush to the bulkhead, he says. Aye aye, candidate platoon sergeant, we say. Scuzz brush to the bulkhead, he says. Aye aye, candidate platoon sergeant, we say. Scuzz brush to the bulkhead, he says. Aye aye, candidate platoon sergeant, we say. Five, four, three, two, one, zero, he says. Freeze, candidate, freeze, we say. Clean the squad bay, he says. Clean the squad bay, aye, aye, candidate platoon sergeant, we say. Ready, he says. Move, he says. Kill, we say. Kill.

Quantico marks the anglicized word for *Pamacocack*, which marks the Doeg word for "by the long stream." According to the historical society of Dumfries, "the Oldest Chartered Town in Virginia," the first settler building constructed in Quantico was the Quantico Church, a satellite church or "Chapel of Ease." It was erected sometime around 1667, and by the 1700s the tobacco cultivations of enslaved people had made many of their enslavers in the area quite rich.

Before then, poor European colonists had survived as the indentured servants of such plantation owners, but when their rulers embraced the mass import of African slave labor as a cheaper alternative, they bolted westward in search of free land. These searches became violent the moment they began, seeing as such land was already occupied by numerous Algonquian tribes. Colonial governor William Berkeley, fearful of another conflict on par with King Philip's War, tried to rein in the aggressions of the settlers, only to be met by further defiance. In 1676 the wealthy landowner Nathaniel Bacon led an armed revolt of European and African laborers (free, indentured, and enslaved) against Berkeley's government. In response to plummeting tobacco prices and regressive taxation, the workers demanded the full-scale conquest of the indigenous and their possessions.

Although Bacon fell to dysentery and Berkeley succeeded in suppressing the rebellion not long after, the specter of working-class solidarity shook the landowning elite to the bone. Jefferson would later hail the event as a harbinger of the American Revolution, but in the decades attending the insurrection, the ruling class in Virginia passed laws bolstering the power of slavers and criminalizing escaped slaves. They introduced newfangled racial distinctions in the courts, labor markets, and society at large. Those Africans deemed "black" were no longer allowed to employ those Europeans considered "white," no matter their status as enslaved or free. Those belonging to this new category of black people could no longer own guns. Social mingling with this caste became stigmatized, just as prosperous landowners in the royal government cajoled their less fortunate but freshly inducted brethren with white-only headright land grants and white-only support in their crusades against nonwhite Indians.

The strategy was intended to drive wedges between subjugated peoples, and it worked. A majority of those now understood as white came to see their own successes as contingent on the successes of their white betters. By the same token, they came to perceive the successes of those now understood as nonwhite as a threat. In both the lead-up to and aftermath of America's war of independence, this alliance between rich and poor whites stymied cross-racial challenges to an emboldened ruling class not only below the Mason-Dixon Line but also in the seaport towns of Boston, New York, and Philadelphia. The same dynamic repeated itself across the country during the early trade unionist agitations of the antebellum period and the urban and rural radicalisms that followed the Civil War and Reconstruction in the South. The alliance has reared its ugly head many times since, including during the Progressive Era, the New Deal stretch from the thirties to the seventies, and the past half century of bipartisan plutocracy.

At every turn and against all odds, multiracial coalitions have proven more common, resilient, and effective, even if such cooperation has failed to stop the next iteration of racist backlash and capitalist consolidation. But at no point have such partnerships solidified across national borders and between the Global North and South to an extent necessary to reverse international capital's ever-tightening stranglehold. For all the progress made in breaking down barriers within the domestic United States, the bulk of Americans remain disposed to rallying more behind their own national elites than behind their counterparts in Africa, the Middle East, Asia, the Pacific, and Latin America. In that sense, the bargain lives on in ways that implicate more than just the most obvious of bigots.

During the Revolutionary War, Quantico housed a state militia, but by the early 1800s it had become a ghost town. The war had disrupted tobacco markets, and siltation combined with overcultivation had destroyed what remained of regional trade. The area was revived somewhat when Confederates encamped there during the Civil War, leaving hospitals and cemeteries in their wake. The introduction of the Richmond, Fredericksburg and Potomac Railroad helped to reenergize the local economy some, too, as well as a mini–mining boom in "fool's gold" during the fin de siècle. Hundreds were employed on account of it, including members of the nearby free black community of

Batestown (named after the freed slave and community leader Mary Bates). Quantico became a day-trip destination for beachgoers and tourists from Richmond and Washington, on top of a fishing haven and naval shipbuilding yard. But it wasn't until the establishment of the Marine Corps base in 1917 that the quiet alcove along the Potomac River earned its spot on the map.

As the twentieth century unfolded, Quantico would become the home of the Marine Corps University, the FBI and DEA academies, the Defense Intelligence Agency, the Naval Criminal Investigative Service (of prime-time *NCIS* fame), and a jumble of other schools and units, including OCS. The exponential growth of the military-industrial complex during the Cold War and War on Terror would make Quantico, along with all of Northern Virginia, a hotbed of rarefied powerbroker politics, palace intrigue, and sprawling meritocracy.

As I had in the winter of 2006, back at OCS in fall 2007 I bear crawled with my scuzz brush countless times. By the end of each session, the full length of my body, from the hamstrings to the shoulders to the core, was crying out for relief. Sometimes it was the hats giving the orders. Sometimes fellow candidates. It didn't matter. The pain couldn't tell the difference.

Quantico shares with Parris Island a passion for pain. And like the Island, that passion often overflows into less welcome and more intimate domains. The Corps has always prepared for the physical costs of such training. Its bases are well staffed with a variety of medical professionals, and most injuries are baked into their estimate planning. Leadership has also improved when it comes to anticipating mental health contingencies. But by the very nature of the institution, an accounting of the military's psychic burden can only go so far.

On the first Spring Thursday of 2013, long after I had departed the Officer Candidate School on Brown Field for good, a tactics instructor at the school shot dead two of his peers before taking his own life. He'd been afflicted with traumatic brain injury and post-traumatic stress disorder symptoms since dodging an IED explosion on a foot-mobile mission in Iraq in 2007 and having his vehicle hit by a roadside bomb in Afghanistan in 2011. The twenty-five-year-old machine-gunner had recently separated from his wife and was crushed by his onetime nineteen-year-old girlfriend's relationship with another twenty-three-year-old marine. Following an inebriated night in town and a spree of pitiable text messages to his ex (e.g., "See u on the other side... im out," "U could have saved me"), he returned to the barracks and killed them both. According to the *News Leader*, a paper based in Staunton, Virginia, a military investigation concluded the killer shouldn't have had access to his personal handgun on base and shouldn't have been transferred from North Carolina to Quantico for instruction duty in the first place. He should have stayed at his prior station and received intensive mental health care. If all such protocols had been followed, it is less likely the killer would have killed.

CNN began its March 23, 2013, report, days after the killing, with "They were three young Marines, decorated with awards and with seemingly bright futures ahead."

Candidate Bartels, a Virginia Military Institute grad, signaled that golden cross between toughest fella in the room and the fella who will always have your back. Candidate Burns was prior enlisted and a mix of kindnesses, eccentricities, and cynical smarts. Candidates Farrell and Duff represented the best of the Boston Irish—all smiles and chipper chatter (Duff being a fireman in a past life was a bonus). Candidates Sandoval and Shaw were two of the most seasoned priors in the platoon and were always eager to offer a helping hand. Candidate Brewster, despite his name, hailed from Chile, was reading Timothy Weiner's *Legacy of Ashes: The History of the CIA* whenever he could find a minute, and was as sharp as a stiletto. Candidate Donahue was eminently nice and a scion of the notorious Donahue ancestral line, a dynasty of patron saints on the Catholic Right.

Unlike during my earlier bouts at Quantico and Parris Island, I developed a lasting friendship, with a candidate named Jake Walton, who ended up graduating first in academics and second overall in a class of hundreds. We were paired up during a weeklong leadership evaluation where he assumed the position of platoon commander while I held down the right-hand-man post of platoon sergeant. I had never been pressed into such a relatively high-level billet, but thanks to his fastidiousness, things went well.

Walton was a rare specimen. One meets hyper-competent types in the Corps, as well as thoroughly decent ones, and occasionally those with a sincere intellectual curiosity, too. But rarely does one stumble upon a marine who embodies all three at once. What impressed me most about Walton, though, was that he didn't appear to be overcorrecting for something. I couldn't help but believe he was in it for the right reasons, from a communitarian love of country to an egalitarian sense of duty. He epitomized the mantras Americans have become accustomed to repeating to avoid having to acknowledge the ambient rot. He really was a hard-working American, a generous American, a wise and noble and brave American.

My final three-mile run time at OCS was 19:27 (one guy ran a 15:35), but because of overuse, my pull-ups dropped from their usual twenty to a still-respectable eighteen. When things slowed down toward the end of the training cycle, I reserved a moment to exult in my achievement. I'd lived my life as a dilettante, a flaneur, a luftmensch, an entitled descendant of the least grounded of my people. Or, as Alain Brossat and Sylvia Klingberg once put it in *Revolutionary Yiddishland: A History of Jewish Radicalism* when describing the pious traditionalists and casual laborers of Russia and eastern Europe who gave birth to their more practical, trade unionist children—I lived as a "Chagallian [character] suspended in air."

And yet here I was, hardly a disciplined, organized worker, but among some of the most hands-on, down-to-earth people on the planet. Still, the immediate pride of having surpassed myself in strength and vigor continued alongside a growing skepticism about the context in which I was maturing.

The commissioning ceremony, held at the National Museum of the Marine Corps on a Friday afternoon, brought to light other dawning fissures in myself and the organization to which I was now committed. A friend of the writer Christopher Hitchens was a member of the graduating class, and Hitchens showed up to applaud him. By November 30, 2007, I could no longer speak in such supercilious terms about an apocalyptic battle between civilization and its enemies, and the fact that Hitchens was still doing so puzzled me.

When Major General John F. Kelly rose to the podium to deliver his remarks and administer the oath of office, my puzzlement—at the mission, at what I had gotten myself into, at what I had become and what I was unbecoming—only increased.

Kelly spoke of the Halls of Montezuma and the Shores of Tripoli, of Belleau Wood and my grandfather's Iwo Jima, of the Chosen Reservoir and Khe Sanh and Hue City and "a million unnamed jungle fights in Vietnam."

He spoke of the "liberation" of Kuwait and Baghdad and Tikrit and Fallujah and Ramadi. Of how our "nameless and selfless predecessors" fought the British and German fascists and communists, and how we were now being trained to fight "a new kind of adversary we've never known before, one who fights by no accepted rules of conflict." The fight today, Kelly said, is in Iraq and Afghanistan:

> America is at risk in a way it has never been before. Our enemy, the one these young people will soon meet on the battlefield, fights for an ideology based on an irrational hatred of who we are. We did not start this, and it will not end until the terrorists understand that we as a people will never lose our faith or our courage.... Marines, just like these lieutenants before us today, have for four years fought this enemy around the world and never for a second wondered why. They know why, and they are not afraid.

Given the fact none of the US government's strategic objectives were being met in any determining manner, and hundreds of thousands were dying on the US government's watch with no end in sight, just as millions were being displaced and those fighting us were skyrocketing in numbers and support, I *was* beginning to wonder why. And I *was* afraid.

Marines, Kelly said, would never let up their "unceasing pursuit, day and night, into whatever miserable lair Al-Qaeda might slither into to hide." That marines "have never lost faith in their country, or doubted the correctness of their cause." Marines like me knew that the United States did not go to war "to build empires, or enslave peoples, but to free those held in the grip of tyrants while at the same time protecting our nation and its citizens."

Except I'm not sure that's what I knew. I didn't know what I knew, but I no longer knew that. And when the general praised us as "men and women of character who continue to believe in this country enough to put life and limb on the line without qualification, and without thought of personal gain," I could no longer speak in such an unqualified fashion about patriotic faith and selflessness.

I pondered how the general's formulation that the "enemy will stay forever on the offensive until he hurts us so badly we surrender, or we kill him first" guaranteed anything other than endless war. And when he proclaimed that the US armed forces have "never known defeat on campaign" and that "when America lost, it lost at home, when others declared surrender—not us," I recoiled at Hitler's stab-in-the-back myth returned to life.

Finally, Kelly related his care for us junior officers to his care for his two sons, both of whom were serving as combat marines, and he finished with this:

> Rest assured our America—this experiment in democracy started just over two centuries ago—will forever remain the land of the free and home of the brave so long as we never run out of tough young Americans like those before us today who are willing to look beyond their own self-interest and comfortable lives and go into the darkest and most dangerous places on earth to hunt down and kill those who would do us

harm. God Bless America, ladies and gentlemen, and success to these young Marines. Semper Fidelis.

I didn't have much time to consider those parting words before the oath of office followed, but the superlatives "darkest and most dangerous" discomfited me for reasons I had yet to grasp. On my feet, right hand raised, I recited the following with my classmates, General Kelly leading us line by line:

I, Lyle J. Rubin
Do solemnly swear
That I will support and defend
The Constitution of the United States
Against all enemies
Foreign and domestic;
That I will bear true faith and allegiance to the same;
That I take this obligation freely
Without any mental reservation
Or purpose of evasion;
And that I will well and faithfully
Discharge the duties
Of the office on which I am about to enter,
So help me God.

When the general congratulated us, the forest of mildew-green alpha service uniforms broke out in rapture. Before heading off to find Leah and my family, I flipped through the program in a fit of unease. In the back our names were listed, along with the colleges or universities we'd attended. I thought back to boot camp graduation, where none of our high schools were listed. In fact, I doubted whether even our names were listed, or if there were any programs at all.

As to General Kelly's "tyrants," who were they?

The founding members of the Taliban, many of whom had been trained, armed, and funded by the United States and its allies, including Saudi Arabia and Pakistan?

The Taliban that had offered Bin Laden to George W. Bush after the attacks of September 11, which Bush rejected?

Saddam Hussein and those fighting in his name or in the wake of his departure, most of whom had never contemplated anything other than how to thrive in and out of power? In the same way the House of Saud contemplated its own sustenance or enrichment?

Saudi Arabia's Gulf neighbors? Tyrants all?

What of Hosni Mubarak in Egypt? The War on Terror's torturer-in-chief?

Was it only those being tortured who were savages and monsters, the genocidaires-in-waiting? The ones who were plotting to nuke or gas or poison the entirety of the civilized West?

Was it the Khomeinist government of Iran? The same government that owed its existence to the United States' overthrow of the democratically elected Prime Minister Mohammad Mosaddegh in 1953 and to the United States subsequently propping up the dictator Mohammad Reza Shah and his CIA-backed secret police? That the United States armed throughout the eighties during its dreadful war with Hussein's Iraq (whom the United States was also arming)? That was wrestling with reformist dissent in its chambers? That had shut down its nuclear weapons program in 2003 under Mohammad Khatami and had made repeated attempts to deescalate through piecemeal negotiations ever since?

Or was it the tens of thousands of armed peasants or city dwellers of Afghanistan and Iraq who had no designs of rule or domination but only mere survival?

Leah was cold toward me the rest of the late fall afternoon, which was the norm since things had taken a turn when I was still at the Palms.

She was even cold with my family, my parents, my grandparents, and Sherry and Beany. I had never seen a chill like that from Leah emanating out so far.

I couldn't get a read on her reactions to the whole scene, but I do recall her being intrigued (with a dollop of disgust) by Hitchens's presence. In any case, she started laughing and goofing a bit when we went out to eat afterward with my little brother Ethan, to a degree that almost made me think I still held her affections. That night we retreated to a hotel room in the area, presumably because we had too much to drink to make it all the way back to DC.

Leah began with a mundane rundown of work updates that ramped up into an argument about my lackluster response when she had fishtailed her sedan into a highway curb during a storm earlier in the season. I had just put my phone aside and was about to call it a night, but the escalation caused me to raise my back up against the headboard in a state of alert.

"I mean it, girl! I really wanted to be there for you! I felt fucking awful about it!"

Leah emerged from the bathroom, flossing her teeth. I wondered if she would even join me in the bed. It almost looked like she might storm out.

"Those are just words, Lyle. It's all just words with you."

That one hurt and I almost replied in kind, something about how I was the one actually committing to something and putting my life on the line while she was still dithering about. But I knew if I said that, she really would leave and I might never see her again. And I still loved her. And I still wanted to fuck her. And I could never figure out where those two truths overlapped and diverged.

"I'm so sorry. Just get in the fucking bed and let's cuddle already. It's been a long day and I love you."

Leah resisted at first, withdrawing to the restroom to finish the rest of her nightly routine. When she returned she looked a tad calmer and prepped the opposite side of the bed for lights out.

We were talking on our sides with a good two feet between us. I was still hoping we'd fuck. She had been mad at me the last liberty weekend I'd gone into DC for a visit, and she'd made it clear then sex wasn't in order. I got the sense it wasn't this time either.

"I'm so jealous of you, Lyle," she said.

"I know, you always say that."

"But seriously, the way you used to talk about your family—and your dad especially. You made it sound like a fucking war zone. I can't tell you how angry that made me. And how angry it still makes me."

"Because that's how it felt, Leah. I was being honest with you!"

"You were trying to impress me! You were trying to convince me you knew what it was like to . . . to . . ."

"To what? To lose a mom? Are you serious?"

"Yes! I am! You were so fucking melodramatic about it, Lyle, and I'm not sure I can ever get over that."

That word: EVER.

She saw my hurt and backed off, even going as far as to touch my shoulder.

"I'm sorry. I shouldn't have said that. I don't know—I just think it's important to be honest about this feeling I have. It's better than keeping it inside, you know?"

"It's a hell of a feeling, Leah. I mean, yes, be honest, but I really don't know what I'm supposed to do. It seems like what you really resent is where I come from—and there's just nothing I can do about that.

"And I do think you conflate my present dad—never mind the dad you see in social company—with the dad I actually grew up with. He really was bad. And I really was scared. He and Brett really did get into fistfights and I really did have to pull them apart. Just like I had to get between him and my mom so things wouldn't get too physical."

"I know, Lyle, I know! And I'm sorry I sometimes make it seem like I don't know that. It's just that—"

"Everything I said to you in college—even if you're right that it might have been motivated at some level by what you're saying—came from a real place. And, yes, my mom is still with me! And my dad grew the fuck up and he's still with me, too. And they love me and are always there for me and I couldn't have it much better than that. And you don't have any of that. You lost your mom and—"

"And?"

"And you pretty much lost your dad, too! I know that. And you don't even have a single other family member to lean on. But all I want in this world—all I've ever wanted—is for you to lean on *me*. To trust *me*. And just let me love *you*."

I wanted to cry, but I couldn't, and I wanted to stop wanting to fuck her, but I couldn't do that either. And because of that, I started having doubts about what I just said. Maybe she was right and I couldn't give her what she needed. Maybe I was too selfish and sex-obsessed and—most of all—hadn't suffered like she had and probably never would. Even if I went to war. Even if I saw some combat. And maybe what she needed was someone who really suffered like her.

But before I could sort any of that out, she started to cry enough for both of us. So I brought her to my chest like I always did and told her I loved her. That calmed us both down, and when the calm settled, she broke herself from my embrace to pick up the glossy magazine that had just fallen from the nightstand and resettled at the foot of the bed.

"Lyle, come here. Sit next me."

I followed the order like a good marine.

"You know this isn't working out, right? And no matter how hard we try, it's probably only going to get worse, right?"

"I really don't want to say yes to that question, but yes. I think that's probably right."

She put her hand on my shoulder. For a brief second I felt infantilized by the gesture, like we'd just rewound the tape to the taqueria back in college, and I was that kid all over again, like I'd gone nowhere. But the touch was warm and sincere, even if mixed with resentment, so I held her hand on my shoulder and let out a tear.

We held each other that night, and the next morning she drove back to Washington and I drove back to New England.

By going in the hole twenty-plus days, I was able to stretch my leave period over a month. Much of that break was spent catching up with people and emails. Along with a *Times* article from Bill celebrating "vulture funds," an officer from OCS had forwarded an unhinged chain email to every member of our platoon. The subject line read, "FW: this woman should run for president." It amounted to a bigoted rant from a "housewife in New Jersey" who, among other things, cheered on a marine corporal's 2004 murder of a wounded and unarmed man in a Fallujah mosque.

The Fallujah incident was caught on tape by war reporter Kevin Sites, and the tape was aired in full around the world. In the United States, however, it was censored. At least three other unarmed men were killed in the mosque that day, all shot by the same marine. The Corps cleared the corporal of all wrongdoing within a year of the shooting, and there is no public record of any others being held accountable. Over a decade later I'd find mention of the episode in *The Sacking of Fallujah: A People's History*, coauthored by Ross Caputi, Richard Hil, and Donna Mulhearn. Caputi is a friendly acquaintance of mine (and fellow historian) who fought in Fallujah as a marine grunt. He claimed his command told the troops all noncombatants had already left the city and everyone present was fair game, meaning they could be assumed hostile. Another petty officer confirmed the same, saying Fallujah had been declared a "free-fire zone." Sites, hardly an anti-war type, said something similar.

Before I returned to Quantico for the Basic School in early January, I planned a trip with Rosen and our friend Josephs to my parents' summer place in the South County of Rhode Island (Josephs and I met at Emory while doing pro-war activist work, and he had introduced me to Rosen).

After considering a gig with the Rudy Giuliani presidential campaign, Rosen decided to return to his previous position at a think tank where he helped translate the Arab or Muslim world in the least flattering of lights. His combat tour in the Israeli Defense Forces, along with his current occupation, appeared to have made him more confident about Israel's policies. I never got a read on what happened to him in the Lebanon war, but it was clear it had been scarring. Casualties were high, and he was close with soldiers who were maimed or killed. Unlike me, he had a visceral connection to the Jewish state that must have made most critical discussion of it sound like a rarefied parlor game. I had come across men like that in the Corps, too, and I got it.

Still, I wanted Rosen and Josephs to hear my political doubts, and I wanted them to tell me why I was wrong. I sprinkled stray remarks about how everlasting preparation for "tomorrow's wars" risks resulting in an ever-expanding battlespace and how a Lockheed Martin–fueled jobs program or aggressive democratization agenda abroad were the furthest things from small government. And many of the guys I'd sweated with the past year and a half, I pointed out, didn't seem all that interested in civil liberties, human rights, or democracy anyway.

Rosen and Josephs responded with care.

"Part of the issue, I think," Rosen said, "is that I was never all that enamored with the humanitarian justifications for the War on Terror anyway."

"Right," said Josephs. "It's more about simple survival. We have a group of people intent on killing us or replacing our way of life with theirs—in the United States, in Europe, in Israel—and it really just comes down to doing what we have to do to keep living our way."

"If perpetual—and well-funded—vigilance is what's needed to keep the Islamists and other threats at bay," said Rosen, "so be it."

This struck me as a reasonable argument then. It was, at minimum, less blinkered than what I was accustomed to hearing from the rest of my right-wing college friends or my fellow marines. Even so, I found it myopic, like a bargain with the devil I had yet to altogether comprehend.

I wasn't ready to smash the holy grail of national virtue, the faith that for all of America's mistakes, America was still right. At its worst, the United States had become for me a well-meaning if clumsy giant. Moving into the new year, I couldn't move beyond that safe compromise. To reconceive my country, my compatriots, and myself as complicit in something worse than an unfortunate if understandable series of mistakes or wrongs, as implicated in something more like a horror—a horror spanning continents and centuries—that was asking too much.

On Friday we headed for Newport and spent an ungodly number of hours at the arcade. I kept rolling the skee-balls into the center slot, and after earning enough tickets to buy a trinket, moved on to the video game with the rifle. I'd hoped now that I was a marine I'd be good at that kind of thing, but I wasn't. Rosen was better. I cashed in my tickets for an unmemorable tchotchke and we left.

I drove my friends around the prettiest parts of the coastline. We had plans to attend Shabbat services that night at Touro Synagogue, but I don't think we made it inside. Touro was the first established in the colonial era, making it the oldest surviving synagogue of its kind in the United States. Like Beth Elohim in Charleston, it was founded by Sephardim. And like Beth Elohim, its history was mixed. On the one hand, its congregants are said to have housed escaped slaves. On the other, the temple had been built by slaves, and its richest member and backer, Aaron Lopez, was a scrappy nobody turned slaver who profited greatly from the slave trade. Among other things, he shipped slaves from the very West Indies many of Touro's membership or ancestry had passed through when fleeing their own oppression.

On August 18, 1790, George Washington paid his respects to the Jewish community in Newport, and after the visit wrote in a letter to the congregation's superintendent:

> It is now no more that toleration is spoken of, as if it were the indulgence of one class of people, that another enjoyed the exercise of their inherent natural rights. For happily the Government of the United States, which gives to bigotry no sanction, to persecution no assistance...May the children of the Stock of Abraham, who dwell in this land, continue to merit and enjoy the good will of the other Inhabitants.

I'd read the National Historic Site plaque before, the one that featured Washington's words about giving bigotry no sanction and persecution no assistance. How could Washington, I wondered, utter such words as a slaveowner, and with teeth in his mouth that may have belonged to his own slaves?

Liberal Supreme Court justices like Ruth Bader Ginsberg and Elena Kagan and renegade Republicans like Lincoln Chafee had delivered keynote addresses on-site during the annual reading of Washington's missive. So had Wes Fastiff, chairman emeritus of the largest union-busting law firm in the world. A syrupy online in-memoriam video for Fastiff ends with a refreshing candor:

"You gotta believe in the firm, and believe in yourself, that we are the best lawyers you can ever have," Fastiff says. "As I keep saying all the time, I am not a competitive person, I don't really try to push things, but, for the record, no one has beaten me yet." Fastiff smirks, and in cuts Nancy Sinatra's most famous tune:

> One of these days these boots are gonna walk all over you.

I had been raised to draw connections among the Jews who had helped escaped slaves and the Jews who had marched alongside Martin Luther King and the Jews today who support Black Lives Matter and other progressive causes. But in the years ahead, I would begin to draw less comfortable connections relating to my intersecting identities as a marine, an American, and a Jew. I would begin to see the heterogeneous legacies in all traditions and all groups, and how some of those legacies win out at different points. And how the spiritual descendants of those legacies most tolerant of the boot—the racist boot, the capitalist boot, most of all the *racial capitalist* boot (for starters, many of the labor organizations busted by Fastiff's law firm have comprised nonwhite workers)—had been walking over quite a lot of people for quite some time.

When I arrived at the Basic School in Quantico on January 23, 2008, I figured I was well positioned to pick up with the next class. Superiors at OCS had told us about half would need to wait until the next cycle and implied that the determining factor would be our PFT scores. Since my physical fitness was top-notch, I imagined I'd test well enough to earn myself a spot. More attentive minds, however, such as my friend Walton, had made sure to separate the good scuttlebutt from the bad and learned that the policy would amount to first come, first served. Walton had arrived in the wee hours of the morning and was awarded his pass. I strolled in well after sunrise, so I, along with a sizable chunk of my OCS peers, would be granted no such pass for another three or so months.

Those months constituted the easiest chapter of my marine career, and one of the easiest of my life. We had to show up for formations and field day at the barracks, as well as attend to working parties, and I'm sure there were other nuisances I've since forgotten. But by and large we were left to our own devices.

The majority of those off hours were spent hanging with my new roommates. One was an Annapolis grad who'd managed to make it to the top of every class he'd ever been in. He was a star sailor at the Naval Academy who also had a lifelong dream of flying jets, and last I checked, he's done very well as a Red Devil fighter pilot. For an overachiever, he never made anyone feel inferior. A real mensch.

Another was a frat boy and prior enlisted. I believe his job had been in a combat arms trade. Maybe artillery. No matter his past, all the two of us did was one-up each other with the standard-fare content. I'd talk about how much I wanted to spew all over some Navy chick's face and he'd introduce me to a viral gross-out like *2 Girls 1 Cup*. What was nice is that even though he was all Maxim and dip, he wasn't one of those shock-jock marines who wanted to chat about blowing off hajji heads, and neither of us was a fan of the video of a marine in Iraq throwing a living, breathing pup off a cliff.

The third roommate was Pat Farrell. He was one of the two Boston Irish candidates I'd gotten to know at OCS. Not the sharpest tool in the shed, but he was one of those you liked to have around. Farrell would laugh at everything you had to say, no matter how lame or asinine, and he seemed to enjoy life in a way that reminded even cerebral oafs like me that there was a great deal to enjoy.

The rest of the time, I was reading. My ideological journey was still in full swing, and the conservative Catholic historian John Lukacs was the latest to catch my attention. He had been born into a family of Jewish converts to Catholicism in Hungary in 1924, but his parents' conversion wasn't enough to save them from the Nazis. Lukacs nevertheless managed to escape a Hungarian labor battalion, survive in hiding, and reach the United States in 1946, intent on fleeing his home country's communist takeover.

Lukacs's politics followed naturally from his biography. He made a name for himself as one of the most eloquent critics of the modern Right and Left both. In his aristocratic disdain for "populist" majorities, he shared much with Ortega y Gasset. But in his critiques of the Cold War, US supremacy, and the nationalism and militarism of mass media, he helped me make sense of my incipient misgivings without feeling like I was betraying my friends, my past, and my country. Lukacs was part of a dying generation of literate conservatives who understood how "pro-American" enthusiasms were inimical to a salutary commonwealth. He knew how a society ruled by philistine businessmen and their military-industrial partners rendered any conservations impossible, and how war ripped apart the social bonds and trusts required of any humane people. Because these complaints were couched in a traditionalist vernacular favored by most Republicans, I didn't feel like I was going too far out on a limb by invoking them.

Lukacs would impel me to take a second look at the work of his friend George Kennan, the diplomat whose writings like the "Long Telegram" (1946) and *The Sources of Soviet Conduct* (1947) were responsible for shaping US "containment" policy toward the Soviets and other leftists. Although I knew Kennan would turn against the policy apparatus he inspired, I was unaware of how thoroughgoing his criticisms would become. And just as Jonah's beefs with social democrats were beginning to usher me into the arms of social democrats, Lukacs's and Kennan's critics on the New Left were drawing me toward radical scholars like William Appleman Williams and Noam Chomsky. Although they still struck me as too dismissive of real national security threats and the need to manage those threats through surveillance and force, their argument that the national security state itself represented the gravest threat to average people was looking more reasonable. I wasn't prepared to accept most of their claims. But I was prepared to entertain them.

Not all my extracurricular readings were so political. Oscar Wilde's poem *The Ballad of Reading Gaol* includes insights about the brutalization of the stigmatized and criminalized. But it was his meditation on how we all "kill the thing we love" that gripped me. Whereas I had rushed toward a spiteful misogyny after my first breakup with Leah, and again during the worst parts of our second try, I was now moving toward something more introspective.

This time I was bearing some blame for what had happened, and what was still happening. In ways big and small, I had been killing the girl I loved. As Wilde would be the first to point out, love and hurt can't be separated. They are the two wings of the dove. But love and hurt, like the people they embody, can exist together in some semblance of peace. And I had failed on my side of that bargain, regardless of whether Leah, too, had failed on hers.

Why it had taken me more than twenty-five years to start hobbling toward that discovery is complicated. A neuroscientist might point to maturing brain structure. A certain kind of psychologist may suggest that something about my military training, or the social cohesion of the uniformed service, was helping me build self-esteem and resilience, in turn allowing me to relate in more healthy ways to those I cared about. The layperson might say I was growing up like everyone else, and accumulated experience was leading me to learn from past errors and seek a better balance.

I *would* say I was being humbled. I could have been humbled without so many risks to myself and others. The humbling didn't need to constitute a scarring, at least not the kind of needless scarring I believe so much of military life and the wider culture of empire ensure. I didn't need to be trained to maim and kill. I didn't need to help those doing the maiming and killing. I didn't need to police others, never mind some of the most impoverished, subjugated peoples in the world.

I was reminded of William James's "moral equivalent of war" that could assist individuals and communities in a nonviolent humbling. James had in mind a peaceful socialism that was nonetheless infused with martial discipline and solidarity. His contemporary admirers and future readers, including John Dewey, Jane Addams, W. E. B. Du Bois, Dorothy Day, Richard Rorty, Cornel West, and Franklin Roosevelt's labor secretary, Frances Perkins, the leading spirit behind Social Security, a protégé of Dewey and Addams, and something of a Jamesian thinker once removed, all put forward their own versions of this moral equivalent. These grew more and more distant from James's recommendation of a national service requirement and its most militaristic features, especially from his emphasis on the purported masculine virtues of hardness, obedience, and the idolatry of pain.

Debates can be had about the proper equilibrium between hardness and softness or obedience and resistance, just as there can be about the relationship between pleasure and pain and how these ought to play out in the public sphere, the workplace, and the more private or sexual realms. James was, at his best, a committed pluralist, meaning he understood these questions can gesture toward a host of favorable possibilities depending on time, place, and individual or collective desires. But in the early months of 2008, looking inward and outward, at myself, my country, and my world, I increasingly felt that almost everything was running off-kilter. A disequilibrium, an all-encompassing chauvinism, was shaking me to my core.

Not that I knew what to do about it, or even if I had known, had the will to do it. Every so often I'd return to badgering Leah. Sometimes I sent her a text with a fantasy. Other times an email with a list of fantasies. She would erupt, I would apologize. And then I'd do the same thing a few months later. I continued thinking and talking about women as if they were, first and foremost, mine to be thought and talked about. Despite my growing uncertainties about the war effort and the political culture that sustained it, I continued to conceptualize whole groups of people, beginning with those I would soon be assigned to police, and maybe even kill, as somehow not deserving the same protections I had been afforded from birth. I kept holding tight to a creed of superiority, of exclusive deserts, that mandated not only my own occasional manly discomforts, or the abuse of those I held dear, but also, of most import, the literal deaths of others.

I was determined to become not only a marine officer but also a good one, irrespective of the politics surrounding my commission. I had no control over the stratagems of the Defense Department or the machinations of the CIA, but I would take command, in the not so far off future, of my own little platoon. I intended to conduct myself with the utmost proficiency, and so I set about perusing the relevant literature.

When flipping through the Corps' *Warfighting* manual, commonly referred to as MCDP 1 (Marine Corps Doctrinal Publication 1), I was struck by its philosophical influences. It was a stealth crash course in modernity that began with a Pragmatist tutorial on democratic deliberation:

> War is thus a process of continuous mutual adaptation, of give and take, move and countermove. It is critical to keep in mind that the enemy is not an inanimate object to be acted upon but an independent and animate force with its objectives and plans.

It proceeded through the mirage of dualism, the hard-nosed counsel of the Nazi legal theorist Carl Schmitt, the poststructuralist iconoclasm of Michel Foucault, the strategic chaos of the situationist Guy Debord, the right-libertarianism of Friedrich Hayek, on the one hand, and the left-libertarianism of Noam Chomsky, on the other. Next, the spurning of the McNamara Fallacy, the Ivy-educated faith of business executives and government officials—from Robert McNamara to Donald Rumsfeld—that success can be secured through the aggregation of quantifiable data. And, finally, somersaulting backward to hints of Leo Tolstoy's pacificism and Friedrich Nietzsche's will to power. If the goal was to survey competing twentieth-century visions of the modern predicament from the white male canon, the Corps could scarcely have done better.

My highlighted sections in the *Leading Marines* pamphlet were just as telling: "There is yet another element of being different that defines Marines, and that is selflessness.... Any man in combat who lacks comrades who will die for him, or for whom he is willing to die, is not a man at all. He is truly damned.... Marines, far flung, performing dangerous—sometimes apparently meaningless and often overlooked—missions find strength and sense of purpose simply knowing that they are Marines in that mystical grouping they know as the Corps."

I still wanted to live up to the legend then. More to the point, I didn't want to let my fellow marines down, specifically those who would be relying on my leadership. But I was also in the process of understanding many themes that would later preoccupy me: the paradox of achieving self-worth and self-aggrandizement through self-sacrifice; the highest form of mutuality, of existence even, necessitating carnage. One's willingness to take life—one's own or another's—counts as life's most precious benediction. In the absence of this ethos one becomes condemned, and that Longfellow got it backward. It doesn't matter the cause of the slaying, or even its ultimate end. What matters is the slaying itself. To kill a brother, or to be killed by a brother, is not to violate the covenant of brotherhood but to affirm it.

The curse of Cain is a blessing.

Documents like these not only contain an unfiltered honesty about the theology or religiosity suffusing US militarism at the level of the warfighter. And they don't just unmask the blood-minded versions of manliness and masculinity that pervade American society. They also let slip the presumptuousness of the empire itself. In *Leading Marines*, one of the didactic vignettes involves a veteran of the barracks bombing in Beirut in 1983 getting assailed with questions by what General Kelly would call the effete chattering class. The reporters ask the corporal, "Should you be here? Should anyone be here?"

The corporal responds, "Where else should I be? I'm a United States Marine. If anyone must be here, it should be Marines."

When reading this in Quantico in 2008, I can't say I comprehended its tragic totality. I sensed there was something out of sorts in the young man's answer, something grim about him having nowhere else to be. Not in a stateside bowling alley having a good time. Or hiking up a mountain. Or working in a field devoted to nurturing communities rather than policing or pulverizing them.

No, the point of the story is he belonged right where he was, in Beirut, killing or being killed. This despite him just witnessing so many of his comrades get killed, or *because* he just witnessed them get killed. The reason for the destruction was immaterial, and the demand for a reason offensive. This marine's purpose in life was to be wherever distant powerbrokers ordered him to be, for whatever reason they gave or didn't give. It wasn't a job but a calling. He was proud to wait for whatever it was he was waiting for.

Later in *Leading Marines* we find this:

> The man who will go where his colors go, without asking, who will fight a phantom foe in jungle and mountain range, without counting, and who will suffer and die in the midst of incredible hardship, without complaint, is still what he has always been, from Imperial Rome to sceptered Britain to democratic America.... As a legionary, he held the gates of civilization for the classical world... he has been called United States Marine.

In publications from the Department of Defense's tract *The Armed Forces Officer* to the Marine Commandant's Reading List, claims to inclusivity coincide with a decidedly white colonial gaze. Though I have yet to find an official reckoning with the racial implications of this ancestry, that the capitalism spanning the globe today descends from the European racisms of the past, those with the guns tend to know the racial nature of their missions. But running through these texts is an awareness of a shared strategic and tactical heritage with prior empires, as is the primacy of maintaining Western supremacy. And in all my years scouring the annals of modern barbarity, nowhere have I seen such a frank admission from the horse's mouth.

The last book I managed to skim before picking up my TBS class was Dave Grossman's *On Killing: The Psychological Cost of Learning to Kill in War and Society*. Grossman served over twenty-three years in the Army, and a portion of that time as an Army Ranger officer. He also taught at West Point and, despite never experiencing combat, would become the most respected authority on the psychology of killing, or what he termed "killology." His writings appear often on Marine commandants' reading lists, and when I was a boot lieutenant, *On Killing* was a big hit.

One point that intrigued me was how most Americans prove to be as simultaneously prudish and consumed with killing as they once were about sex. For an empire saturated in boundless, commodified transgression, never mind one whose most self-satisfied members pride themselves on being plainspoken and telling it like it is, this seems counterintuitive. But interest in the role of this ambivalence and repression in the endurance of expansionist aggressions led me back to Freud and Herbert Marcuse. My nation's libertine openness was superficial and failed to wrestle with the most uncomfortable instincts at work and with how these instincts merge, again and again, with denial and shame into ruinous fates. The American origin story comprised Puritanical strictures, on the one hand, and limitless rape and pillage, on the other. From our zealots to our prisons, our missionaries to our hired guns, this remains the story of America. And not so much as counterposing poles but as reinforcing drives.

In *Eros and Civilization*, Marcuse writes:

> The exploration of [the tabooed and subterranean history of civilization] reveals not only the secret of the individual but also that of civilization.... the primal father, as the archetype of domination, initiates the chain reaction of enslavement, rebellion, and reinforced domination which marks the history of civilization.

Marcuse went on to declare that "repression from without has been supported by repression from within: the unfree individual introjects his masters and their commands into his own mental apparatus." Most pertinent is how the empire avails itself of repression. Not just repression in the basest, most material sense. Not just through checkpoints and terror. But through offering aspiring men a release from their pious upbringings by way of licentious barracks life and death-dealing. By advertising military service as an escape from the secular zealotry of the lifeless market, the sexless workplace, for those who seek virile adventure. Most of all, by granting the public a perennial respite from Calvinist boredom, in the form of hypersexualized violence. And then recycling the guilt (conscious or otherwise) that comes of this violence by packaging America's next war not as a continuation of the horrifying one that came before but as a noble course correction, as a return to America's birthright as either a Christian or a liberal protector.

Grossman's book didn't just set me on a path to psychoanalytic abstraction. It also nudged me toward more mundane realizations about military training and, in due course, larger frames of conditioning, such as S. L. A. Marshall's study concluding that fewer than one in four US troops in combat during World War II fired their weapons at the enemy. This figure would later be brought into question—along with Marshall's embellished claims about his own and others' service—but the greater part of the relevant research parallels these takeaways. Marshall deduced that killing does not come naturally, and barring intense deprogramming, most people will resist taking another's life even when under threat. For the future brigadier general, this meant the US government had to invest in such deprogramming, and Marshall got his wish.

A slew of exercises were introduced in entry-level training and beyond, all designed to dehumanize "the enemy" while engendering an instantaneous obedience to orders. I would learn these methods well, with bayonet or pugil stick in hand. Trainers have moved from an emphasis on civilian-style target practice to combat marksmanship, in which recruits (now in foxholes or mock urban settings) shoot at moving, human-shaped targets in full battle-rattle. Those with the quickest trigger finger reap praise; those with the slowest ridicule. Much of the training cycle is devoted to knifing or shooting anonymous effigies of one kind or another, all of which are made out to be terrorists, hajjis, the monster who raped your sister. And all of this takes place in a loop, over and over, until the violence itself is reduced to a mere reflex.

Years later, I would shudder through an episode of the TV show *Black Mirror* titled "Men Against Fire," a direct homage to Marshall's study of the same name. Set in a futuristic hellscape, it centers on a soldier tormented by guilt and with some of the personal costs of military dehumanization described in *On Killing*, though it goes much further. The operant conditioning that followed Marshall's study becomes a metaphor for a much wider, postwar desensitization, where it isn't just the warfighters who have been conditioned. The viewer is forced to contemplate the possibility that they, too, have been blinded from the carnage and domination that reside at the heart of empire and global capital.

Neither Marshall nor Grossman ever arrived at a similar place. Marshall died a belligerent flagbearer for the Vietnam War who had disowned his own grandson for his conscientious objection, and Grossman took on a second career instructing warfighters and cops alike in playing the role of killer sheepdogs in defense of the sheepish masses. He makes a lucrative living on the speaker circuit convincing his audiences wolves are everywhere and those best equipped must always be emboldened to put them down.

Today's marriage of the military-industrial and prison-industrial complexes has historical resonances that reverberate from the approximately thirty-six-year war against the Apache Nation (from around 1850 to 1886) and the Fort Sill prisoner-of-war camp to the over twenty-year occupation of Afghanistan and the Guantanamo Bay Detention Camp. The most famous Apache prisoner at Fort Sill was Geronimo, whose name was Bin Laden's military-assigned codename. The official history of the Field Artillery School at Fort Sill suggests that Geronimo's confinement might amount to "the post's most glamorous responsibility." The fort later served as a Japanese internment camp during the Second World War and, under the Obama and Trump administrations, a detention center for undocumented migrants fleeing US-fueled drug wars and economic despair in Central America.

Professional guidelines for modern law enforcement were written by early-twentieth-century veterans from Cuba to the Philippines, and its earliest ranks were stacked with like-minded vets. They and their protégés would erect, in the mold of the counterinsurgencies they once participated in, a transnational doctrine of centralized training, funding, and authority combined with decentralized discretion. Newfound agencies like the Office of Public Safety—founded as the policing arm of the US Agency for International Development in 1962—assembled a vast network of proxy policing spanning seventy-seven countries, while, in time, supermax prisons were bought and sold in the international marketplace.

In a very material sense, the local despotism of racial policing in the United States and its territories went global. Black and brown freedom movements have drawn clear lines between the demonization of dark-skinned communist guerillas abroad and black or brown gang members or radicals at home, and a similarly reciprocal demonization of Muslims and Arabs has taken hold in recent decades.

Little of this was on my mind as I readied myself for TBS. I didn't even know most of it. But I was already becoming more open than Grossman to considering how his argument implied a wider desensitization to US-led violence and injustice. I was also mulling over the differences in training between officers and enlisted marines. At boot camp we would chant mild classics like:

Li'l yellow birdie with a li'l yellow bill
Landed on my windowsill
Lured him in with a li'l piece a bread
Then I smashed his li'l fucking head
Blood and guts!
Good for me!
Good for you!

Military cadences like this spoke to a deeper divide between the officer class (and the political class it works for) and the rank-and-file troops. In 1989, for example, a senior drill instructor at Parris Island had his recruits march beside a picture of a naked woman and a guidon flag emblazoned with the words *rape*, *kill*, *pillage*, *burn*. When a distressed mother brought the graduation photograph to the attention of Senator John McCain, the hat was forced to write an apologetic letter to his just christened marines explaining the words were never meant to be read literally.

The anecdote touched on a certain cultural gap between those at the top and bottom of the uniformed or civilian hierarchy. Such conduct would have been unthinkable at my OCS or TBS schoolhouse circa 2008. At Quantico I saw far less degrading language toward Muslims, Arabs, women, or anyone who wasn't a straight white male than what I was accustomed to on the Island or in the Palms. There were no cadences about raping girls and grandmas or murdering babies. Sometimes we'd greet one another in a hallway with a shout of "kill" or call a roster or list of any kind a "kill sheet." And if instructors did emphasize a kind of instantaneous obedience to bloodthirsty orders in the beginning of OCS, the brief interval was meant to give us an ephemeral taste of enlisted life—not turn us into automatons. To the contrary, officer instruction concentrated on honing our discretionary capacities as leaders, up to and including our willingness, when appropriate, to rein in our marines.

As far as I can gather, the letter of apology marked the extent of the boot camp instructor's punishment, and the incident speaks more to tolerance of the behavior in question than intolerance. As I became aware in the three years that followed, it also tells us something quite damning about the perpetual avowal and disavowal loop of the very racial, gendered violence that keeps the war machine—and the empire—rolling.

While waiting to start the Basic Officer Course (TBS also runs a course for warrant officers and a follow-on course for infantry officers),

I prepped for the coming storm. Walton was kind enough to pass along another lieutenant's BOC "gouge," five pages of chiseled bullet points that told us everything the author thought we needed to know, extracurricular and practical, about the schoolhouse.

- Keep iPods for the infrequent lull
- Look out for your buddies when attacking the bar scene
- Keep USB drives and 550 cord on hand
- Buy new canteens instead of relying on the issued ones (which are grimy)
- Use a carabiner to secure your gear during the endurance course
- Keep tweezers for the ticks

The best bit, though, was the simple warning that it was all going to be very fucked, it was designed that way, and the most you could do was mitigate the worst of it through nonstop anticipation. Also, to keep your fellows as informed as you can about everything and continually volunteer so you'd do well on your peer evals.

By early April I would begin what amounted to six months of down-in-the-dirt grunt training in infantry tactics for squads, platoons, reinforced platoons, and companies. I'd learn how to call in indirect fire and close air support and how to compose complex orders that take hours or days to write and fragmentary ones that take minutes. I'd pull the string for a 155mm artillery piece, build terrain models from sand, lead security patrols, execute cordons, and orchestrate support by fire missions with live ammo. I got tested on first aid, combat lifesaving, and arranging a casevac, as well as combat water survival and combat comms. I operated with a handful of night vision devices, from infrared sensors to thermal imaging to laser sights, and I assembled, disassembled, and fired crew-served weapons from the 240 to the 50-cal to the Mk 19. I studied the ins and outs of IEDs and combat engineering and dodged paintball-like simunition rounds on the military operations and urbanized terrain circuit. I detained mock enemy prisoners. Somewhere in the mix we took a few classes on the rules of engagement and cultural awareness. The details were as much of a haze then as they are now; I learned to the tests and moved on.

For all my grunt-like training, though, I was never being trained *as a grunt*. The distinction is a crucial one for anyone who's worn the uniform, and one I'd already come to respect as an enlisted marine. No matter how many times I heard the aphorism "Every Marine a Rifleman," I knew what the marketing obscured. We all did. There are two kinds of marines in the Corps—those who are groomed to do the killing and be killed, and those who are groomed to support them and (for the most part) live. The first are the grunts and the second are the pogs.

The etymology for "grunt" is convoluted and contested, but suffice it to say the grunt does all the grunt work up to and including the deathwork. They dig holes and sleep in them during rainstorms, they put up tents and take down tents and scrub or brush everything with Pine-Sol or bleach. They are browbeaten, hardened, and scarred. It's as if boot camp never really ends, or only ends when you end. That's the life of the grunt: punctuated by little deaths and big deaths and then just death (far earlier than a nongrunt life punctuated by the same).

The pog is the Person Other than Grunt. But the term's definition was retrofitted to complement *grunt*, and its usage has deeper roots. First there was *pog*, English slang in the late nineteenth century that derived from the Irish word meaning "kiss." Then *pogey bait*, WWI-era military (and possibly prison) slang for sexual lures or jailbait. Around the same time, sailors and marines suspected of homosexual activity were slurred as "pogues" for their perversions or readiness to play the role of the woman.

In 1919 the first major national scandal about gay men erupted in Newport, Rhode Island, when it was revealed the Department of Navy had dispatched numerous detectives as a sting operation to have sex with pogue sailors. The operatives and their bosses justified their actions by claiming that if the undercover agent was the receiver of the oral and the giver of the anal, they didn't count as "fairies."*

*The reputation and leadership of the assistant Navy secretary at that point, one Franklin D. Roosevelt, was nevertheless called into question, however fleetingly.

Rumor has it the word *grunt* itself originated during World War II, to refer to the general replacement unit, *not trained*—the GRUNT—who would resume the course of their better-schooled dead on the front lines. To be trained as a grunt, then, meant to be untrained. To be thrown into the ring to deal death or die, like game dogs in a dogfight. To the extent the grunt was trained at all, it was in opposition to the domesticated training of the pog. The grunt looked beyond survival and whimsical thriving, beyond kisses and queer pleasures, beyond limp-wristed joie de vivre. Beyond life itself. No matter how much a pinched part of me wanted it to be otherwise, I was never trained as a grunt.

Early on at TBS I ran the obstacle course in 1:16 and was hoping to run the Double-O in a perfect three minutes. I was running six in a row then and feeling unstoppable. But I choked on judgment day, had to remediate, and ended up with a mediocre final score closer to four than three.

I did well on both the day and night land-nav tests, considered some of the most challenging evaluations at the school. I shot the pistol for the first time. I was one of the "anticipators," tensing up right before the round was released from the chamber, throwing off my aim. Even so, I managed to eke out a marksman badge. Same with the rifle. Not much had changed since boot camp.

My academic scores were good, though, while my leadership scores started strong but declined. Given the two-front war in Iraq and Afghanistan, TBS was producing an oversized number of lieutenants, which meant five to six officers to a room. Quarters were tight, and everyone was at one another's throats. I knew how to work hard, plan and communicate well, and make clear-sighted decisions, even under taxing conditions. I got along with most of my fellows when everything wasn't going haywire. But sometimes I got flustered. I was the furthest thing from a swaggering jock or machine-like military man. Despite my efforts, I still thought and spoke like a bookish Jew, an alien life-form to many I was now spending my every waking minute with. I screamed and howled in my sleep, rolled and kicked. The more I fucked up, the more I fucked up, and the less inclined I became to assist others. I wasn't mature enough to excel in adversity, and there were moments I lashed out and grew sour. All of this amounted to subpar peer evals.

Ironically, it was my steady fall from grace that helped me get my preferred job of signal intelligence officer. The Corps divvies up their junior officer talent by thirds, making sure each specialty is occupied by an even number of TBS all-stars, middle-of-the-roaders, and shitbags. I'd begun at the bottom of the top and ended at the top of the bottom. The former was a terrible place to be because it meant your preferences were the least prioritized among your all-star third. The latter was ideal because your preferences were most prioritized among your shitbag third. So being the least shitty of the shitbags earned me a slot in SIGINT.

Toward the end of BOC we were assigned Eugene Burdick and William Lederer's *The Ugly American*, a hokey but classic novel that argues the United States would have to become more culturally sensitive, crafty, and diplomatic if it wanted to keep ruling the world. John F. Kennedy was inspired by its messaging, and as president, he spearheaded the Peace Corps, counterinsurgency, and special operations across the Global South. Marlon Brando starred in a film version of the book in 1963.

We were also assigned General Victor "Brute" Krulak's *First to Fight: An Inside View of the U.S. Marine Corps*, which put me to sleep every time I picked it up. The author was one of the Corps' few in-house intellectuals, the man responsible for creating the "inkblot" strategy, the attempt to win the hearts and minds of the Vietnamese by securing one village at a time through a light but wise military footprint. He also advocated heavy, LeMay-like "strategic bombing" in North Vietnam.

As the legend goes, the Marines first rejected Krulak for being too short, but he later earned a commission after graduating from the Naval Academy. Despite distinguishing himself in battle during World War II and—throughout his career—being decorated with almost every medal, from the Navy Cross to the Navy Distinguished Service Medal,

Krulak didn't make it to four stars. Nor did he become commandant. This is because he irked Lyndon Johnson for criticizing his "overregulation" of the military in Indochina.

Meanwhile, when one of Krulak's sons arrived home three minutes late, he grounded him for a month. Another son, Charles C. Krulak, would be awarded a Silver Star for his combat service in Vietnam and in the nineties would fulfill his father's dream of becoming Marine commandant, where he'd keep alive the elder Krulak's counterinsurgency aspirations by devising terms of his own, like "strategic corporal" (low-ranking warfighters who know how to fight and, through restraint, gain the trust and respect of locals at the same time) and "three block war" (modern conflict that necessitates simultaneous killing, peacekeeping, and humanitarian relief within three contiguous city blocks). Tom Clancy romanticized the genius of the younger Krulak in his book on the Marine Expeditionary Unit, and that romance was wafting through the halls of power when I wrapped up TBS in the fall of 2008.

Krulak Senior's parents were Jewish, and his grandparents were Orthodox émigrés from Ukraine. He denied this until the day he died, claiming he was raised Episcopalian and that his ancestors had served as Confederate soldiers during the Civil War. Two of his sons (one the tardy teen) became Episcopalian ministers. His biographer wrote that, for all Krulak's newfound Christianity, it was the Marines that had become "his new tribe."

Before moving on to our MOS schools, my roommates and I posed in our dress blues in the Hawkins Room, the cocktail lounge in O'Bannon. We looked sharp but miserable.

We continued to call rosters kill sheets.

The feeling of being judged at every turn, and of being caught in a high-stakes zero-sum struggle with one's peers, relaxed beyond Quantico, but it didn't evaporate. Military life can furnish rare feelings of mass belonging for people who sense they were born into a nation that scorns them, never mind a nation that scorns any instinct toward large-scale sociality. But those feelings are not smoothly distributed.

The camaraderie of the enlisted ranks adds up to a latent class solidarity. As enlisted marines are fond of remarking, they represent the majority of the military—the majority that "works for a living." The officer corps, on the other hand, is made up of strivers, at once distinguishable yet of a piece with their civilian professional counterparts, who learn to compete with one another at an early age and attend colleges and universities that double or triple the reputational stakes of the contest. Officer schooling mimics this pedigree in a way enlisted schooling does not. Marine officers are pitted against one another as individual equity, from the cutthroat peer-review process to the promotion system that follows. It is for this reason I never felt like I was part of a lieutenant whole the same way I knew I was a member of the lance corporal underground. There was an earnestness to the enlisted existence, a conviction of collective duty and sacrifice, however barbaric its realizations, that was never allowed to congeal among the brass. Staff officers who'd signed off on recruiting slogans like "Army of One" or "One From on High" were operating from experience, and that experience cut across all branches.

A stark individualism among the officer ranks made the training all the unsightlier. Spending months on end learning how to murder strangers can prove revolting enough. But at least the enlisted experience comes with an insistence that we are all in it together, and that we are equals in our willingness to kill or be killed. Camaraderie in blood is still blood, but it's hard to deny its romantic appeal. But when learning the art of, let's say, calling in an air strike, the competition-minded officer is typically divorced from any higher mutuality. The underlying nihilism of the education and the "upwardly mobile" rat race that buttresses it, therefore, come more into focus. Even more when such artistry is given not only a grade but a grade that, attached to a million other grades, determines one's standing in much the same way a grade in business or law school does.

In any event, it was at the Navy and Marine Corps Intelligence

Training Center at Dam Neck that I allowed myself to let my guard down a bit. There were about twenty in my Signals Intelligence Officer Course, and much like our initial arrival at TBS, we were forced to wait a few months before picking up. Occasionally we were assigned a minor task or two, but we tended to go about our days as we pleased. It was another cushy interval, and we had a good time. I became close with my two roommates in a rented condo on the beach, and both before and during the coursework, I had fun with the rest of the class, too. Sometimes this happened at a cage-fight viewing night in a nondescript basement in downtown Virginia Beach. Other times while sharing running space with SEAL Team Six up and down the musket-shaped Sandpiper Beach.

The grotesquerie of the training itself came to a head during our two-month sojourn at the headquarters of the National Security Agency (NSA) in Fort Meade, Maryland. Here I learned about how my government was intercepting commercial signals spanning from the internet to satellite, as well as about the dragnet collection programs Edward Snowden would later reveal. I was shocked how easy it all sounded: a single satellite placed here; a single wiretap room positioned there; a single breaking-and-entering op or cover-up op conducted here or there or anywhere. Judging by stray comments from briefers, it appeared anyone who needed to get extorted for a mission was getting extorted. And whenever they needed a fall guy, they found a fall guy.

I also learned about the uses of international intelligence-sharing partnerships like the Anglospheric "Five Eyes" (the United States, the UK, Australia, Canada, and New Zealand) and how they could commission foreign partners with otherwise illegal or unconstitutional activity, like the surveillance of one's own citizens. This practice amounts to the signals intelligence equivalent of extraordinary rendition. Just as the US government has employed third-party governments for torture, it has done the same for SIGINT collection.

I learned about unmanned aerial vehicles my own unit would later use to hunt peasants in Afghanistan, like the ScanEagle, based on a drone designed to spot schools of fish, and about the specifications of old warhorse assets like the Guardrail, a manned SIGINT aircraft that worked overtime in my area of operations to help geolocate our targets and shape the offensive ground operations of infantry or reconnaissance marines. I learned about the massive carbon-intensive energy required to maintain ludicrous and counterproductive loads of data storage. I experienced pattern-of-life analysis of random Afghans on a Top Secret watch floor and godlike omniscience through voice-monitoring systems like ONEROOF.

This area looks like the bridge of *Star Trek*'s USS *Enterprise*. It looks like the International Space Station Flight Control Room. Except the objects of your gaze are real and reside here on earth. The ultimate effect is to make the human a thing. A routine, bureaucratic thing. But they are humans. Sometimes they are humans at risk of death. Sometimes immediate death. At the hands of men like me.

The Fort was also where I was briefed on Real Time Regional Gateway (RT-RG), an elaborate multinational interface designed to make kill-or-capture missions as user-friendly as possible. It would be used thousands of times during my deployment to finish off alleged enemy combatants, many of whom investigative reports have now concluded were civilians.

Part of its user-friendly charm involved its circumvention of standard oversight and control, which allowed it to eradicate anyone holding an earmarked SIM card. Even though the commanders we were chasing switched out their cards as a regular security precaution.

None of this risked threatening the market yields of the program. Battle damage assessments continued to list virtually all military-aged males as the enemy, and RT-RG has been deployed on the US-Mexico border.

When I wasn't soaking in the spycraft and killcraft being used profitably and with abandon across the globe—and questioning these uses—I was holding on tight to residual habits. I couldn't bring myself to vote for John McCain in November, or any Republican for that matter, but I couldn't bring myself to vote for Barack Obama, either. I remained convinced the main crime of our time was state overreach. What had changed was now I was prepared to accept the obvious—that US militarism counted as a principal part of this problem.

Then again, social democracy no longer struck me as frightful, as it once did. I read with interest the philosopher Samuel Freeman's acclaimed article "Illiberal Libertarians: Why Libertarianism Is Not a Liberal View" and noted the consonances between capitalist and imperialist cultures, the shared drive to defeat, dominate, and expand. But I still figured some ideal version of market society could deliver social goods without the obtrusions of big government, even as that faith was put under increasing strain. I couldn't comprehend in full the unified (and unifying) culture that had made me. And for that reason, I couldn't turn against it.

For all America's sins, I told myself, we were still the good guys. I was not ready to fess up to the most wretched ramifications of my slow-going disillusionment. I was not yet equipped, mentally or intellectually, to see the empire, but I was becoming more sensitive to my own status as both its product and its guarantor, a crossroads fraught with conflicting excuses, self-deceptions, and escalations. In Virginia Beach I became the proud owner of a Walther PPS, a sleek .40-caliber pistol I referred to as a souped-up James Bond gun. I was sworn in as a concealed-weapon holder, and I wisecracked about how Israelis shouldn't be the only Jews to play with firearms.

Despite my growing doubts about US foreign policy, I went on relating to my buddies as a fellow conservative. When Bill mocked a billboard encouraging black people to use condoms and get tested for HIV, I kept my mouth shut. When Micah went on about Muslims, at most I gently pushed back. When Josephs shared a chain message celebrating the construction of the USS *New York*, an amphibious warfare ship fashioned with seven and a half short tons of steel from the fallen World Trade Center, I found the religiosity excessive but still relatable. The ship's motto, which still resonated with me, however faintly, was licensed and sold as a challenge coin by the Department of the Navy: "Strength forged through sacrifice. Never forget."

In April I attended a birthday party for Luntz at the China 1 nightclub in the East Village. It reeked of Polo cologne, and soon-to-be-rich (if overworked) corporate lawyers dominated the scene. I couldn't hear most of what anyone said, but I know everyone thanked me for my service.

I woke up late the next day at my grandparents' place on the Upper East, downed the remaining tap water from the refrigerated pitcher, and after reading another chapter or so of Edward Skidelsky's biography of the German Jewish philosopher Ernst Cassirer (whose even-keeled humanism was comforting at the time), taxied with my dear octogenarians to a belated Passover seder in Brooklyn. Our hosts were my grandfather's younger brother and his Cuban American wife. They'd fallen in love as young leftists in the sixties and, unlike so many others of that era, never renounced their politics. Instead, they became public school teachers, trade unionists, and parents of two sons just as engaged and engaging. I'd always respected that side of the family for their knowledge and passion, even if I had strayed elsewhere. I remember as a child attending a concert for the New York City Labor Chorus and feeling like I'd stepped into a parallel dimension as alluring as it was indecipherable.

The homemade Haggadah included a verse from a Jewish critic of the Israeli occupation, alongside a photograph of unjust suffering, a home demolition. The verse may have been Avot Yeshurun's "Passover on Caves," a fabled Israeli poem published after Israel's founding in 1948. Yeshurun juxtaposed the Holocaust with the Nakba—the catastrophe of Palestinian dispossession. The meal service incorporated Paul Robeson's "Go Down, Moses." Robeson's deep baritone moved me, set me on a certain course.

Someone that afternoon had alluded to imperialism. Whereas before I'd dismissed such verbiage as left-wing hysterics, now the language beckoned me like voices of prophecy from another era. Driving back to Fort Meade, my mind ran circles around that encroaching revelation.

I began thinking about all the hit TV series with empire in mind. They seemed to be everywhere: the swooning liberal nationalism of

The West Wing, the frontier rapaciousness of *Deadwood*, the superpower paranoia of *24* and *Battlestar Galactica.* Crime dramas, from *The Shield* to *The Wire*, sublimated the torments of the inner empire for mass consumption, just as *The Sopranos*, *Mad Men*, and *Boardwalk Empire* made entertainment out of more local or private conquests. Although Americans would keep refusing to see what was right before them, their favorite diversions, their collective unconscious, would keep trying to reveal it to them.

As I prepped for my own war, the empire was all around, closing in and bounding out, cutting through in ways big and small and measureless. Out of fear, inertia, and self-interest, I proceeded on my course, as if the surrounding premonitions meant nothing. The officer pay was good, the reverence limitless. The prospect of giving up what I'd strived for, in addition to risking a dishonorable or other than honorable discharge—or just the stigmatization that would come from applying for conscientious objector status—was inconceivable. But I had a strong inkling at that point, for all my equivocations, I was marching in the wrong direction.

The summer of 2009 I was granted a long stretch of leave between completing MOS school and reporting to my first duty station at Camp Pendleton. My brothers and I planned a road trip to Pendleton. I led the charge. I also footed most of the bill, with some reimbursement assistance from the government. Brett was about to start his first semester of law school at Tulane, and Ethan a semester abroad in Cape Town. We hadn't been together for an extended period since childhood. We missed each other, and seeing war might be in my future, that longing had become more intense. Our lives had proved comfortable and safe, and we'd never had to consider, in any urgent sense, the prospect of that changing. Although the actual odds of me getting hurt or killed were negligible, the prospect still hung over us like the Sword of Damocles.

The first week of June, we set off on the road from Bloomfield and took a brief stop in New Rochelle, where Bill and his grandmother treated us to lunch. The next day we made it to DC and spent much of the evening at Kramers, where I bought Jack Kerouac's *On the Road.* For all my misgivings about the war effort and even the United States writ large, I was still entranced by my nation's mythos. Especially its swashbuckling ego and id, from Huckleberry Finn to Augie March to Dean Moriarty to me. I still wanted to be one of them. All of them. All at once.

Courtesy of an Emory newspaper friend who let us crash at his place, we enjoyed two full days in and around the nation's capital. Our itinerary included pigging out on milkshakes and burgers—twice—and passing around our favorite Belgians at Beck's Brasserie. We walked across the National Mall and up the steps of the Lincoln Memorial before making a drunken appearance at one of Ethan's GW frat parties.

Brett drove us to Savannah the following day, his first time behind the wheel in years. He steered across a majestic bridge at sunset, where the sky descended on us as boss and beauty, painting everything else it touched with splendor.

We dropped our gear off at a Hilton and headed over to the Pink House, an eighteenth-century mansion where Bill had recommended we wine and dine. We ordered a South African wine in anticipation of Ethan's upcoming adventure and Bill's honor. He'd visited the country over thirty times and clearly had sympathies for the former apartheid government, though I clearly didn't care enough yet to call him out on it. We rounded out an elaborate meal with cheesecake, custard, and chocolate mousse. The total damage came to over two hundred dollars.

The waiter was a handsome thirty-something with a thick Southern lilt. He was born and raised on the Savannah coast, and he reminded me of some of the more calloused hands from the Island. In that sense he made me feel small, even though I was big then, even though I'd been trained to look and feel and act big. Tour groups walked past as they learned the mansion's history: the Olde Pink House, built around the 1780s, first went by the name the Habersham House, in recognition of its owner, James Habersham Jr., a wealthy slaver.

A whitish-blueish mist hovered over the high grass of Middle Georgia during its mornings and above its low roofs at night. When making my outings to and from Sherry and Beany's home as an Emory undergrad—a temporary Yankee import plopped on the upscale outskirts of Atlanta—I'd marvel at the surrounding vapors, just as I would those enveloped by them.

Joe Wilkinson was the town's most respected elder. As a former mayor and church cofounder, as well as one of the area's more prosperous farmers, he knew everyone, and everyone knew him. Sherry called him Mr. Joe, which meant I did too, and when he taught me to fish my freshman year, I was calling him Mr. Joe every other breath, on top of mixing in the occasional, facetious Southernism.

On the day I arrived with my two brothers, Mr. Joe was in characteristic form. "Mr. Joe done fix yuh a mightuh fi'day at the pon', yuh hear."

We used crickets as bait, and the only thing I snagged that afternoon was the sagging canopy of a slim-trunked evergreen. "Got myself a big one, Mr. Joe," I shouted across the pond. "I done caught me a branch!"

Mr. Joe was once a military man, having served in France and Germany during the Second World War. But by then he was all red cheeks of joy, and sitting on his stool, rod on his lap, he chuckled and asked how much that branch weighed.

We feasted on hush puppies and fried fish at the water's edge, and Mr. Joe led us in prayer. After lunch, the affable patriarch recounted an anecdote I'd heard before about the time he and his now ailing wife visited Hitler's retreat, the Eagle's Nest, up in the high sky as postwar tourists. He invoked the name of the closest down, Berchtesgaden, and how, when the war was done and they needed a place to rest and calm down a bit, they went there, to the Fuhrer's vacation spot up in the mountains. When he returned some six decades later, he met the kind local folk, and on his way out, fumbling, old-man-like, for his wallet to buy train tickets, the young man at the entry said, "You already paid, sir, in 1945. Come on in." It made him cry right then and there, in front of his wife and everyone. And then he cried again, and we were ready to cry with him, witnessing the poignant moment of an elderly man, who had done something in his life, something that hurt but that meant something, remembering.

We went back to fishing after that, and I still didn't catch a thing. When the sun started setting and the Georgia forest took up its strange evening chant, Mr. Joe guided me to a quiet corner and said, "I'm fixin' to invite you an' the buhs to my ol' Caboose Club."

The Caboose Club was a breakfast club for the town's elder men, set in a refurbished train car right off the main road. The next morning, we showed up at Mr. Joe's door at 0530, to find him waiting in his overalls, fingers gripping the suspenders at his breast.

"Lordy, Lordy. Mightuh fine day."

"Yes indeed, sir. Yes indeed." Our repartee had become a shtick.

We hopped in his pickup truck, me in the passenger seat and my brothers in the back, with their feet dangling off the bed. At the caboose, seven other cars were parked on the grass.

"Smaller crowd than reguluh. They prob'ly heard y'all was comin'," he said with a chortle, shaking his head.

The red train car had small wooden staircases leading up to entrances on each end, and its interior was adorned like a museum: glass-protected paintings, sketches, awards, plaques. Obscure descriptions were printed below each object, but before we could inspect them further, we were greeted by the current mayor and sheriff, along with a man who introduced himself as "John Quincy Adams of South Carolina. No connect'n to that Bost'n sap!"

John Quincy Adams of South Carolina wore a hunter's cap, camouflage green with mesh in the back. He was a kind, jovial soul bursting with witticisms. We chatted some about our military experiences. Most of the ten men there had service backgrounds, which helped carry the conversations forward. Everyone shared their stories, and when the biscuits were gone, we said our goodbyes. Since Mr. Joe was excited to give us a tour of the decorated walls, my brothers and I were the last to leave. He even let Ethan film the artifacts, including a homemade wooden signpost with "Table of Knowledge" on one side and "Table of BS" on the other. That and an encased flag of Old Georgia.

We visited the Huey helicopter, the decommissioned Bell UH-1 Iroquois that stood just a street away from the caboose, still fitted with stretchers and other medical instruments in the rear. I tried my best at explaining its relevance to the Vietnam War. I had forgotten the name of the chopper type but knew it was featured in the movie version of *We Were Soldiers Once... and Young* (starring Mel Gibson).

When we drove out one early morning, Mr. Joe waved goodbye from his yard, mower in hand, beaming. I felt so blessed as a secular Jew to have built a bond with a man like him, and with all the rest. Like we were all somehow the same, even though we weren't, and that we were all somehow reconciled, even though the histories defining us were still rushing in less reconciled directions. I was still grasping on to histories (or myths) Mr. Joe and—on the other side of the Mason-Dixon—my gramps embodied, of goodness and greatness and no conflict in between, where the United States, its people, its legionaries, guarding the gates of civilization, could still stand proud.

In Chattanooga we drove to the top of Lookout Mountain, encircled by riches, and gazed at the feudal scene below.

In Nashville, the "Athens of the South" (for all its institutions of higher learning), we stopped by the Parthenon replica and took in its tacky magnificence. It was designed by William Crawford Smith for the Tennessee Centennial Exposition in 1897. Smith had fought as a Confederate in the Civil War and died fighting on behalf of the United States in the Philippines in 1899. We drove down Music Row, ate fish tacos and drank microbrews at Big River Grille, and listened to live honky-tonk at Robert's Western World and the Station Inn. We rode the mechanical bull at the Cadillac Ranch. I took three turns and held on the longest of the bunch, for a total of twenty-two seconds. I thought of my old boot camp rack-mate, Rundle, and how I would have made him proud. I wondered what he was doing now. If he was still getting hounded.

In New Orleans we took the first city bus tour of our lives. Our driver, Harry, was born and raised in the city and spoke from a heartfelt place about every block and street corner. He knew them all like a neighbor, and he told us their stories. When we passed through the Lower Ninth Ward, he directed us to the red spray paint on what was left of the doors. The numbers denoted how many died during the hurricane, and therefore how many bodies had to be removed by FEMA or local and state governments. Whenever we drove by anyone without flood insurance, he'd tell us so, which amounted to everyone we drove by. We saw steps to nowhere and whole rows of houses that had vanished. Harry told us the word *jazz* comes from "jackass music" and rhapsodized about his hometown's burial procedures. When we made it back to the rich parts and passed John Goodman's house, he said, "John Goodman is a good man. His wife? Not so much."

At Pete's Dueling Piano Bar in Austin we threw twenties upon twenties toward the musicians, who played every song everyone requested. "Sweet Child of Mine" and "Sitting on the Dock of the Bay," "Brown-Eyed Girl" and "Moon Shadow," long before Van Morrison would sing about the oppression of masks and social distancing during a pandemic and after Cat Stevens became Yusuf Islam and was denied entry in the United States because of his last name.

At the University of Texas campus, we stared at the Main Building Tower with a casual vacancy. In 1966 a marine had stabbed his wife and mom to death and climbed to the tower's top, where he proceeded to shoot dead thirteen people below. It was the deadliest single-perpetrator mass shooting in the United States until 1984, when a domestic abuser who'd been a gun-obsessed recluse since childhood mowed down twenty-one at a McDonald's in San Ysidro. In 1991 that record was beat by a Navy and Merchant Marine veteran who killed twenty-three in Killeen, Texas. The murderer drove his Ford Ranger into a cafeteria and then shot up everyone within shooting distance. He was a racist and a woman hater and he came from a military family, the son of an orthopedic surgeon who worked on countless bases across the country. The last base they moved to before the parents' divorce was

Fort Hood, the biggest in the nation. Killeen was the town over, and at the time of the massacre, UT-Austin's Main Building Tower, a little over an hour south, was still standing tall.

The sun was an explosive blast the size of America, and it lit up the "Fireworks for Sale" signs and the gas stations for miles on end. The oil rigs bowed to the sun in the distance, through Oklahoma and Kansas and into Colorado. For a fugitive moment, the sun set behind textured clouds, radiating the crown of Libertas.

We sputtered up the Rockies and descended from the snow caps to the least forgiving deserts.

We hiked up Angels Landing at Zion National Park. I froze toward the top, like I always do when I get too high. Ethan took a shot of a condor perched nearby.

In Vegas we gorged on steak, and in San Francisco, visiting yet more cousins, we did the usual: Coit Tower, Kerouac's and Ginsberg's old stomping grounds in North Beach, Vesuvio Cafe.

Next to the Pacific Heights mansions we snickered at a big-cocked robot named Goliath, born of scavenged scraps.

I made it down to LA to see my brothers off at the airport around July 4. Saying goodbye before heading off to war requires a certain dis-association. There's no way to issue farewells under this circumstance with anything approaching full presence of mind, but we were in rel-atively good spirits. Assuming we stayed lucky, we had bright futures ahead. I checked in at Pendleton a few days later, after moving into an apartment with a fellow lieutenant. We roamed across San Marcos and Escondido and Carlsbad like they were ours to roam. For all our faults and embarrassments, we still owned the world.

PART FIVE
TURNING POINT

Countless coal-black bodies, the men and the animals alike, both infinitesimally small from the sky, the black bodies of men and animal bodies, the body called mine, or man's, mines, men.

—*C. E. Morgan*

I

All the world's a stage. But when you're in uniform, that fact becomes heightened. And when you're staging for war, it's the only fact that matters. Military operations require staging areas, and before then, warfighters perform full-dress rehearsals. Military practitioners call their areas of operation theaters of war, and their counterparts bad actors. Up until recently, promotion boards required headshots of each candidate (as it was explained to me, leaders of marines must have good stage presence and look the part). Military ceremony involves costumes, plotting, mise-en-scène, and monologue or dialogue, and the Marine Corps Birthday Ball would make any theater kid blush. Even combat operations themselves entail a myriad of scripts, from the orders to the debriefings to the radio etiquette. Martial superiors don metaphorical masks of command, just as troops share their etymology with the theater troupe.

In FM 6-0, the Army's Mission Command field manual, much of this has been laid bare. The tract is padded with dramatic "historical vignettes" and instructions on "the role of the commander," the "role of liaison," or "the dual roles of religious leaders." Military intelligence staff "plays the enemy commander" during rehearsals while a "rehearsal director... assesses and critiques" the rehearsal. The director is advised to work off a "rehearsal script." Since the manual's original publication in 2003, an entire cottage industry of military role-playing has cropped up. Hundreds of millions of dollars are squandered on the recruitment of role players and the construction of mock villages. The villagers hail from the countries the United States and its allies war against, and an NBC report described one such village in the Mojave Desert as

> elaborate and carefully designed as a Hollywood set. It features more than 500 buildings, signs with Arabic writing hanging on several walls and a central market complete with barrels of fake fruit. From a hilltop control center, training officials can pump smoke and audio into the dwellings to simulate the real thing.

The Hollywood analogy only touches the surface of militarism's cinematic universe.

Theater and war grew up together. From the Greeks to the Romans to the Elizabethans, they have shared the same heroes and adversaries, the same settings and props. And the tradition carries on with Pentagon-backed television and Langley-advised film. Security-state consulting fees and funding sources now constitute a considerable portion of Hollywood's annual budget.

At its most shameful, war does more than just entertain, it arouses and titillates. When the Defense Department's *Dictionary of Military and Associated Terms* defines *assault* as "the climax of an attack," the dramaturgical nod might have been conscious. Its sexual undertones almost certainly were not. If people speak words, it is just as true that words speak to people. Put more sharply, certain words are drawn to certain people, like iron nails to ore.

The words that cling to war and its participants—its performers—gather around the same motif. We all became, at one point or another, fucknuggets or fucksticks. We fucked the shit out of our girls back home and fucked shit up in training or in Afghanistan. When things got fucked, we called it a clusterfuck or a circle jerk. We humped with a load, hoping to get some action. If you were a virginal newbie in the Army, you were a cherry. If the bad guy was wounded and bloody and dying to escape, he was a squirter. Sometimes warfighters were inserted. Sometimes they withdrew or pulled out. Sometimes they harassed others with their bang-bangs. Sometimes others harassed them with theirs. There were frontal assaults and rearguards, bombshells and cruises and straight shots. Deployed marines destroyed the enemy. Stateside marines destroyed their conquests. If you conquered an Air Force girl, she became a cockpit. Everyone was sucking the big weenie in the suckiness and the suck. Everyone was getting fucked by the green weenie in the suck. It was all fuck-fuck games before the suck and after the suck and during the suck. And everything worth anything was war porn.

Radio Battalion, or RadBn ("RAD-BIN"), was the signals intelligence unit where I would spend the rest of my military tenure, headquartered forty-five minutes up the road from San Diego at the sprawling Camp Pendleton. For the first few months, I served as the "S-4 alpha," the go-to lingo for the assistant logistics officer. Walton, my OCS buddy and someone who had already established himself as a top lieutenant, told me the odds of staying in the billet for long were 30–70, and to "bloom where I was planted." So I put in my all as a jock captain's errand boy, just as I had developed rapport with the enlisted guys in the supply shop.

By late September, a little over two months after I'd become the

S-4A, the battalion commander released the officer slate for an upcoming deployment to Afghanistan in February or March of 2010. I had been tapped as the assistant officer in charge (AOIC) for one of the two operational control elements (OCEs). I would be paired with a senior first lieutenant in commanding a small unit in and around the Helmand Province. The length of the pump was uncertain, but we were expected to be there for at least six months. The size of the OCE was also bound to change as needs shifted, but it was clear I'd be leading somewhere between eighty and ninety personnel comprising marines, civilians, and occasional soldiers.

Thirty to forty men—everyone in my OCE was a man—would conduct analysis of leadership and insurgent cells behind ample monitors in a windowless room on a spacious base. The rest would be linguists and collectors (those gathering insurgent signals) spread across an area of operations the size of my home state of Connecticut. The second category would be divided into four- to eight-man teams, and to the extent I would experience anything resembling what most Americans think of when they think of war, I would experience it with or en route to the team marines. They would be the ones attached to squads or platoons of trigger-pullers, where their intel would sometimes help drive or shape coordinated company, battalion, or even regimental missions. More frequently, though, they would accompany the front-liners on regular foot patrols, eavesdropping and geolocating radio (mostly generic ICOM) chatter while providing indications and warnings: that is, instantaneous heads-up on the location, size, equipment, and intent of those their supported units hoped to close with and destroy.

That summer, before being notified of my assignment, I had gotten the hang of rattling off the jargon and doing so with ostensible confidence. I could name the equipment with aplomb and list its specifications and functions without pause. My short stay in the supply shop, where I went out of my way to get to know my marines and them me, seemed to have proved a success. Even the paternalism of that routine phrase—*my marines*—was starting to make sense at a more affective register. Over a few months, we had built a mutual respect, one based on professionalism and precision, but also silliness and candor. Whether transferring expensive gear or staging it, we had fun doing what had to be done and bitching about it afterward. Of course, they were the ones tasked with the heavy lifting, and it took me a while to fess up to that and stop joining in each haul. But I guess that was the point. I was taking ownership of my managerial responsibilities just as much as I was entrusting them with theirs. If they had become my marines, it was only because I had become their lieutenant. And no matter how contrived that sounds now, I really was looking forward to putting it to the test with a new, forward-deployed platoon.

My optimism was nonetheless accompanied by unease. Sure, it appeared I had gained the trust of a few supply marines, and my command appeared to have faith enough in me. But would it be the same with eighty or ninety SIGINTers, many of them of the more critical, unruly variety? How about the handful of thirty- or forty-something civilian linguists, most of whom hailed from Afghanistan or Pakistan and had endured lives far harder than mine?

For all my training I still felt like I hadn't the slightest clue what my deployment might entail. Others told me I had just been handed the most prized spot for RadBn officers, a position that would bring me as proximate to the action as pog officers can get. Not only that, but one that offered the possibility of a back-to-back deployment, with the chance to fill my senior lieutenant's shoes, assuming he was sent home at the half-year mark. But I still couldn't picture what this meant in practice. I had been selected to take part in one of the more daring rides in the park after more than three years spent studying incomplete sketches of the ride. But the preparatory materials had been redacted, and every other instructor assured me they didn't come close to capturing what it was I was getting into.

I can scarcely think of an analogy more offensive to the final truth of war, never mind a war of empire. But if there is one thing a good many marines will admit, it is their wish to experience, if not death itself, then brushes with death.

Despite my cavalcading questions about Iraq, Afghanistan, and the wider crimes of the United States, I, too, wanted a little death. Not only that, but I still felt I had a right to it. At least I didn't dwell on the alternative proposition that I didn't. That no one had a right to thrill-seek at the expense of others. At the *lethal* expense of others. And that a society that didn't just accept such an enterprise but idealized it was a society that had already forfeited any claim to virtue, much less supreme dominion.

My pursuit came with an underlying dread. I was overwhelmed by thoughts of my own death or near death, petrified about the prospect of coming home without a leg or half my face, or with a brain injury or mental illness. But such possibilities were often suppressed by ones that felt—and still feel—even more terrifying. I became an expert in an array of possible futures, ranging from getting someone on our side hurt or killed to crapping in my trousers to freezing up during a hairy second. I was racked by fears of humiliation and inadequacy, and the barks of my Officer Candidate School instructors came back with a vengeance.

"Someone lied to you, Rubin!"

"You're gonna get someone killed, Rubin!"

"Something's gonna happen to you, Rubin!"

"You're weak, Rubin, you're weak!"

Aside from worrying about any destined incompetence, I perseverated over mere bad luck. Walton had been poised to seize a billet in one of the two OCEs, until a marine in his recon-trained SIGINT platoon, in a freak accident, almost died during a pool exercise. The marine incurred severe and lasting disabilities, and Walton had to remain at Pendleton through the completion of the formal inquiry. Although I had never met this marine, his sudden misfortune disturbed me. For more self-interested reasons, so did the predicament of my OCS buddy, the most squared-away marine I'd ever known. If something so fateful could happen under his watch, it could happen under anybody's.

Rosen, my Israeli Defense Forces pal, assured me I had everything it took to lead and hold my composure. My parents told me the same, though they had long demonstrated a pattern of wishful thinking, and once they'd realized they couldn't coax me (or, in my father's case, berate me) into giving up my harebrained quest to join up, they carried on with convenient self-deceptions: That I'd never get deployed. And if I did get deployed, it wouldn't be in a combat zone. And if it were in a combat zone, it wouldn't be anywhere near the actual combat.

Granted, I'd strung my folks along. I never told them straight-up that I wanted to experience the front lines like most other marines I knew. Nor was I on the level about the deployment tempo of Marine units at that point, including the ones where I was likely to be stationed. To do so would have meant confronting the situation I had put loved ones in and the terrible selfishness of my journey.

The pre-deployment training cycle at Pendleton started off slow. The OCE commander, Lieutenant Waldron, a quiet New Zealander American, put me in charge of much of the initial paperwork, medical checkups or shots, scheduling for the rifle qual, first aid, and other unit-wide requirements. I taught classes on COIN—counterinsurgency theory—and tested the platoon on what they'd learned. They memorized capsule histories of the major ethnic groups in Afghanistan, particularly in the southern portion. After familiarizing them with the most common insurgent tactics in use at the time, from bait-and-ambush to recycling ambush sites, I had them war game a series of case studies. I assigned news articles and, on a tip from one of my men, organized a unit-wide viewing of a *Frontline* documentary called "Obama's War." Some of the guys groaned—they wanted to break things and get some—but most were respectful and at least appeared to appreciate my earnestness. Besides, a little shit-talking behind my back, I figured, was a small price to pay to feel like I was still doing something defensible.

In between the lessons and box checking, the marines treated me to small and tall tales. About drunken stupors on booze cruises in Bahrain, Dubai, Kuwait, Jordan, Spain, Italy, and Guam. About super-secret assignments in Norway. About their involvement in medevacs in Iraq, anti-piracy ops off the coast of Somalia, coming to the aid of victims and survivors of Al-Qaeda's USS *Cole* bombing in Yemen's Aden Harbor in 2000.

Some were just as inclined to talk family history. One marine descended from military royalty. He was the grandson of a lieutenant colonel in the British Royal Army during World War II. His grandfather on the other side got tossed into one of Vichy France's POW camps in northern Africa. After making it out, he served a stint in the fifties at the bomb-testing facility in Nevada.

Another marine was the son of a retired Navy pilot. When he asked his pops what Naval job he should sign up for, his father said, "Don't be a pussy. Become an enlisted US Marine."

I had the son of a retired sergeant major in my platoon, and the son of another marine who had just retired after twenty-two years and who now worked for various intel agencies. A conspicuous number came from households where at least one parent was hooked into the war machine, from the NSA to marksmanship training companies like Beamhit. Another noticeable batch were raised by devout Christians. A handful were homeschooled.

Gauzy sentiment has a way of draping over anything that's yours, especially when they're other people. When they're no longer yours, or when you grow up and realize they were never yours to begin with, you're pushed to speak about them even more tenderly. Because you feel stupid and ridiculous for feeling anything so paternal for people who had already at such tender ages labored in ways that bring you to shame. Because all you were doing at that tender age was reading books, smoking weed, and jacking off.

Free riding on the jibber-jabber became my favorite fringe benefit in the Corps. Marines were always woofing and wagging, warping and wefting. I'd get lost in their alternations. They'd taunt one second and cozy up the next. Grandstand, then confess. I'd listen to them, on and off, for hours, goading them with a word or two whenever they hinted at a stop. And it wasn't just the badinage. It was their personal narratives. Their talents. Their victories and disappointments. Their struggles, most of all. How they came to be. Even those who held their backstories closest to their chests had a certain charming mystery to them.

Kwon was my age. He had a bachelor's degree in sociology and was working on a master's in government. He'd done Christian missionary work across China and Central Asia. Like most marines worth their salt, he knew how to string a few words together.

"I enjoy long strolls on the beach with voluptuous women, followed by copious amounts of liquor and other questionable activities that may be banned in thirty-nine states."

Asner was the other Jew in my platoon. He was pimply and respectful, but he had a bite when he felt it necessary. I found most like him often did. One can be only so respectful.

"I'm from the Jersey Shore, sir," he told me. "Been working my whole life, sir. Started landscaping for rich people in Cape May County when I was fifteen. My mom was a house-watcher there."

"What's that?"

"She watched the houses of rich people. Their summer homes. Kept them all tidy, everything in order. Kept the plants going. Made sure nothing was burning. Smoking. Stolen."

"Hey, Baptiste."

"Good afternoon, sir."

"So tell me about yourself."

"I'm from Queens."

"Cool beans. And?"

"I exited the womb with a full-grown handlebar mustache..."

"No shit."

"...and the tenacity of a Bengal tiger..."

"That's something."

"I speak French in Russian."

"And Russian."

"*In* Russian."

"No shit."

"I'm basically Ron Burgundy."

"Good flick. But seriously, tell me something real about you. Just one thing. Whatever comes to mind."

Nothing. Just the sound of the oblivious fan.

"One thing, Baptiste."

"I need to dominate and excel in areas new to me."

"See, was that so hard?"

When it came to Gunny Lee, bells and whistles were not included. Last I heard, he'd finally made it to JSOC, the Joint Special Operations Command. He was taciturn and exact, the paradigmatic secret squirrel. Although *Secret Squirrel*, the sixties-era cartoon, parodied the spy genre. And marines, most of whom didn't seem to be aware of the phrase's origins (myself included), tended to wield it in a similarly sardonic fashion. But Lee was the genuine item. Not so much squirrel as cheetah. I'd never met a man with a more feline manner. His build was sturdy and slim, and so was his speech. There was a wryness to him that almost made me uncomfortable, like he was prepared to ruin me with a single syllable, at a time of his choosing. But for obvious reasons of career advancement, that time never arrived.

"My father was a pipefitter and my mom was a crackhead." So said Staff Sergeant Morris. "Born and raised in Mississippi. Mom left when I was two. Dad raised us. Older sister. Younger brother. We never had much money but always seemed to have everything we needed to get by."

"Tell me more, if you don't mind."

"Oh, this is all I do, sir. I'm a real talker if you haven't noticed. Our first car in Monterey at DLI—that's the Defense Language Institute, sir—is this shitty putrid green '73 Plymouth Duster. After leaving Monterey in that car, my pregnant wife and I went to San Angelo, Texas, for five months for crypto school. West Texas is the pits of hell, sir. Straight up. And being in a one-bedroom trash apartment with a pregnant emotional wife I didn't even like was definitely a battle. But I graduated first in my class."

Later he talked about the birth of his first kid, William, in Lejeune in North Carolina. He lit up when he said his kid's name. So many of these guys had kids. Some didn't light up, but most did. And they made clear it was for their kids that they were turning their lives around. Most were older. In their mid- to late twenties. Maybe even thirties. Mostly senior enlisted. But plenty were just out of high school.

Everyone with a high-speed résumé liked to drop intermittent details. Most drenched you with them. Some harped on their survival, evasion, resistance, and escape (SERE) or combat lifesaving qualifications. Or their three weeks in the Jumpmaster course and twelve weeks in the Basic Reconnaissance Course (BRC). Others hewed closer to their geeky essence, going on about Digital Network Intelligence (DNI) or Tailored Access Operations (TAO). Same went with their language chops, which ran the gamut from Korean to Spanish to French to Russian to Arabic to Farsi to Dari to Pashto. They conveyed their linguistic versatility with the same pride they did their past or present gigs.

"I'm something of an electrician, sir."

"If you ever want to know anything and everything about sys admin, programming, networking, hacking, I'm your guy, sir."

"I did some car work. Installed audio. Good side hustle, sir."

"I've waited tables, bartended, opened the store at a fast-food joint, you name it, sir."

"I've done everything from assistant manage to selling mortgage-backed securities. And yes, sir, I know it was guys like me that tanked the economy. Lesson learned!"

Most got animated talking about their hobbies (photography, videography, gaming, ballroom dancing) or athletic triumphs (captaining the lacrosse team, commanding the rifle team, destroying it in the local rec league, BMX biking like a madman, impressing the ladies as a swimming instructor, powerlifting). A few spoke with contentment about their hopes and dreams, from attending culinary school to settling back at the family farm.

I suppose most of it was true. After all, they appeared just as eager to relay stories of perceived failure, which were boundless and pensive, disordered and proud.

"I can't control my liquor."

"I dropped out of college."

"I used to be over three hundred pounds."

"My wife cheated on me during my last deployment."

"I have at least one kid on every continent. That I'm aware of."

"And that's when I reevaluated my life, sir. That's when I turned it all around."

The recaps of their previous pumps vacillated between the heart-warming and the scornful and the absurd. If their deployment added up to a hill of beans, they said so and moved on. If it was exciting, you could feel the excitement. I rarely came across anyone in RadBn with the thousand-yard stare or the silence. That would come later, in Afghanistan. And even gruntland would greet me as a more jocular and effusive affair than I expected. At least when the mourning wasn't immediate.

Marines love to shape-shift and change course. In the military vernacular, they are masters of the erratic attack, the dynamic defense, or the Rhizome maneuver. There is nothing they hate more than to be pegged or pinned down (in public, anyway). Semper Gumby, they say. They are the movers, the shakers, adapting and overcoming. So much of their flanking maneuvers, their pincer movements, their feints comes from a need to flout external expectations and standards. To trick authority—or any condescending parties, for that matter—into a state of panic and defeat. But if defiance marks a badge of honor, what comes first: The regimented orders marines react against? Or marines in search of regimented orders they can defy?

That paradox leads to a holding pattern of sorts, one that requires a predictable if idiosyncratic rotation between submission and rebellion. Some enlisted marines go officer, and therefore become mustangs. The rest remain workhorses. Better yet, they remain racehorses. Day in and out, around the track, earning their trophies and plates and cups—as commanded. But they never stop rearing, to remind those who ride them who's really the boss.

Race horsing constitutes a hell of a performance. And like war, it constitutes one without much care for those involved.

Marines, too, need paychecks. Some more than others. And to excel in the Corps, one must perform, no way around it. But what's remarkable is how invested marines are in their performances, in their climaxes and anticlimaxes, their buildups and denouements. And how invested I was in mine. How I yearned for my own confounding ambiguities, to evade the categorizations of those who thought themselves better than me. With it came a need for narrative tension. And in that tension, an addiction to plot twists. There was a romance, a sensuousness in the desire, a desire that seemed to be shared by those around me. Leah was right when she said I lived my life as if I were a protagonist in my favorite novel—maybe even more than she recognized, in the sense that I wasn't alone. So many of us marines, us men, played the part of the unshrinking wender of our own plot, and everyone and everything else its auxiliaries.

During our five-month sojourn in California, I tried to drag my platoon toward an enlightened view of their mission. But this gesturing proved somewhat fraudulent, and not just because I couldn't help but suspect the war's advertised humanitarianism was serving to obscure and prolong the inexcusable. It was also that I couldn't help slipping out of the nation-building mindset at various turns.

This became most evident during a few weeks of field exercises back in the Palms, where combat units trained in mockup villages before heading off to Iraq or Afghanistan. The program was called Mojave Viper, and it was known as a notorious ball-buster for grunts. My RadBn guys were just providing SIGINT support, but still they put in long and demanding hours. Whether our hypothetical intel was helping to drive hypothetical infantry assaults, hypothetical drone assassinations, or hypothetical surgical raids, the rush that came from these simulations was real. The team marines exhibited a sincere exhilaration in attempting to pinpoint the origin of shortwave HF signals: a difficult task involving the most precise stationing and use of various antennae and equipment that, if achieved, promised the instantaneous liquidation of strangers.

To claim I maintained immunity to such exhilaration would be a lie. Of course I didn't. I was just as much a marine as those to my left or right. And yet, I wanted to believe I was somehow different. More importantly, I wanted to impress others with my difference. Most of all, I wanted to impress Leah.

On the rare occurrence she'd respond to my attempts, I tried to keep the conversation going with interminable evidence of my maturation. For me, that meant talking books and ideas.

"Seriously," I said to her once from the parking lot of a Verizon shop somewhere in SoCal, "*The Golden Notebook* is incredible. The way Lessing covers the lives of estranged communists and socialists—Jewish leftists! Incorrigible, cold leftists! Warm, confessional leftists!—"

Leah, somewhere in the Caucasus, delivering aid and relief to internal refugees, answered, "Uh-huh."

I already knew she wouldn't be engaging, but it was nice just knowing she was there—on the other side of the virtual wire that existed between us. I took a seat on an empty parking lot curb.

"Some of the trade unionists were racist, and the black nationalists had a point—"

"Lyle, what does this..."

"It has do with you and me because she's got such an eye for men like me and..."

"Why does every book you read need to be about you?"

"No, it's about you, too!" I said this with a grin, knowing I'd set myself up for another of her favored put-downs.

"That's even worse."

"No, it really is. About how we're all so lost and broken, trying to put the pieces together."

Even though I'd already resigned myself to Leah's disapproval this round, I experienced a momentary glimmer of hope as a bird I couldn't name passed above.

"And that's about me? In particular?"

"It is! We're both so obsessed about how broken everything is... inside... outside..."

The bird was gone and the hope was gone, but I waited to hear something—anything—from Leah.

"Lyle, I have to go."

At other times, I'd talk about how I might see some action in Afghanistan. Or I'd boast about how I'd just earned the expert badge in the rifle and my sharpshooter in the pistol. I'd talk about my Bond gun, which wouldn't be accompanying me to Afghanistan. That would be the Beretta M9. Or I'd email her my sick fantasies. Occasionally she'd respond with justified rage. Once she responded in kind. But she cut me off again when I asked for more.

I was large. I contained multitudes.

"Go from strength to strength."

Mom's arm was tucked in mine, her head nestled on my shoulder, as we strolled past the galleries of La Jolla on a late afternoon in January, my last with the folks before reporting, in a few weeks, to a reserve base in the Inland Empire.

Dad gazed through each windowpane for something, anything, amenable to being bought. I had the lavish painting they'd just purchased for me folded into my side. Its carnal acrylics, cadmium red, bringing me back to Leah.

"What's that?" I asked.

"It's from the Bible. We talked about it at Kol Hamishpacha. I thought of you. How you just need to go from strength to strength this year. That's how you're going to make it through."

I knew she was talking about herself as much as she was me.

"That's the study group, right, with Rabbi Moser? Something like 'our family'? 'All the family'?"

Dad rolled his eyes. He might have been down on Kol Hamishpacha then. He always liked to always be down on something, just for fun.

"You know, it's funny," Mom said, ignoring him. "I've forgotten the exact translation, despite going for so many years!"

"The whole family?" I suggested.

"They all work," she said.

"No, they don't."

Mom looked up at me in confusion.

"Oh, I was just being a wiseass," I said. "Suggesting most families do not in fact work. But I know you were saying all the translations work."

"Our family is working better these days, wouldn't you say?" She gave Dad a waggish look.

Dad cackled, "Who woulda thunk it?"

Were it not for the painting, I would have put my other arm around my old man. I was a solid four inches taller than him now. He was still biking and in good shape. But I was in better shape, and I'd learned how to hold my own.

"I can't begin to say how much I love you guys." I realized the day was almost up and I wanted to get everything out. "And I'm sorry for sometimes being such a spoiled brat."

My eyes settled on Dad, but Mom responded first.

"Oh, honey," she said, giving me another tight squeeze, "you have nothing to apologize for. You're the world to us. All I want from you is to come home safe."

"Lyle," Dad said. "We're so proud of you. Just, please, do what you can to stay behind a desk, okay? I'm saying that not just for selfish reasons but also because you have so much to give."

"Like I said, I'm going to go where I have to go, but I will do everything I can to stay safe. I promise you that."

The moment I said it, I knew I'd lied. I wanted action. But I couldn't tell them that. I couldn't even really tell myself. It was too vain a thought for my self-image, as someone above the frivolous fray.

"I do think we've come a long way," Dad said. "I'm sorry for my temper. I wish I'd done it differently."

"You and Mom were always loving parents. Even when you were an asshole, Pops, I knew you loved me."

"We did always give you that. I mean, things were so stressful back then, Lyle. I was working eighteen-hour, twenty-hour—"

"Darling," said Mom, "I love you, but so was I. *And* I was taking care of the kids when I came home."

I was in between them. And Mom knew Dad had already committed to being on his best behavior on such a precarious occasion. I imagine those two facts empowered her to say what needed to be said. Still, before Dad could respond, I intervened.

"Everyone could have behaved better, no doubt," I said. "And yes, Mom, you were incredible. I don't know how you did it, but—I mean, sometimes you broke. Just like sometimes—okay, lots of times—Dad broke." I glanced at Dad with a forgiving humor. "But the point is, I had an amazing childhood, and I have an amazing family, and I'm nothing but grateful."

I wonder, in hindsight, if there was a connection between the way my parents treated my ponderous road to war and the way they treated their own marriage, particularly in its earlier years. They knew it wasn't ideal, maybe even something that could get dangerous, but they needn't confront the problem in any conclusive sense because, well, we would all survive and it would get better. And they'd been right in the end. Just like they ended up being right about me and my war. But on some level, I still resented them for not trying hard enough to keep me unafraid as a child.

I guess what I'm saying is, in the most repressed and mischievous recesses of my subconscious, my madcap scheme to go to war was an attempt at forcing a familial reckoning, and it was all so fucking petty. So pathetic. So self-absorbed and entitled: my deepest, darkest reason for killing or being killed.

II

In February of 2010 the British colonel Richard Kemp announced that "Afghanistan has seen a turning point." Kemp had in mind the purported successes of an International Security Assistance Force offensive in the Taliban stronghold of Marjah. The offensive had been christened Operation Moshtarak, a Dari word meaning "Together," and in its early months every important person involved in the US-led occupation of Afghanistan was singing in unison. Marines and other warfighters had become accustomed to "mowing the grass," a phrase denoting the cyclical seizure and loss of Talib-controlled areas—and one that would later become popularized by Israelis when referring to their periodic assaults on the denizens of Gaza. But the newly minted ISAF commander, General Stanley McChrystal, insisted the war may not have "turned a corner" quite yet, but operations had made "significant progress." From here on out, a new model of counterinsurgency would be embraced, where the Battle of Marjah would function as a nation-building prototype. The days of taking turf without keeping it were over. "We've got a government in a box," said McChrystal, "ready to roll in."

Marine Brigadier General Larry Nicholson added to the chorus when he emphasized to a group of incoming marines that "the population is not the enemy." Rather, "the population is the prize [and] they are why we are going in." Nicholson's conceptualization of an entire people as prize betrayed the contradiction of the mission, just as much as McChrystal's assumption that these same people would be happy to accept a foreign invader's offering of a boxed government. But it was Colonel Kemp, more than anyone, who would come to epitomize this contradiction.

Having served as the commander of British forces in Afghanistan during an opening chapter of the war, by the end of the decade, Kemp was still treated as a neutral expert by mainstream outlets like Channel 4 News. But in the years ahead, he would become a harsh critic of those attempting to hold British soldiers accountable for suspected war crimes in Afghanistan and Iraq, and in Northern Ireland during the

Troubles (Kemp himself took part in Operation Banner as a young officer of the Royal Anglian Regiment). He would levy an incendiary and libelous charge against Sayeeda Warsi, a Muslim politician in the Conservative Party, suggesting she was making excuses for the terrorism of the Islamic State of Iraq and the Levant. He claimed Islamists had infiltrated the British military and became a strident defender of the Israeli occupation, particularly the very lawnmowing operations Operation Moshtarak was marketed against. And he would play a significant part in smearing critics of Israel as antisemites.

It wouldn't take long for President Obama to realize his surge of tens of thousands of new troops in Afghanistan was a mistake. By 2011, he was eager to "wind down this war" through de-escalation, and by 2014 to "turn the page" by hailing the end of major deployments. The president declared the drawdown a new kind of "turning point." Obama, to a large extent, was following the lead of his vice president, Joe Biden, who opposed the surge from the get-go and had announced a similar "turning point" at West Point two years earlier. Biden, as it happens, would be the one to end the war altogether in 2021, a decision that Kemp, along with most of the transatlantic establishment, would not take to kindly. For Kemp, Commander of the British Empire (CBE) and honorary doctor of Tel Aviv's Bar-Ilan University, Biden's withdrawal from the Central Asian country didn't just mark a surrender to the Taliban or signal a win for their professed backers and sympathizers in Pakistan, Iran, China, Russia, and Palestine. The withdrawal, above all else, signified a humiliating loss for the West. "I don't believe President Biden should be impeached," Kemp said. For his civilizational betrayal he "should be court-martialed."

FRAGMENTS FROM A CIVILIZING MISSION BETRAYED

Sojourned in an air reserve base in the Inland Empire, sometime in February 2010. The hangar returns to me as Leviathanic, like the hollowed sanctum of a great white whale. Red stanchion rope bordering our anxious forms, we wait in a long and winding queue. Up front an industrial freight scale, the heavy steel floor. I watch as each aspirant struggles to lift their gear onto the formidable block, with a false and exaggerated ease becoming of a marine. An olive-drab sea bag, coyote-brown rolling trunk, Improved Load Bearing Equipment rucksack ("Ill-Bee"), and smaller woodland assault pack or personally owned, nonissued alternative (in my case, a kangaroo-colored 5.11 pack). Each tagged with blue, red, yellow, or orange tape, depending on the section. My OCE rocks the orange.

Those whose net poundage exceeds the limit congregate in a separate file. They are dour, sweating, panting, anticipating orders to rummage their effects. The rest of us make our way to a mass of folding chairs, assembled as if for a college graduation. We gobble up peanut butter and jelly sandwiches in the rear, exchanging swift and cheerful pleasantries with the women provisioning them. A cacophony of hip-hop, country, and metal leaks out from dozens of iPods as a conspicuous number cast around for spaces in the colossal pale to talk dirty with their partners. Some give up and talk dirty in place. I think about sending Leah something awful. But I'd already emailed her an apology for the last time.

I grow weary of the commotion and retreat to the head. The toilet's face is clean but for one drop. A graffiti collage coats the stall walls, overlapping boot-green hopefulness with salty disillusion.

Outgoing: Cpl Jax was here. 1/22/08. Off to Iraq!

incoming: fuck afghanistan fuck my country i want cunt

• •

On the commercial airliner attendants greet us with mostly forced grins. If you're an officer or senior enlisted, you enjoy some limb room. If you're junior rated, you're crammed tight with your baggage. The boxed-up entrées are indistinguishable from the civilian fare, but free. I can't sleep and I'm too exhausted to scan my Kindle. So I give in to the in-flight movie: *Transformers.*

"No sacrifice is too great in the service of freedom."

• •

We stop to refuel in Bangor. Off the flight line Vietnam vets greet us with hearty handshakes and heartfelt thank-yous for our service. They're tatted, grizzled, white-bearded, pierced, and patched up in black biker leather. When we shake hands, I hold my grip stiff and thank them back. I make the most direct and fervent eye contact I can marshal.

• •

At the Manas airbase outside Bishkek, Kyrgyzstan, marines pronounce it "Man Ass." We stand by for haircuts in the wet snow as some from another unit debate whether soccer is gay. The Kyrgyz woman who cuts my hair tells me she likes my face. She chuckles with the unhappy coworker to her left. None of them seem happy. On the way out, Walker, one of my top linguists, lets me in on the relevant intel.

"They were speaking Russian, sir."

"I thought that's what that was. You speak Russian, right?"

"I do."

"Along with ten other languages."

"Not ten, sir."

"Forgive me. Nine and a half. I rounded up."

I get a perfunctory laugh out of him.

"They're racists, sir."

"Oh yeah?"

"They were badmouthing some black soldier for giving a bad tip. They called him a nigger. Their word for that is *negr*. Spelled N-E-G-R."

"Good to know, Walker. I'm not surprised. And I'm not sure there's much we can do at this point. But I do learn something new from you every day."

"Anytime, sir. There's more where that came from."

Walker was brought up a third-generation Polish American in one of the Jackowo neighborhoods in Chicago. He managed to earn a full scholarship to Loyola University, study abroad in France, and graduate magna cum laude with a major in political science and a minor in international studies. He did some business school, but it wasn't for him. Then, against the wishes of his folks, figured it best he follow in the footsteps of his grandfathers on both sides—WWII vets—and become a marine. I can't make sense of his mixed academic prowess and vaguely plebian aggression. He sometimes talks about what it was like growing up in his small corner of the world: weaponized baseball bats, junkies. But still I wonder what has driven him to war, in the same way I wonder what has driven me.

• •

We latter-day Jonahs have entered another whale, riding the C-17 into country.

If you're junior enlisted, you're stacked in the central rectangle of the cargo hub, hunched over with your plate carrier (flak jacket), Kevlar helmet, rifle, and assault pack, on portable seating fastened to pallets beneath. Senior leadership lines the cabin's walls on each side, facing inward toward the rabble. Every arm is suspended in awkward diagonals, every neck crooked to one side, every foot and leg wedged into a blood-constricting pretzel. Whether or not you're sleeping, your eyelids are clamped shut.

During the turbulent descent, each bump guarantees a forward thrust of the palletized seating, crushing limbs. Windows are fixed too small and high, like in a submarine, so no one knows how close we are to land or when this will end.

Then green neon suffuses the scene, the aircraft's curved girth made visible, the whale transmogrified into an ark. As the vessel's stern opens to the chilling Afghan blaze, we are shepherded to a warm tent in Camp Leatherneck to suffer paperwork.

• •

We receive a mandatory brief on the base rules:

1. No alcohol
2. No having sex unless you are married to that person (there are married couples here)
3. No porn
4. No drugs

A first sergeant clarifies the rule about no sex.

"No vaginal sex, no oral sex, no anal sex, no digital sex, no dry sex—no doggone sex, you understand?"

"Yes, First Sergeant!"

Another cursory brief on the laws of war and the rules of engagement. We can defend ourselves when facing a hostile act. A hostile act is defined as an attack against us, coalition forces, and our property, or as any use of force designed to preclude or impede our mission. We can also defend ourselves when we identify hostile intent, which is defined as any threat of the imminent use of force against us, coalition forces, and our property, or as any threat of force designed to preclude or impede our mission. We should have reasonable positive identification (PID) of a military target, which is defined as an enemy combatant, unlawful combatant, or unprivileged belligerent. We should deescalate when time and circumstances permit, warn and give opportunity to withdraw. We should respond decisively to hostile acts or demonstrations of hostile intent, but the response should be reasonable in nature, duration, and scope to the perceived or demonstrated threat. This is the rule of proportionality.

We are handed red laminated ROE cards that summarize what we've just heard. My marines have already received similar instructions from me and whoever came before me. They yawn and fidget. So do I. I'm also regretting never finishing Alistair Horne's classic *A Savage War of Peace: Algeria 1954–1962*. All the smart COIN experts have recommended Horne, and because of time constraints, I'd barely made it past the hundred-page mark. How can I be expected to help win over hearts and minds while barely breaking one hundred pages of Horne? I feel the same pang thinking about the pages left unread in David Petraeus's *Counterinsurgency Field Manual*, David Kilcullen's *The Accidental Guerilla*, and David Galula's *Counterinsurgency Warfare*. Everyone serious agrees with the Davids.

Back at the transient tent I flip through Aisha Ahmad and Roger Boase's *Pashtun Tales* from the Pakistan–Afghanistan frontier. The first epigraph reads "It is not the running around but that which is written on the forehead —Pashtun Proverb."

I can't make heads or tails of it, and in my frustration my mind flees toward the macabre; something about it not mattering how much you run this way or that because the fated headshot is coming your way regardless. In my dismay I race forward:

> The Pashtuns...trace their descent to Qays bin Rashid of Gor, a tribal chieftain of the seventh century AD, whom they claim was the thirty-fifth lineal descendant of Afghana, son of Jeremiah, whom they say was son of Saul, the first king of Israel. However, modern historians believe that they are descendants of the Aryan horde that had moved down from Central Asia....
>
> The stories reflect the Pashtun code of honour, known as Pashtunwali. This code is based on three obligations: revenge, hospitality and forgiveness....Tribal feuds over zar, zan, and zamin (gold, women, and land) are a constant drain on the economy.

The Pashtuns think they're descendants of the Jews. Historians think they're descendants of the Aryans. They can't stop fighting over gold, women, and land.

I nod off on the green cot, too worn out to ruminate upon the world-historical ironies.

I'm tasked with supervising a live-fire training at the machine-gun range. Many of my marines haven't used a 240 since Marine Combat Training, and a handful may have never used the 50-cal or Mk 19. They're having fun now.

I peer over the berm and catch a glimpse of the cold, empty desert.

So this is Afghanistan.

• •

It's early March and I'm already putting aside the desert Gore-Tex most days. Today it's in the forties, though, so I've got it on. I'm sitting in on an unheated mission debrief at a battalion headquarters in Delaram, an outpost about ninety kilometers (fifty-five miles) northwest of Leatherneck, right over the Helmand's border in Nimruz Province. You could easily mistake the debrief for an after-action with the DEA. It's clear that the grunts in my area of operations have spent the past six months mainly raiding drug labs. They know everything you can about opium, morphine. But they don't seem to know or care much about the intricacies and contours of the insurgency.

The most conspicuous war is the drug war. But there isn't just one war. There's a slew of them, many overlapping. The standard narratives hold up: tribal, subtribal, ethnic, religious, geopolitical. There is also a war of memory. Villagers every day, especially where I am, wrestle with this or that traumatic Scylla and Charybdis. Infidel intrusion on the one hand, Taliban or anti-Taliban governance on the other. They all carry bad memories. Most farmers are simply left by the powers that be to scrounge at any given moment. This usually means giving the thumbs-up to the Americans one day—a gesture I'm told was derogatory in Pashtun culture not too long ago—and running drugs for the Taliban the next. Or just nodding in agreement with everyone who happens to pass by.

• •

About 40 percent of my time is spent convoying, flying, and patrolling to and around remote combat outposts (COPs) or patrol bases (PBs) north of the main effort in Marjeh. The other 60 percent of my stay is spent on a watch floor, behind a series of variously classified laptops, reading and producing intel reports, attending meetings, occasionally offering a brief or two. Most of my intel work centers around conversations among those planning to murder and intimidate the local populace, coalition forces, outsiders (NGOs, journalists), and even competing or floundering insurgent leadership.

I am thus of two worlds: the sequestered desk jockey, on the one hand, and the more austere traveler, on the other. This is a strange place to be, seeing that most marines currently in Afghanistan occupy only one of these two spaces. Thousands reside at large command hubs, where a majority have not donned a flak jacket or Kevlar since landing in-country. Thousands more expend virtually every day of their six-month tour toe-stepping around mines and ducking fusillades. My team marines patrol so many poppy fields their trousers turn charcoal-colored from the juices.

My split living results in a splintered psychology—a distant, almost textbook reading of events (the watch floor experience) at stubborn war with a guilty conscience about what lies beneath the synthetic narratives.

• •

Settled on the back of a roofless up-armored seven-ton "armadillo" for a mid-March convoy, I have a nice view of everything. The bad guy probably has a nice view of me, too. The first thing I notice on the way out is a downed Russian tank from the 1980s, on the opposite side of the Hesco barrier—the glorified sandbag that lines my unit's compound. I had no clue it was there. I spot more monuments to the Soviet–Afghan War on the way, somersaulted or buried beneath heaps of sand, but this is the first one that really raises an eyebrow. Then there is the stream of camel caravans, usually led by a woman pulling on a rope, her face glazed with exhaustion and dirt. Our convoy must be split up seven different ways by caravans zigzagging across the patches of pavement. Young men on motorcycles stare us down as they speed across the road. Little kids (mostly boys) chase after our vics as we drive by, miming requests for food or water, or just offering a thumbs-up. There are cities of sheep, a solitary shepherd somewhere in the middle. A lone gas station on the outskirts, with two pumps, no food mart, no employees, no customers. One green highway sign, in English: "Herat: 300 km."

Once off-road, nothing but the haloes of sand our trucks kick up as we skate across the desert. And then, two hours in, a couple of tents, staked in no-man's land, massive dogs, and three boys watching at a distance as we halt and a marine or two pisses off the flanks.

The first COP I stay at is typical. You crap in a "WAG bag" and piss in a tube—a simple, narrow cylinder that juts out from the ground—in the open for all to see. You dip industrial tape in honey and hang it on the ceiling to divert the bugs. You call it a fly ribbon.

You ponder metaphors concerning the fly ribbon: the enemy is the fly; I am the fly; I am the ribbon; the enemy is the ribbon; and so on.

The village lives right next to you. You can hear it going about its business on the other side.

You learn from marines. You are always learning from marines.

"That's Purdah, sir."

"What's what now?"

"What you were just talking about—the practice of concealing women from men—it's called Purdah."

You spot marines learning on their own. One lance corporal keeps reaching for Kierkegaard's *Fear and Trembling* whenever he has a minute.

Another is reading *The Journey: The Study Bible for Spiritual Seekers.*

You're surrounded by all the porn you're not supposed to have, and no one, including the commanders, gives a shit. Most of the mags were left by the Brits, some from other US units. They get mixed together in every hut and hooch: *Nuts, Maxim, Loaded, Playboy.*

You wonder how publications so salacious could also prove so bougie. The British rags come off as less prudish than their American complements, but they're both obsessed with what you can and can't do.

You hear or watch IEDs go off in the distance and then watch kids, old men, poppy farmers—everyone—go about their day like nothing happened. Except for those it happened to.

"Like fire trucks in the States," says one marine.

You run through every piece of gear, checking for damage. You make sure every dollar, ranging into the hundreds of thousands, is accounted for. You are constantly asking your marines about room for improvement in each device ("It would be better if the switch was positioned here"), or about anything they might need or want ("More cigs, sir, definitely more cigs"). You are asking endless questions. But you are also relaying everything you have learned from other team marines about best practices or relevant pieces of intel that might help them better navigate their human terrain. You are building relationships with the unit's leadership and adjacent supporting elements like human intelligence (HUMINT). You want to ensure RadBn remains a crucial component of their operations. Otherwise, your whole lousy unit is worthless, and no one wants to be part of a worthless unit. When you have your own minute, you read whatever it is you read. And you tend to have many minutes. In this one its Sylvia Plath:

> I don't believe in god as a kind father in the sky. I don't believe that the meek will inherit the earth: the meek get ignored and trampled . . . it is the bold, the loud-mouthed, the cruel, the vital, the revolutionaries, the mighty in arms and will, who march over the soft patient flesh that lies beneath their cleated boots.

You jot a haphazard thought in your latest Rite in the Rain weatherproof notebook: The friction of their voice (Sontag, Lessing, Plath)—the confessional mode—to disrupt, to interdict, but never to hold.

You watch arm wrestling tournaments.

• •

The first patrol: fifteen of us, thirteen of whom have risked similar patrols for six months straight, every day and into the night. A smart, disciplined young corporal who lost a friend in an IED blast a few months prior, and with whom I will later share an hour passing intel (he is determined to avenge his friend), leads the charge. We step off at 1600. The first hour is desert. Wadis. Ditches. Trash. They warn us to avoid the trash. At one point, we take a knee as the squad leader and another marine pull out their metal detectors and sweep a patch of suspicious dust. They mark a portion with the outpourings of an opened-up chem light so that when we return that night, we will know which side to walk on. Then the farms, and the farmers standing still with their shovels and scythes. A pair of worn slippers lies on the edge of the green. The farmers are all shoeless and I glance at their feet, wondering who the slippers belong to. I wave. One mimes back, asking for food and water.

We're in the first village. More like a compound: three mud huts, a circle of waist-high sand that keeps in two camels. We're on our knees again, providing security as the corporal and the interpreter (the "terp") consult the white-bearded village elder. Vast poppy fields surround us. Three brothers watch, a couple meters away, a tall teenager in the middle, the younger two leaning against him on either side, smiling, miming. I pull out a candy bar. They smile some more and wait. The questioning proceeds.

"How many wives do you have?"

"Thirty."

"What are you, a pimp?" The corporal cuts me a smirk.

The terp, a local national, asks, "What's a pimp?"

"I'll explain later. Ask him where he sells his poppy."

About an hour later the questioning is complete. The kids are still spectating. I get off my knees (now sore) and approach my lance corporal, a linguist.

"How do you say, 'We want peace'?"

"*Muj hram quarum*."

(This is what I hear, at least.)

I walk over to the three brothers and hand the bar to the oldest. I've been waiting an hour for this.

"*Muj hram quarum*," I say.

He smiles and nods. Not quite sure if I said it right. Not quite sure if he understands. In any case, he removes the gum from his mouth (a gift from another marine on patrol, for sure) and offers it back.

"No, thank you," I say.

I wave goodbye. He waves in return, puts the gum back.

One of my marines reports bad-guy traffic to the squad leader during the patrol back to base. A couple insurgents have eyes on us. They have night vision goggles. Likely marine gear. No signs of them planning an assault or ambush, but they're observing us in green. My marine gives the squad leader a rough idea on the map where they're at. The sergeant adjusts our return route slightly.

The best part is being able to finally let out a piss. I do it while providing security in the prone. Unbutton and let it rip. Might have just gotten some on my trousers.

I am using the single-eye NVGs of one of my marines, a leftie, so my weak eye isn't prepared for bearing the whole effort. I should have thought about this before stepping off base, but I didn't.

The dispersion among each marine back to base is impressive, and there are times when I feel like I am all alone in the desert, with nothing but NVG green and barking dogs as comfort. A few nights earlier, one of the dogs was put down, with a 5.56 round, by a marine who claims the dog attacked.

I fall in a couple water-filled wadis. Just miss a six-foot ditch. Walk on the right side of that chem light–marked IED, though. At one point a few marines spot movement about fifty meters out, marking it with their infrared. I get on my knees and point the barrel in that direction. Then a woman's voice, screaming. And children. And a father. All rushing back into their hut. They likely don't see us. They do hear us.

Late that evening, when I return to my living quarters, one of the HUMINT marines is booming Mozart's "Magic Flute." It reminds me of the Wagner in Coppola's *Apocalypse Now*.

The second patrol: we file through a small village thought to be housing a suicide bomber. There are about fifteen military-aged males on each side of the fields, all of them farming poppy, and two children in the distance, who disappear within minutes of our arrival. This in stark contrast to the day before, when the village was full of children who approached with open hands and the fields were tended by a mix of young and old. I post security about five meters away from the farmers. Whenever one of them reaches down the stalk of the plant, I imagine a weapons cache hidden by the long green vertical, soon to reveal itself in fateful glory. A man glares at me with the eyes of Medusa, sporting an unusually classy cashmere top in the hot spring swelter. I imagine a vest underneath, lined with explosives. During the debrief, all the grunts voice similar thoughts. They, and to a varied extent, my marines, will endure this paranoia most days for a total of six months.

The second COP I stay at borders a bazaar. We are allowed to head out there with just a handful of marines. It's in a town that's been battered relentlessly for the past eight years and is still recovering from its latest clearing, so it's not flourishing, to say the least.

Still, things are being sold. Delicious nan (we bought stacks), live chickens (the head was cut off in front of us, though we were given the option to twist it off ourselves), communication devices, et cetera. Children everywhere, asking for gum or cigarettes. One teenager, training to be a policeman, is reported by my marines to have described the experience of smoking American cigarettes as "ice in his mouth." He is also reported to have shown them a nasty scar on his leg from those "Taliban bastards."

In general, the street population falls into three categories: children (mostly boys), old men, and young Afghan policemen and soldiers. The tragic logic is that if you are a young man and not a policeman or a soldier, you are somehow involved with the Taliban. So when young men on motorcycles stop by, unfriendly and aloof, our rifles are raised. No women. A few girls, quiet and shy.

Later that day, standing atop the Hesco barriers bordering our compound, unarmed (except for a pistol at my thigh) and unprotected (no flak jacket, no Kevlar helmet), throwing chow and candy to a dozen or so kids on the other side. At first, they fight for every piece that comes their way. Walker tells them they will only get more if they share, so that stops the fighting. A few girls stand patiently in back, wearing beautiful sparkling Sabbath dress (it is Friday). We ask them to come forward and throw them the best we have. They smile fleetingly and return to the rear. A few boys approach them during the hour-long giveaway, discreetly passing them a pencil or a pound cake. Otherwise, they are spectators. Toward the end, a woman (the first I've seen in the village), dressed in a black burqa that covers her face, including her eyes, walks through the crowd with a little girl. Everyone goes silent. One of my marines welcomes her. She continues to walk, no acknowledgment. Once she is a safe block away, the kids resume their game of who can win the most bounty. In the distance, past the mud huts, just off the path to the mountains, two young men on motorcycles watch. I advise my marines, once the giving is done, that this is not something they will be doing regularly.

That night the marines huddle around a minuscule laptop to watch the original *Red Dawn* starring Patrick Swayze, the Reagan-era cult classic about a counterfactual Soviet invasion of the continental United States and the ragtag guerilla resistance it inspires.

"You know we're the imperialist invaders this time, fellas."

"Oh hell yeah, sir," Walker says. "We watched *Star Wars* the other night. Same deal. We're all about it."

"That's hilarious. Didn't Lucas write it as a protest movie against the Vietnam War? The Viet Cong are the freedom fighters and we're the stormtroopers?"

"Yut!"

My marines haven't showered in a month and a half. They've relied on baby wipes, water bottles, and a miniature water bladder system they hang on whatever they can find. They wait for the sun to warm the water in the bladder, then let a few drops drip down on their naked bodies. Sometimes there is not enough bottled water to make this happen, so they settle for rainwater.

A cute East Asian doc from the Shock Trauma Platoon shows up and no one can stop talking about her. Some use the bladder system more than usual. Some spend more time in the jack shack. I write a poem about the jack shack: "they call it the jack shack— / the place we go / to rub off all that's left / of our dying love. / most of the time / it's shared with the shitter, / where it belongs."

I write another about how "writing mediocre poetry / while brothers die / just in the distance / (and by brothers I mean all good-willed things) / is much more fucked than fucking / rough and drunk / those nights in the city / those no name girls / while those sirens breezed by."

Later I hate myself for still being a blowhard prick, but I can't stop thinking what I'm thinking and writing what I'm writing and at least I'm sublimating my awfulness.

I overhear the doc speaking about her three-year-old son and her other son, who's eleven and almost finished with his first year of middle school.

I wonder what she must think about all the ogling. I once met a marine at the Palms who told me she loved all the ogling. But that marine was young and fresh out of boot camp and I doubt her love lasted. Maybe it did. Or maybe she wasn't being entirely truthful with me. Anyway, I wonder if the doc has faced anything worse than ogling.

I envy her for saving lives.

Boom!

"Was that a controlled det?"

"None that we know of..."

Turns out it's a goat that stepped on it this time. Two days ago it was an Afghan cop, a member of the ANP.

A chaplain handed me a Bible the other day, a thick black rectangle with the bald eagle flying through a hoop that spells "Operation Enduring Freedom." I'm done with Plath, so now I'm reading God. I'm starting to think a lot more about God. I'm flipping through God's book for the part in Leviticus where I think the term "scapegoat" comes from. Eventually I find it. It's Leviticus 16:20–22:

> When Aaron has finished making atonement for the Most Holy Place, the tent of meeting and the altar, he shall bring forward the live goat. He is to lay both hands on the head of the live goat and confess over it all the wickedness and rebellion of the Israelites—all their sins—and put them on the goat's head. He shall send the goat away into the wilderness in the care of someone appointed for the task. The goat will carry on itself all their sins to a remote place; and the man shall release it in the wilderness.

I write another bad poem about the goat and jot down in my notebook: "What if God grows up with us?"

• •

I'm back in Delaram by late March, spending a day with one of my teams. We're op-checking gear and our vic, staging everything, receiving briefs from higher, only to be told the mission we're prepping for is postponed. We spend another full day doing the same thing, except this time we spend around nine hours outside the wire on the way, only to be returned to base ("RTB'd") at the last second because of what we are told are weather concerns. We then spend a third day doing the same thing, except this time we are RTB'd at about the ten-hour point.

The element is led by your standard-bearing grunt officer, a bulky-chested lieutenant with eternal sunglasses, a permanent dip compartment in his mouth, and a countenance that never makes it past freezing point. The crowd he shepherds isn't much different, as far as the dip. But not all of them have the sunglasses, and a few are less fit. Before stepping off, we get in a circle for a chaplain-led prayer. It includes phrases like "Please, Lord, allow us to track down and kill those cowardly little pricks" and "Loan us the force and fury of your almighty power, to be the instrument of justice, in finding the snares—IEDs—where they may lie and destroying those who laid them."

Once complete, a few of the grunts take a picture in front of their vic, cigs at their crotches, the other hand with the middle finger up and toward the sky, pointed upward to God Almighty.

Despite my doubts, the COIN part is what I keep telling myself has brought me here in the first place. The part about means and ends, rights and wrongs. The pursuit of something, if not righteous, then at least not ignoble. But when I learn from Waldron (who is still something of a cipher to me) why the op was really terminated, I start questioning my motives. He tells me McChrystal had determined the risks of alienating the locals with another bloody raiding op was too high.

I have lunch with Bartels, my old OCS buddy, the VMI grad. He once told me if anyone ever gives me shit, to place my hands around the back of their scalp and up-knee them in the nose.

When it comes to the canceled op, Bartels tells me he's been in this shithole for six months and he's on his way out and the juice isn't worth the squeeze. I guess that's his way of saying the blood ain't worth the effort. And while I know he's right, and McChrystal was right, and we need to fight a lot less rather than a lot more, and that I'm the guy who used to tell my marines this every chance I got, and I'm the guy—I keep telling myself—who's different from the other guys, the fact is, I want to get some like everyone else. And so I'm disappointed as fuck.

• •

In late April, during the height of the opium harvest and fighting season, I attend a dinner hosted by the battalion commander in Musa Qala ("Fort Moses"). The commander has invited an Afghan National Army colonel, a couple staff officers, and all SIGINT and HUMINT marines and their linguists. It is hot and crowded in the tight stone-walled quarters, and most seem anxious for the exit. But I'm grateful for the bread, okra, and potatoes, as well as the chai. I'm especially appreciative of the watermelon at dessert. And I've enjoyed sharing notes with the Afghan full bird, who warns me not to jump into the whirlpool when I make my way to Kajaki Dam.

"Don't worry, I'll just give my marines the order."

I've also enjoyed my side conversations with Jon, an Afghan American linguist I've had a few chats with during my periodic visits to his area of operations. As we walk out together, he tells me about being born in southern Afghanistan and fleeing to Russia during the Soviet–Afghan War. And then somehow making it to the United States, becoming a citizen, and earning a security clearance as a government employee.

"That's quite a life. You should write a book."

"Why's that?"

"Well, you've lived under the two great superpowers, for starters."

"Plenty have."

"Right, but you were also born in the graveyard of empires. And you got the hell out of Dodge because of the proxy war that would end up burying the Soviet Union."

Jon responds with a mischievous grin.

"Thing is, if I were to write a book, it would be a very dangerous book."

"How so?"

"You know, sir, a few people planned all this."

Shit.

"Planned what?"

"All this death and destruction. It's all the result of one race."

Fuck.

"None of this would have happened if they didn't exist."

Does he not see my name tape? Does he not know who he's talking to?

"You have to be more specific than that, Jon. Spell it out for me."

"They come from a small but very influential country. But that's the most I'm going to say."

"I sure hope it is. Doesn't sound like a convincing theory, to be honest. And you should be careful about who you tell it to. You know what I mean?"

"Yes, sir. That's why I stopped."

"All right, I need to get back with my guys."

"Understood, sir. Goodnight."

"Goodnight."

I tell Jon's staff sergeant about our conversation, and he says he's already aware of his beliefs, which apparently involve every conspiracy theory in the book. Jon also won't stop complaining about civilian casualties. The staff sergeant says Jon's too soft, and the other day flipped out when the staff sergeant told his marines to unload if some suspicious kids got too close. He's too friendly with the people he's talking to and he constantly insists this guy's not Taliban, that guy's not Taliban. I say that might all be true, but those are way more legit concerns on Jon's part than his bigoted conspiracy theories. I mean, this is a COIN mission, right? We should be avoiding civilian casualties, especially child casualties, right? The sergeant says sure, but there's something fishy about Jon and he knows this and he's working on finding out what to do with him. But he's short on linguists at the moment and he needs the Talib-sympathizing shitbag.

I walk away wondering if the jahood-hating bastard ought to stay, if only to keep his hajji-hating colleagues in check. Then Anwar, my Afghan American linguist on base, approaches me. He seems to have gotten word of what's happened.

"I knew you were Jewish, sir. The first time I met you. There was a brightness. Noor."

"We're not all so noor, I promise. If you don't believe me, I'd be happy to arrange a meeting with some of the non-noor members of my tribe."

That night, in the sleeping quarters of the human intelligence exploitation team (HET), I shoot the shit with some OGA guys. That's short for Other Government Agency, which is open code for the paramilitary wing of the CIA. They're bearded and tatted and they're usually sleeping like babies. But right now they're telling stories about how on Christmas they used to gift their Russian counterparts with alcohol and were gifted in turn. They'd play lighthearted games with them, too, but they don't get into specifics.

When they think someone is a good killer, they call them "talented," and they're confident it's the government, not the insurgents, that "always wins."

This baffles me given the historical record, but I keep my mouth shut and we move on to bitching about the local command caring more about punishing marines for wearing nonissued white socks than rewarding those doing civil affairs work.

Eventually they hit the rack again and I'm left watching a couple marines watch a Lady Gaga video while one of them skims an *Esquire* piece on Lady Gaga at the same time. At some point I chat with them a bit. They keep saying "jigga-jigga" when they mean money, and they keep telling me all the Afghans love fucking boys.

As I try to fall asleep, I stare at the stuffed dog hanging from the lamp above me. Then I stare at the "Karachi 555" embossed on the steel ceiling. I've seen that embossment elsewhere and all I want now is to be elsewhere, maybe in Karachi, with a stuffed dog come to life.

The next morning I make my way to the closest jack shack early enough to catch an opening. Someone has posted the weekly ministry right on the jack shack door.

Tuesday 0900–0930 Prayer Warriors Chow Tent
Wednesday 20–2100 Bible Study Chow Tent
Friday 2030–2130 Worship Service Chow Tent
Saturday TBD FOB Worship Rotation Chow Tent
Sunday 1000–1100 Worship Service Chow Tent
2030–2130

I consider what it must be like to pray so much when waging a war of aggression. Or being informed of your next appointment with God immediately before or after jacking off. When I'm in the hot box (this one's made of wood), I stand in place while conjuring the most reprehensible fantasy imaginable. I'm done within ten seconds. It's done the trick.

As I make my exit, a cocky marine approaches. He seems to think I know him. He's excited to show me a mouse in a mouse trap, but when he realizes I'm not who he thinks I am, he offers a goofy smile and so do I. Then I go about the rest of my morning chores, and he goes about his.

I stroll around the base, happening upon Afghans coloring over the British Gurkhas' coat of arms with white paint. One Afghan is standing on a ladder in his slippers while another Afghan stands on the first's shoulders. A younger Afghan is hanging from the roof with a rope or cord of some kind while the one on the first's shoulders holds his ankles. The hanging Afghan with the ankle support is the one doing the painting, and he smiles the whole way through. Since I was brought up with Jewish slapstick, I end up joining him in his seeming mirth, especially when they decide to quit a couple minutes into the routine, leaving more than half the coat of arms still visible. I'm self-aware enough to recognize the racist slapstick trope, but I don't care. I laugh along with my fellow onlookers.

Minutes later I realize a monstrous cross in memoriam I'd been used to passing by has been dismantled. Was its Crusades-like effect too on the nose? The iconic marker has occupied a central place on the base since my inaugural visit a couple months earlier. And now it's gone. Poof. Before I can mourn its passing, I come across two marines making a fuss about an Afghan who lives in a residence with an observation tower built on top of it. He had lived there well before the British or Americans showed up, and it wasn't until recently he had been granted any compensation for the inconvenience. He was provided with free electricity, but according to the marines, that wasn't enough for the man. He still wanted more.

"Fuck him. He should be grateful we're helping him."

A couple months ago I might have given a hip-pocket lesson on COIN. But I know now the intervention won't go well; I'd have a target on my back the rest of my time on the base, and were I to make a habit of such interventions, I'd be intervening every second of every day. So instead of belaboring my cowardice, I move seamlessly to the next thing. I marvel at the real buildings and real trees. Musa Qala is a real city and I'm comforted by that. I haven't been in many real cities since I've arrived in-country, and so far, Musa Qala has functioned as my most reliable stop for real multi-story housing and real sprawling green.

But then the rotten stink passes through, as it always does. And I wonder if it's the piss or shit or burn pit or death or just the general stench of war. Perhaps the reek of the cosmos. Maybe it's narrower than that. Maybe it's humanity. Maybe it's America. Maybe it's me.

• • • • • • • • • • • • • • • • • • • •

As I depart on my convoy to the new location for Walker's team, I try for something more healing. I breathe in the trees and hillocks. I breathe in the beautiful clearing and its sea of glinting puddles. I know for all its verdant exceptions, what we have here is still a desert, and so I bless the desert. I bless Fort Moses, from the woman walking across her farm in her sparkling gold to the daughter's sparkling purple beside her. I bless the sprinting children, the scintillating jamboree of motorcycles and bikes. I make a silent blessing for the ornamental trucks and the little boy raising two thumbs up.

I am in the passenger seat of the lead vic, the seven-ton with the mine roller, and so I bless every pebble and speck of dust before us. Those planting the mines have gotten smarter. They know the commander is likely siting in the third or fourth vic. I make a special, wordless blessing for the commander, too. But the blessing isn't quite wordless. Its words flash through me:

Shema yisrael adonai eloheinu adonai echad.
Hear, O Israel: the LORD our God, the LORD is one.

The Muslims have something similar in the Quran.

I am a Jew in the spirit of Baruch Spinoza, meaning I am a pantheistic

Jew: God is everyone and everything and everyone and everything is God. We are all the same substance. Amen.

We take a piss stop at COP Edinburgh. I'm reminded of Adam Smith.

As I hop back into the seven-ton, I strike up a conversation with the driver, someone I've gotten to know from past excursions. His name is Galloway, and he's your standard-issue hoot.

"Tell me what's on your mind, Galloway. It's been a quiet ride so far and I'm in the mood for some amusement."

"Permission to speak freely, sir."

He always says this and it's always ironic.

"Shoot."

"Our battalion commander is crazy, our sergeant major is crazy, and our executive officer is the stupidest man I've ever met."

"Now that's the Galloway I remember. You still a 9/11 truther, or was that more Neel's thing?"

Neel and Galloway are besties in the motor-T shop. Last time I rode with them they wouldn't stop trying to convince me 9/11 was an inside job. I asked them why they were risking their lives for such an evil government and they said they still love their country and that has nothing to do with it. And it's just a job anyway.

"I'm telling ya, sir, check out the dope on Flight 93. It's wild!"

"Oh, now I remember. It was Neel who was skeptical. You were all in."

"Still am, sir! Still am!"

"How's Neel doing these days, by the way? He's been hit... what... three times now?"

"Four since a week ago, sir."

"Holy shit, Gallo. That's steep."

"That's what I keep saying. Man has done his part. Send him home already."

"That's for sure. I get we've learned to armor the fuck out of these things, every single one of them, from the armadillo to the MRAP to the MATV, but it's still not good for the brain. Never mind every other part of our body. And I can't tell you how many marines I know who are still going out after their third or fourth blast. It's batshit."

"I'm with ya, sir."

We end up with Zeppelin's "Stairway to Heaven." Later, Eminem and Biggie.

Around Biggie, we get caught in traffic as we pass through a surprisingly bustling hamlet. The kiddos run up to us, so we throw them some of our MRE goodies: pound cake, Skittles, peanut butter, whatever care-package candy remains. And of course, a good many waters.

Once everyone has something, we make absurd faces and play Simon Says. It's the first time I've played that one out here, but Gallo has done it a few times now and he likes their reactions.

"Simon says put your right hand on your head."

"Simon says put your left hand on your belly."

It's the same as it is in the States, except you need to go slower and be much more exaggerated with your body motions since they don't speak much English.

Before we can get to the next command, though, an IED goes off well within a klick and the kids disperse in nine different directions.

We find out over the radio that it's an Afghan soldier who's been hit this time. He's been killed in action. ANA KIA. The convoy commander says, "We're gonna push. He's dead already."

But the traffic is still bad and now there's a random number of kids—probably some of the same ones we were playing with earlier—running up to the trucks and jacking whatever they can find on their exteriors—foodstuff, water, you name it. So that slows us down some, too. Someone on the radio says, "Fuck these kids. I hate these motherfucking kids."

Gallo and I look at each other, and he says, "You know what, though? If I were in their shoes, I'd probably do the same thing."

"I sure as hell would. Who wouldn't?"

As the traffic clears and we're moving again, we talk some more, and as I scan his iPod, I find out he doesn't know who the Boss is. Someone else put him on there and Gallo has no clue who he is. So, as punishment, I make sure that's all we listen to from there on out. We start with "Born in the U.S.A."

We spend the night in a tiny PB, and the next day, I end up on the bed of an armadillo with another HET sergeant. His name is Davies and he's a thoughtful type. He tells me about his grunt deployment to Iraq and how he didn't see any action, and he gives me the rough lowdown of his source and asset work in the district.

"Basically the Talibs we're working with here are just like the gang-bangers back home. They've got no jobs and they're pissed off. Especially since we've burned all their poppy fields and raided their refineries."

"That's changing now though, right? With Obama and McChrystal?"

"It's supposed to be, sure. But honestly I'm not seeing much change yet where I'm at. The DEA guys are cowboys. They treat everyone here like FARC."

"No doubt. Saw some of that at Delaram when I first showed up."

We try to get some shut-eye, but one of the vics ahead of us hits a mine. The plume cloud this time is larger than usual and we know we'll be here for some time. A man carrying hay ambles by, along with some speeding junkers. While we wait for word from the convoy commander, the armadillo gunner aims in with his rifle RCO at a hill about half a klick out, where there are some moving bodies. So do I and Davies with our sights.

"I think they're digging, Sergeant," says the gunner.

"No, they're playing," says Davies.

We recline on the bed of the truck anyway, just in case anyone out there has any ideas. The sky couldn't be any bluer, its clouds any silkier. They remind me of home.

One sandstorm, a dozen gypsy wagons, and who knows how many ominous, IED-containing yellow oil jugs later, we make it to our destination at Salaam Bazaar, the Market of Peace.

Plastic bags, cardboard boxes, hypodermic needles, and other trash line the road into the marketplace. Walker greets us near the entry point. He's jittery and set on dazzling me with his knowledge and good cheer. He's standing next to Staff Sergeant McKay, one of the more mature and even-keeled team leaders in my platoon. I greet them both as professionals.

"Good afternoon, Staff Sergeant. Good afternoon, Lance Corporal."

Then I tell them they look like shit. They return the favor, and we pat each other's backs.

We make our way to the SIGINT-souped Mine-Resistant Ambush-Protected vehicle where I'm greeted by the other team members. Healy is the youngest, or one of the youngest. He's the son of a firefighter and has the top-heavy build and demeanor of one. He's always spitting, likes to fix stuff, and I get the sense he's fairly Catholic, too. He's told me he's a "Saturday Sinner, Sunday Saint" more than once.

"Sir, you got us our Pines."

"You ask and I deliver."

I lower my pack to the dirt and reach for the cigs.

"Hope this is enough for now."

Walker intercepts the handful.

"Absolutely, sir. You've come through on this one. We were worried we were withdrawing."

"You sure look it."

"Damn, sir."

"All right, we need to do gear inventory, but real quick, I've got that Pashto dictionary, too. Courtesy of my little brother, Ethan. It was a tough one to find!"

"You're the man, sir."

"Hey, y'all. Do me one favor and let's get a group photo or something with the dictionary. Something I can send back to E-man when I'm back at a big base. I think he'd appreciate it."

We pose in front of the MRAP and everyone looks like they just shat their pants. Afterward we branch off into side conversations. Pegler—they call him the Skyscraper because he's so towering—approaches me the moment there's a pause.

"So, sir, Descartes walks into a bar and—"

"Oh, not one of these again."

"And the bartender says, 'Would you like a beer?' And Descartes says—"

"Let me guess: *Cogito, ergo* fuck'm."

"That's a good one! Doesn't make much sense, but I like it."

"So, what's the correct answer?"

"Descartes says, 'I think not.' And then he disappears."

"Good to know you're as cryptic as ever, Pegler. Mine was better. Anyway, what's new?"

"You know me. When the ANA aren't trying to convert me and Walker, we're bringing in the good stuff. Wait until we tell you the latest on the police chief and the DG."

The two had a bloody rivalry going and the supported battalion was trying to find a way to exploit it to their advantage. Since the governor's attempted assassination of the chief, command had been leaning heavy on SIGINT for the inside scoop.

"I'll tell you more in the vic, sir, but bottom line is the chief has a whole harem of chai boys and one of them happens to be the governor's nephew."

"Yeah, I heard about that at headquarters. Let's take care of the inventory and then you can give me all the updates. The staff, especially intel—the S-2—want more dirt on the chief. They might be getting ready to make a move of their own."

"It's about time!"

Pegler's father is a classics major turned stockbroker who read *The Odyssey* and *The Iliad* to him as a kid. We'd spent some time on other bases and convoys earlier in the cycle and he'd told me about his latest reads (*A Tale of Two Cities*, *The Victory of Reason*, *Candide*, and *The Rise and Fall of the Third Reich*) as well as the latest exploits of his drug-dealing brother. But before I could get another word in edgewise, Staff Sergeant McKay jumps in.

"Sir, I'm thinking we have a solid two or three hours to go through all the gear while it's still light. Then we can brief you on everything afterward. You good on chow?"

"I'm good."

As we work ourselves through the hundreds of thousands of dollars' worth of classified equipment, the good staff sergeant takes his own turn impressing me with his book knowledge. He speaks fluently about the anti-communist dissidents Czesław Miłosz and Václav Havel just as he does more daring subjects like the IRA, Sayyid Qutb, and Frantz Fanon. I tell him he really needs to go to grad school, and he tells me he's still thinking about it.

"Last time I checked, one dollar equaled eighty-three PKR. That's Pakistani rupees, sir."

"Got it, Walker."

"It's always changing. You know how it is."

"I do."

He tells me how the latest shifts in currency values have been shaping insurgent ops in the AO, with respect to both the harvest and the fight. I ask what this means for us, and he's already ready with a five-paragraph response about how the main effort, when it comes to following the money—and therefore mapping the local and regional command structure and associations—needs to remain with the PKR.

"One dollar amounts to forty-seven Afghanis, but that's unstable. The bad guys mostly deal in Pakistani dime for drugs, since it's more reliable."

Once we cover the necessary ground, he makes the same joke I've heard before about meeting his Polish grandmother halfway on his back tattoo, a gigantic Eastern Orthodox cross. He's never been all that fond of the Christian thing, but whatever makes her happy. I doubt a gigantic cross tattoo makes her happy. I suppose that's the joke. I laugh like I always do because the deadpan way he delivers it is so funny. He's got this earnest look on his face that's hilarious.

We hop out of the vic and Sergeant Somerset greets us each with a Pine, the most satisfying cigarette in all of Salaam Bazaar. Then Somerset recaps their first firefight.

"Everyone dropped and then laughed."

"Really?"

"Until someone bleeds—until it becomes real—everyone is upbeat."

"Just a heads-up, gents: Jon doesn't like the Jews. Thinks they're running the world. That sort of thing."

"Could have called that one a mile away, sir," says Walker. "They're all like that. We had a game at DLI with the teachers. Probe them out. All of them ended up believing that crap."

"That's interesting. Maybe it's because I'm Jewish and they're smart enough not to say anything to my face, but I've had great working relationships with all the Cat 3 linguists across the board. And unless he's the best actor since Marlon Brando, Anwar is all about the Jews. The man loves me."

"Nah, he's playacting, sir. If anything, it's an exception to the rule. Probe the others. You'll see."

"I doubt it, man. Anyway," I say, "had a great conversation with the OGA guys the other night."

"Look at you! Our lieutenant is going all high-speed on us now!" says Somerset.

We chuckle.

"They were telling me about how they used to send drinks and other gifts to their Soviet counterparts during the Cold War."

"That's old hat, sir. Russians still send Russian-English dictionaries to DLI grads, thanking them for learning their language. Psyops at its best!"

"No shit. Do we do the same thing?"

"I sure don't!"

We watch a boy with a shovel approach one of the berms asking for a cig. The grunts shoo him away.

I make sure to check in on Healy and Pegler in the vic—the mobile sensitive compartmented information facility (SCIF). They've been collecting plenty lately. It's windowless and dark, and I still feel special whenever I find myself in one.

"The insurgents are having problems with their suicide vests, sir," says Pegler. "They're troubleshooting."

"Troubleshooting suicide vests?"

"Just like we troubleshoot a bad radio or a damaged MATV, sir."

"Makes sense. And Gunny Lee, Lieutenant Waldron, and the rest of the watch floor are working the situation?"

"That's an affirm, sir."

"All right, what else?"

"The LNs resent us for bringing the Taliban to their villages."

He's referring to the local nationals.

"Tell me something I don't know."

"Sir?"

"I'm kidding, Pegler. I just don't see how we can have any military presence and win the locals. It's a Gordian knot."

"You know how I feel about this war, sir..."

"Oorah, amirite?"

"Rah."

"What else?"

"Coalition forces have asked the LNs to cut down trees that Taliban use for hiding, but the Taliban is now threatening to kill any LN who complies."

"Fuck. I'll talk to the captain here about that. Thanks."

"Anytime, sir."

We talk some more about the Taliban's expected mass public executions, but that's mostly above our pay grade. I read through the team's transcripts of Talib traffic. Some of them tickle:

Tx [Transmit]: You see that? Shoot! Allah Akbar!

Rx [Receive]: Why are you saying Allah Akbar? You're missing!

It's clear that Talib morale is down in the area and the leadership is increasing internal beatings, threats of beatings, even threats of more suicide bomber assignments if they don't complete their more conventional missions. I make a detailed note about it that I plan to bring back to the regimental intel shop. This presents both military and political opportunities.

Walker dominates the rest of the night, the consummate entertainer.

"We got to watch the snipers kill, sir. It's kinda like watching your older brother fuck."

He recounts a farcical exchange with the battalion commander when they passed through headquarters:

> Sir, we've given you the two best Pashto linguists in the Marine Corps.
>
> That's great. Are they wearing real boots?
>
> The sergeant major checks.

Yes, believe it or not, they are wearing the right boots.

How about in Now Zad. They also get the right boots mailed to them?

They have, says the S-2.

Great, no excuses now.

Walker moves on to the porn he's trading with the ANA.

"They like it real crude, sir. Rough sex, gang bangs, that sort of thing."

"Don't we all."

"And they love the extremes. They like 'em really young and really old. Anything in between bores them."

"You're trading them kiddie porn?"

"Nah, teen sex. And they really love the old fogy shit."

"Seems like child rape is the main problem in this part of the country."

"Pashtun culture is like prison culture, sir. The Kandahar and Helmand Talibs abduct kids from orphanages. They're literal sex slaves. Haven't you seen *The Kite Runner*?"

"Have yet to see that one. Haven't read the book either. What you trading the porn for?"

"Sometimes other porn. Mostly cigs. Chow. You know."

Then he shows me the recent *Playboy* centerfold for a marine they all knew at DLI.

"She got around at Monterey, sir. And we all knew she was going places."

The world is spinning on a strange axis now, and I am having a hard time keeping my bearings. Voices are merging, too. I hear the words from a typical lance corporal in unison with the words of another lance corporal on a convoy saying he loves to fuck with the kids.

He loves to bait them with food without giving them any.

Or throw rocks at them.

Or aim in on them.

Or shout at them, "Fuck, no, I'm not gonna have sex with you, but I'll fuck your little sister!"

Or make himself a hood ornament of them. I have that in my notes: *Make myself a hood ornament of them.*

These are words in the air, like a harsh, passing breeze, and I cannot grab hold of their precise meaning. Another marine heading to a memorial at battalion headquarters for one of his fallen buddies picks up an actual rock on the bed of the armadillo. One of his fellows dresses him down before I do, then assures me his peer was just kidding, that he would have never thrown it. It was just a bit. Putting on a show for the laughs.

I can't recall how I've responded the other times. It's harrowing not knowing what I did or didn't do, but knowing I never did enough.

Sometime, somewhere, I imagine objecting, reporting everything I've seen through the proper channels. But when I think about what I've seen, everything turns to mist. What have I seen? What have I seen that is worth reporting? And how would the people guarding the proper channels react? Would they mock me? Penalize me? Cover their asses and let me hang my own rope? What evidence do I have of wrongdoing? Other than vibes. Hearsay. Intimations.

I have a hard time distinguishing the playacting from the real item, the fantasies from the facts. I forget what I've seen, or I tell myself what I've seen is what one always sees at war. In its proper context, I've seen nothing at all.

I tell myself I will continue to contain the damage. Whenever. However. Subtly. Slowly. Surreptitiously.

Couldn't have been long after that two explosions blast a kilometer out. You can see the plumes and feel the vibration. Someone suggests they are controlled dets, but the suggestion dissipates at a stroke. And once the birds appear in zone, everyone knows someone is hurt. Atop our SIGINT vic, I peer at the aftermath with my binoculars. All I see are points moving every which way. Or not moving at all.

Walker relays the enemy traffic.

"Yes, brother, the birds are in the air! They're singing! They have felt our power! Our electricity!"

Someone mutters, "Our own little Al Anbar in Afghanistan."

My new HUMINT pal, Davies, had joined the grunts on the fated patrol, and I embrace him upon his return. His blouse and face are now stained in blood, his hands shaking. And now all my onetime garrulous interlocutor can say is "It was bad. It was bad. It was bad."

Those hit turn out to be two explosive ordnance disposal techs and the squad leader, a marine my team guys had been working with for some time. He'd sometimes borrow their satellite phone to call home. The squad leader loses his legs, along with one of the techs. As for the other tech, a grunt from the patrol says to me, "He's fine. Just some metal in the face."

Whenever a marine is seriously wounded or killed, every base and outpost within the immediate area of operations reverts to River City condition 1. This is the codeword for reduced communications, in which all long-distance interfaces with the civilian world are dropped, sometimes for days. The intent is to ensure the proper authorities are the first to notify and offer condolences to the victims' families.

For me, River City obtains a religious quality, a moment of reflection amid a bureaucratic or amoral routine. But now that Salaam Bazaar, the marketplace of peace, has been thrown into another state of solemnity, I do not brood. The platoon wants revenge, and they want SIGINT to hand them a time and place for the vengeance.

I meet with leadership for consecutive nights to plan a raid, and SIGINT plays a central role in the planning. One marine exults, "I feel like we're cheating with ya RadBn guys. BAMCIS!"

(The reviews vary. Grunts in other AOs think we're useless.)

I leave before the raid takes place, and as I write this, I'm not even certain it did. But I have been part of similar plotting on other occasions, under similar circumstances, when they have.

• •

Asner and Kwon on the watch floor, back at the regimental base, watching the feed for the GBU, the laser-guided bomb unit. It's all *pop pop pop. Dot dot dot.* The pop pop pop dot dot dot of imperial war.

"Black turban. ICOM. Shoot him."

"Hide site compromised. Drop him."

"You gotta discipline them."

Where *discipline* means "kill."

SHOT HIMARS / SHOT HIMARS / 2 RDS IN BOUND / SPLASH HIMARS / 1 MORE INBOUND 1 MIN / SPLASH.

mIRC chat, Internet Relay Chat, was invented by Khaled Mardam-Bey. Little is known about Mardam-Bey. Some say he was born in Amman, Jordan, to a Syrian father and a Palestinian mother. Some say he enjoys Palestinian poetry.

The poetry of imperial death.

When I was a kid, I threw water balloons. I said splash.

• •

At some felt crossroads, I write that war is America's main industry and peace its ephemeral by-product, like our pinkish polluted skies.

I relate River City to liquid iron, the point at which your soul either hardens into the surrounding steel or flows more beautifully, furiously, into a river of resistance.

Beautiful resistance is not the story of my war. Mine. I am a paradox from which I will never escape.

A month has passed since April. Maybe two or three. The past, the present, the future—all keeps passing.

When I return to the bazaar for the final time, the site has become even more despairing. An amount of $12,500 has just been divided between three local Afghans as recompense for the deaths of loved ones. A two-star shows up investigating another incident, in which a JDAM was dropped on a nearby compound, incurring further civilian casualties.

I watch the general's helo land and depart. I watch him as he asks a marine if there are any wag bags. There aren't. Everyone is shitting in whatever they can find.

McChrystal is gone, booted a few weeks earlier, after a *Rolling Stone* article revealed his contempt for Obama's top civilian advisers. McChrystal's entourage had some choice words for Obama, too. And the frontliners I've met who like to complain about McChrystal's restrictive ROEs might be getting their way, with rumors of looser ones to come. But I've been in-country long enough to know ROEs are set by local commanders anyway. And the latest command looks to have already done some loosening. Maybe no loosening was needed. These things are hard to parse.

"Kill everyone with a cell phone," Walker relays to me.

"Positive ID nonexistent," says Somerset. "Everyone shoots where everyone else is shooting."

"Kill everyone with a motorbike," says Ross, one of my Dari linguists. The teams have been mixed up a bit since my last visit.

I say that's fucked up and that shit should be reported when it happens and they tell me it's battalion commander approved.

More syringes coat the deck, specifically around the shitter.

"It's funny," says a sniper platoon commander—a fellow lieutenant—after mentioning a handful of ANA soldiers looting the bazaar.

Reports of Afghan National Army and Afghan National Police atrocities are increasing. One Afghan soldier shoots a little girl, who is subsequently medevacked. I don't know what's happened to her. Detainees are executed on their knees, by the ANA sergeant major himself. Someone says something about a beheading.

I overhear jokes about child murders and rapes. I can no longer confront every disturbing utterance. There are too many. And when I do, they evade.

"I'm embellishing, sir. Just shits and giggles. There are other sniper units that kill innocents. But that's not us. Our bolt kills are clean."

I don't know what parts of that are true or false.

A lieutenant no one likes is now in the brig for murdering an Afghan at a checkpoint.

"He's got this ridiculous Southern accent, sir," says Walker.

"Reminds me of Lieutenant Calley," I say.

"Calley, the My Lai dude?"

"Yeah, except I don't think he had the accent."

Walker changes the subject.

"Hey, sir, a Marine Air O was put up as the sexiest marine in *Playgirl*!"

"No shit. What's his name? I might know the guy from OCS or TBS."

He's forgotten, and I tell him no big deal.

Ross approaches us in the ANA's carpeted abode, one of the many erstwhile market stalls.

"S'up, sir. Just was talking to the terps over there."

"In Dari?"

"They're Hazara. One of them reminds me of the shop owner in LA who taught me Dari."

Before Ross can tell me more, the three ANA soldiers who invited us to the hut in the first place—all Tajiks from the north—offer to make us a meal.

"Let me guess," Ross says, "goat meat, rice, and chai." He looks over at me. "It's always the same three, sir. And it's always delicious."

We accept their gracious offer.

Before the sun sets, we take shots of each of us with the Soviet-made RPG-7, the rocket-propelled grenade launcher of choice for the Viet Cong, the IRA, the mujahideen, and the Somali forces that took down the Black Hawk helicopters in Mogadishu in 1993. Egyptians were the first to deploy the weapon, against Israelis during the War of '67. We take a few seconds reciting our shared knowledge.

One of the soldiers, Farrukh, wraps a belt of 5.56 rounds around his diminutive frame and asks me if he looks good. I give him a thumbs-up. All three hold their M16s in awkward sideways or upways positions, always speaking with their hands.

I ask them what they think of the M16s.

"The Kalashnikov is better in battle," Farrukh says (courtesy of Ross).

They tell us about their favorite Pakistani movie star, whose name I fail to record.

Over chai, buttered rice, goat meat, okra, and bread (Ross had failed to mention the especially palatable okra and bread), we have a passionate discussion about Islam, with my marines interpreting throughout.

"Basically they think we're all gonna burn, but they want peace with us in the meantime," Ross says.

I ask them what they think of Iran. I'm curious because both populations are Persian-speaking.

"No, they arrest us," says Hafiz, a short but built soldier and the quietest of the three up to this point. "Plus, they not real Muslims."

Farrukh jumps in while Ross keeps translating.

"India treats us best. India is good people even though they're infidel country."

I ask what makes them so good, and the response is long and both Ross and Walker attempt to paraphrase it for me. Something about Indian movies and the sex. They were thrown in jail in Pakistan. They call Jesus "Isa." It's hard to follow, but everyone gets animated when the conversation turns to "fucking all the time" in Kabul. They "flirt with girls' eyes" in the capital city. Their last time there, on R&R, they fucked a whore together. A man showed them pictures of options. They were mostly foreigners.

I try to follow the conversation, jotting notes to myself along the way. Our hosts keep saying, "*Ho*," which means "yes" in Pashto. But they also mostly seem to be speaking in Tajik and Dari, with a few words slipped in Arabic, Hindi, and Urdu. Ross and Walker keep making helpful asides to me.

"*Manana* is thank you, sir."

"*Shai* is good."

When I hear something I'm not sure about and my marines are too preoccupied to clarify, I take notes.

Kabulki—in Kabul?

Delaramki—in Delaram?

Mohammed looks nervous, and Walker tells me he's worried about what I'm writing. I apologize and put my notebook away.

They like *Rambo* and *Rocky*, and what they've seen of *The Kite Runner*. They like fighting movies because they don't have to read the subtitles. There are three movie theaters Kabulki. All the televisions are Kabulki. They like cricket and California, but they're too poor to go to America. They like visiting Nangarhar. There are good Muslims in Nangarhar. No one is Talib in Nangarhar and they all want peace.

"How about books? You read books?"

Farrukh can't read, but the other two can. Hafiz made it to fifth grade. Both Hafiz and Mohammed read religious books.

"Any books other than religious?"

"Yes," Walker tells me. "They also read seminary books, books that teach them Arabic and Farsi."

I'm curious about what they see their future looking like. Do they want to stay in the ranks? Walker tells me they want to be officers, but I'm not sure if that means all three of them, and before I can ask, they're talking about another ANA soldier named "Smokey" becoming an officer. They call him "Smokey" because he smokes a ton of weed.

Walker breaks out the Pines and offers them to our hosts. We all end up with one as the conversation moves to Hazaras being slave boys.

"We miss home," Farrukh says.

"Yes, we all want to go home healthy," says Hafiz.

Mohammed agrees.

"When we go home, no cigarettes, no hash. Back to being good Muslims."

Hafiz and Mohammed explain to me the difference between a rug and a carpet. I marvel at their knowledge. The Pakistanis and Persians dominate the industry, but the soldiers are partisans of the Afghan rugs in the north.

We start talking tattoos. Hafiz says they're against Islamic law, but some of the soldiers have them anyway.

"How do you feel about the Afghans you're fighting?" I ask Hafiz.

"Every Afghan has Afghan soil in his heart. Can't take it out."

"Do you have hope for your people? Your country?"

"Hope? No, you leave, Taliban take over."

"Won't people fight the Taliban?"

"People here don't want peace. We aren't Iraqis," Mohammed says.

I'm bewildered by the interjection but barrel on.

"Will the Tajiks fight?"

All three nod yes.

"Well, at least that's something."

"When you leave," says Mohammed, "will be just like when the Russians left. Taliban come to power."

They start debating among themselves. Hafiz appears to have more faith in Karzai than Mohammed. He thinks Karzai, despite being Pashtun, will face off with the Pashtuns when the time comes. Mohammed is not even sure targeting Pashtuns is wise. Behind them, Farrukh prances around with his ammo belt.

I glance at my watch. Four hours have passed. As we stand up to depart to our own bed net cots a few stalls over, we thank our hosts effusively while following them with our hands on our hearts.

Ross tells me they want us to come back to Afghanistan, keep learning their languages, and hang out with them Kabulki.

"From the heart," says Walker. Despite all his teasing, he means it. He likes them. We all do.

I'm distracted by an oversized ant dragging someone's dead toenail across the carpet.

By the end of my stay at the bazaar, we've agreed to move the team to battalion headquarters at the Musa Qala District Center. They've already halted patrols since my last visit, and the situation has only deteriorated since then. The juice was no longer worth the squeeze, as Bartels once told me upon my arrival to Delaram.

If it ever was.

I promote Walker to corporal and call him a hero.

"Remember these months for the rest of your days."

I'm still in the business of motivating, for the sake of my marines. For the sake of myself.

Our last evening at the bazaar another ANA soldier I don't know sees us packing up and tells us not to come back.

"There's Talib everywhere."

I gaze at the postapocalyptic seductiveness of the burn pit flames and the smoke, the three 4×4 MRAPs wrapped into the pinkish-purple declension of the night. The US flag is hoisted beside the Afghan one. But the

Afghan black, red, and green is ripped at its red center, nothing there but an oval-shaped gash.

I mark in my notebook: Murder hole = glory hole.

I'm still making my way through the Bible, so I add more stray impressions, too burnt out for capitalization:

> god was fearful/jealous of man's achievement with the tower of babylon—hence: divide & conquer; jacob's covenant with god, new rendering of abram's covenant, as esau-jacob is rendering of cain-abel (isaac-ishmael), joseph and his brothers—haunting reverberations; screech of dying, starving cat

---

I loved my men. And I say that because I still feel something deep inside me that requires me to say it. And I loved those men who weren't mine, like Galloway and Neel. They all made me laugh, even when I shouldn't have. I envy those who pick the side of a less complicated gentleness and sweetness early enough in their lives to never have to wrestle with this peculiar exasperation, of both rejoicing and recoiling at your most intimate, cursed associations. And there are few things more intimate and cursed than sharing in war's nihilism. If that war is being executed by an empire, and if you are the imperialist, then the intimacy of guilt and shame can grow into something uniquely uncanny and (for some) unbearable.

I will not deny that such intimacy differs in relation to one's proximity to the bloodshed. Nor will I claim this law holds for everyone in the same way. And I understand my own role in Afghanistan as an officer—a roving, vagabond-like officer—in some ways reduced that intimacy. It might have even allowed me to acknowledge the poison at a much earlier stage in my reckoning. Some will never acknowledge the poison and will hate me for doing so. Their hate may be as close as they come to an acknowledgment.

I was far from a grunt, but I was close enough to them to be close enough to the terrain they were navigating. And that terrain had nothing to do with whatever decency exists in this world. Even the ostensible decency, like handing a colonized child a candy bar, proved nauseating.

On the way back to battalion headquarters my guys wanted to see me up on the 50-cal turret. More to the point, they wanted rest. So I took a shift. It must have been an hour or two before the second vehicle ahead of mine erupted in fumes. The force stunned, and I got some benign shrapnel to the goggles. But I was fine, and I stayed up there as the convoy command had us set up a 360 perimeter. At no point could I see those being medevacked. All I caught was a red flare and mine sweepers walking on line. I glimpsed the hit MRAP, too, its entire engine block blown off.

As it happens, it was Gallo and Neel who guided our vic to the preferred spot on the security circle. I remember worrying about them stepping on a secondary, but their metal detectors worked. And when EOD showed up some hours later, I was impressed with their routine, from their pace counting to their massaging of the dust to the way they had their cigs set in their mouths.

Before the wrecker arrived to haul back the downed vic, a local jalopy attempted to maneuver around the mess and rolled over into a steep indent of dirt. The driver ascended from the rut howling at us, fingers extended outward into a drill instructor's knife hand. I watched at a comfortable distance as another marine approached. And I watched as he exhausted whatever remaining energy he had left. Our vic was repositioned before I could figure out how that situation resolved, and we left not long after. But when I think of the empire, I sometimes think of that.

My notes on the war, once transcribed in a Word document, extended to 159 pages, much of it clogged up by Bible passages or excerpts from the women I was reading at the time to make me feel close to someone not a man. Interspersed are slabs like this:

> talked to █████—double amputee lost one ball (sgt ████)—in shock—panicked—battery, jug, pressure plate—non-metalic tube, still very conductive—our metal detectors are worthless—dogs worthless—████'s ear drum burst; █████—quadruple amputee, ear drums burst, brain trauma, back in the states; 3rd time they went to this compound; same two squads each time; 1st time = 1, 2nd time = 2, 3rd time = 3; DOG TAGS ON GROUND; eod techs running around making sure no one step on IED—end up stepping on one themselves. Oh, and this = ssgt ███ lost both legs here, demonstrates an imaginary line running across the thigh. clean cut. A few lost fingers. OTHERWISE, HE WAS GOOD; ran out of tourniquets—3 used just for sgt ███s leg—if one more person had stepped wrong, he would be dead

I don't know if these notes refer to the incident I witnessed at Salaam Bazaar. Some details line up. Either way, returning to them over a decade after the fact induces in me a feeling not captured by any single word. Or combination of words. It is a feeling of a rage that has outlived its welcome, but also one mixed with an undying warmth.

What to make of this feeling is another question. It comes from a sense of solidarity with my own people, my compatriots, who in this instance also happened to be the invaders and occupiers. I suppose the anecdote of the Afghan run off the road also enrages and inspires an aching compassion in me at the same time, but neither to the same degree. And I don't think that's solely because the latter, as far as I'm aware, resulted in more precipitant blood. It is also because I've spent much more valuable time with men like those maimed in the IED blast than the man run off the road.

What to do with the feeling, then, must be to universalize it, or if that's not possible, which I suspect it isn't, then at least to behave as if the feeling *ought* to be universalized. For every time I feel for myself and those with whom I'm most familiar, I must go out of my way to attempt to feel for those whom I assume to be least like me. And in doing so I continue to see the world for what it is: a world none of us can truly live in and accept but rather which we feel obliged to turn into something in keeping with our love.

After returning from Afghanistan, I came across an explanation for the origin of the term River City, the codeword for the reduced communications imposed when a marine was seriously hurt or killed. It involves the Broadway hit *The Music Man*, about a con man who comes to River City, promising to keep children out of trouble by teaching them how to play music. But first the parents must fork over cash for the instruments and band uniforms. The man's pitch is that "Ya got trouble, my friend, right here, I say, trouble right here in River City."

I don't know how accurate the explanation is, but there's wisdom in it all the same. The musical debuted in 1957, at the height of the Cold War. It suggested trouble in the heart of the United States, trouble parents were desperate to protect their children from, even if it meant handing their children, along with their wallets, over to a hustler pledging a salutary band of brothers. These items add historical specificity to my otherwise humanistic plea. They drive at the mass psychology—the mass pathos—of the decaying imperium. But when combined with one of the musical's most popular songs transmigrating, in metaphorical form, to the gravest corners of contemporary Pax Americana, an even more layered view emerges. The pathos becomes more present and global, a pathos the United States continues to play a leading role at inflaming but by no means monopolizing. And in that recognition the task of doing something with that pathos, of daresay healing it, becomes all the more urgent.

This is where I was supposed to tell the story of my war, some semblance of climax. But I didn't even make it to the act where I earned my combat action ribbon, an act that entailed little to no combat. I haven't included the latter half of my deployment, when I found myself, in anticlimactic form, behind a desk, a weary, disillusioned OIC.

It's remarkable how much of the Hebrew Bible, a peerless drama soaked in the very carnality that tends to make for the most gripping of spectacles, concerns God punishing disloyal whores, or those consorting with disloyal whores, or men behaving like disloyal whores, or most of all, those, in their pitiful viciousness, reminding Him most of Himself.

PART SIX

AMERICAN HERO I

If we had a keen vision and feeling of all ordinary human life, it would be like hearing the grass grow and the squirrel's heart beat, and we should die of that roar which lies on the other side of silence.

—*George Eliot*

In 1922, two years before his retirement, General Joseph Pendleton wrote that political economist Henry George was "one of the greatest men this World has ever produced." Pendleton was a longtime adherent, especially of George's famous proposal to tax unimproved land value at steep rates and redirect the revenue to public investments and a universal basic income. Had the plan ever been enacted, it would have amounted to a historic wealth transfer from the rich to everyone else, which is why George and his followers became such fixtures of the radical scene during the turn of the last century. Pendleton associated with many members of that scene, from Cleveland mayor Tom Johnson to the editor of the San Francisco newspaper *The Star*, James Barry. Even the general's commanding role in the occupation of the Dominican Republic in 1916 seemed to have pushed him leftward. Pendleton spoke about the Dominicans in racist terms (at least once lamenting their "nigger smartness"), but in time became close with the anti-imperialist Desiderio Arias, working to implement Georgist land reform on the island.

Although such reform never took hold, Pendleton did win a policy fight back home. His waning years were devoted to establishing a major base on the West Coast, and after his death in February of 1942, the Department of the Navy announced its intent to build, just north of San Diego, what would become the largest Marine base at the time, and the installation would go on to train troops for the Pacific campaign. Its significance expanded further during the US military occupations of Korea and Vietnam in the fifties and sixties, but by then the complexities of Joseph Pendleton the man were all but forgotten. This included his adoption by the Tlingit peoples amid intermittent assignments to Alaska from 1891 to 1904 and his supposed concern for their well-being the rest of his life (Alaska governor John G. Brady's request for Pendleton's transfer on account of his cruelty toward the Tlingit casts doubt on this alleged concern). It also included his continued interest in the Christian proselytization of Native Americans across the Americas, and his seeming disregard for full indigenous autonomy. Pendleton never recorded misgivings about the fates of the Payómkawichum and Acjachemen were his beloved base to be constructed on their ancestral lands, and he facetiously counted himself, alongside Spanish explorers like Juan Rodríguez Cabrillo, one of San Diego's "discoverers."

As I settled down in Southern California in the lead-up to my war and in the wake of the 2008 financial collapse, a vague anti-capitalist sensibility was taking root, one that approached the ownership class with increasing suspicion while still leaving room for open commerce. It was a politics not far afield from Pendleton's, in all its incongruence.

In those early months, I had plenty of time to devote to autodidactic pursuits, and as Camp Pendleton's brown-grassed hills became familiar, so did the ideological panorama that had shaped its eponymous general. This was a tradition that belonged to Henry George but also, before him, to Thomas Paine and Adam Smith. A once influential version of liberalism—a version suppressed by the 1920s (after the first Red Scare) and further buried during the McCarthyism of the fifties—saw in concentrated economic power an obstacle to liberty, and in monopolistic landowners, bankers, and bosses the rebirth of feudalism.

My reading carried me through the century, well beyond Pendleton's passing, from the French mystic Simone Weil's "The Iliad, or The Poem of Force" ("To define force—it is the x that turns anybody who is subjected to it into a thing") to the critic Dwight MacDonald's "The Responsibility of Peoples" ("More and more, things happen TO people") to Noam Chomsky's homage to MacDonald in his *New York Review of Books* debut, "The Responsibility of Intellectuals" ("It is the responsibility of intellectuals to speak the truth and to expose lies"). Each thinker chipped away at the chauvinist residue of their predecessors, one after the other, like an intergenerational carving of stone. And their dissents were helping me envision freedom as something other than domination.

I was honorably discharged from the Corps in May of 2011. I'd completed my active-duty contract of about five years and had no interest in re-upping. Had I wanted to, I probably could have done all right in the SIGINT world, either as a marine or as a civilian. But I never even entertained the thought.

Before leaving Pendleton, I attended the cloudy memorial service of one of the hardest-hit marine battalions in the Afghanistan war. Lined up across the deck of a helicopter landing zone (HLZ) were twenty-five battle crosses, each made up of a wooden block, combat boots, a downward-facing rifle with dog tags hanging from the back end of the pistol grip, and a Kevlar helmet sitting atop the buttstock. The blocks were adorned with plaques and photographs of each lost warrior.

General Kelly, who would later spearhead President Trump's "zero tolerance" family separation policy, offered a few stolid words. His son, an enlisted grunt turned grunt officer, had been killed in the Sangin District the previous November.

I learned during an intelligence brief at Delaram, weeks before I visited Sangin in December, that Lieutenant Kelly had slipped on a wooden plank while crossing a canal. His foot landed on a waterproofed IED. By that late date, having lost faith in the mission, I'd tried my best to discourage my teams from venturing past the wire. But my second-cycle marines, whom I had never trained nor met in person, saw it differently, and I decided to offer solidarity by committing to patrol with them the morning after my arrival. We geared up before dawn, but my RadBn command wisely determined it wasn't worth the risk and called us back last second.

The general's son had died on November 9, and his friend General Joseph Dunford, then assistant commandant of the Marine Corps, notified Kelly at his home of his son's death that same day. Dunford approached the door in his service uniform, so Kelly knew what had happened before a word was uttered.

The next day, November 10, marines celebrated the Marine Corps' birthday, and the day after, Americans observed Veterans Day. On November 13, Kelly delivered a speech at the Semper Fi Society of St. Louis, where he asked that his son's death not be mentioned. He seemed to have nonetheless found a way to speak about his loss:

> I have the name of the most recent hero, killed in Afghanistan a few hours ago, but I cannot share with you his name because a Marine officer and Navy chaplain have not yet executed their honored duty of notifying the next of kin. That family, right now, somewhere in America, is in the final minutes of blissful ignorance before their entire lives change forever. I know God will help them bear this inconceivable burden—a burden I am told by those who know never goes away or even gets lighter—and help them find comfort in the fact that their son was doing exactly what he wanted to do, was doing it with the finest men on this earth, and for a cause that meant more to him than his life.

In early March of 2011, a couple months before the memorial at Pendleton, Greg Jaffe at the *Washington Post* reported on a letter Kelly had written to his son in October that hinted at a softer, more thoughtful side:

> Do not let them ever enjoy the killing or hate their enemy. It is impossible to take the emotion out of it, but try and keep it as impersonal and mechanical as you can. The Taliban have their job to do and we have ours. That's it.... Combat is so inhumane; you must help your men maintain their humanity as well as their sense of perspective and proportion.

That side was not on display at the memorial the following spring. I'd like to say I at least detected a change in the tenor of his voice. But I'm not sure I did.

Afterward a chaplain gave a benediction, lamenting the selfishness of our society that touched on the news of the day—something about the public's fawning over Kate Middleton's royal wedding—with unvarnished scorn. Hundreds of marines and their family members sat or stood in reverence as each fallen warrior was honored. Two hundred from the unit had been wounded, so the number of limbless in the audience was considerable. Some had hooks for hands. Others sat in wheelchairs. One marine held himself up on his crutches throughout the ceremony, even when it appeared his entire form was about to shatter. I flipped through the pages of the program. Each time I stared at another of the twenty-five fallen faces, an otherwise undetectable vessel running from my navel to my throat tightened. A part of me wanted it to stay that way, as comeuppance for sacrificing nothing.

At the end of the service, I heard a mother say, "We get to take the box home with us. Not the rifle though."

War, for many Americans, is something we can't do without. It defines us at our deepest spiritual center. If there is one thing most agree on, it is that to die at war as an American is to be a hero. To almost die at war as an American is to be a hero. To go to war at all as an American is to be a hero. To be a close relative of someone who dies at war as an

American is to be a hero. Some might dissent on those final judgments, but the main consensus holds: American war is American heroism. All else is negotiable.

There is something about the religion of war, which is a religion of death, that cannot be contested. It can only be surrendered to. Being at that service, in the presence of so much suffering, proved unsurpassably humbling. I felt this same humbling whenever I showed up at a new outpost where blood had been shed. I never dared pontificate about my disgust with the religion of war then. What license do I have to pontificate now?

I came home safely. Save for the concussions, so did all my marines. So did everyone I knew well enough to know if they didn't. I patrolled in a few difficult spots, only a few times, but I never patrolled in Sangin, the most difficult of them all. And Lord knows I didn't do anything else of import.

Yet here I am, pontificating.

The first thing I did once I had my signed discharge papers in hand was pack up my gear and drive across the country. I can't say I took the most direct route. I'd grown close to my cousin and her future wife while living in California and hurtled up Route 1 to celebrate with them in the Bay Area. I was looking for places to stay during my return trek to the East Coast so, before I headed off, they hooked me up with a couple in Portland who turned out to be just as lovely as my cousins, taking me out to ambiguously blue-collar hipster bars and eclectic music venues, as well as a very serious game of kickball on a majestic mountain somewhere (and somehow) within city limits.

This was my first time socializing with civilians since returning from Afghanistan. It was also my first time socializing as a civilian since 2006. There was therefore a strange freshness to my twin excursions into the leisurely lives of San Francisco and Portland. I felt like I was rediscovering certain communities anew, ones free of hyper-masculine hijinks. But I was also bathing in a bitterness that I have yet to, to this day, fully shake off. Boot camp never instilled in me an absolute contempt for the average, overcivilized American. I had too many ties with too many civilian friends and family, and too much awareness of that contempt's purpose as a bond-building tool, for me to swallow the pill whole. But it was impossible not to internalize some fraction of that contempt through osmosis. And when I look back at the antipathy I'd felt toward civilians since my return, I suspect I was in the process of inflecting such trained disdain in a more left-leaning key.

The American civilian wasn't a problem for the reasons provided me at Parris Island, but the American civilian was still a problem. Did the happy young people I was partying with in the Pacific Northwest know their government was still at war in Afghanistan? Could they place Afghanistan on a map? Could they care any less about the tens of thousands of people dying there on the regular, Americans and non-Americans? Why, despite their ignorance, did they continue to thank me for my service? And how would they feel if a JDAM dropped on them?

This was presumptuous, of course, and no one feels anything when a JDAM drops on them. I knew all this when I wasn't basking in my overheated sense of superiority. One minute I would begrudge those around me for their apparent ease, and the next I was praying for a world where everyone could share in it, including those at the memorial service at Pendleton, including those I'd helped torment in the Helmand.

It was this schmaltz, combined with a gratitude for America's great expanse, that characterized the next leg of my trip. I hung with anachronistic grunge enthusiasts in Seattle, and schmoozed with a park ranger on the Montana side of Yellowstone after tipping my Jetta into a ditch while trying a quick park to take a shot of a passing wolf pack. He'd served as a secret service agent for four presidents, from Reagan to George W. Bush, and didn't mind telling me he wasn't very fond of the Clintons. When I glided through South Dakota, I reveled in the sunset behind the far-off, bobbing oil rigs, just as I had done during my drive through Nebraska, Kansas, and Oklahoma with my brothers.

To fall into a state of unchecked nostalgia made sense. To do so while driving across the country, in a desperate, subconscious attempt at recovering my lost faith, made even more sense. I was inhabiting a space of liberal fantasy, where the best of America—the America of quiet nobility—still existed in the interstices of everyday life. It was an America that might have been overrun by an anti-Obama opposition, but the phoenix would rise again, and when it did, all that had made America great would be restored. The fact that the basic structure of this fantasy, once shorn of its partisan superficialities, was indistinguishable from its conservative opposite was the punchline. Both the American liberal and the American conservative pronounced with Langston Hughes (but without the poet's irony): Let America be America again.

For a moment I saw the Dakota sky as the Afghan sky. I remembered the barks of the Afghan dogs and the texture of Afghan hair, thickets of dirty hair on our heads, hints of shared humanity.

The time, while pissing on a small outpost before heading off to the next base on a convoy, I spotted a detainee crouched in a makeshift wooden box not much larger than his crouch. I found the sight wretched enough to jot it down in a notebook, but nothing more. Or the time I was asked to make sure another detainee sharing a back seat with me in an armored vehicle wasn't allowed to pull his shawl above his forearms, for fear he would find a way to remove the zip ties from his wrists. I watched him, a teenager really, shiver for fifteen minutes—it was wintertime in the Helmand, and at an altitude of well over three thousand feet, the temperature was in the high twenties—before allowing him to cover up. He looked too much like my marines.

Fifteen minutes was a long time to discover the humanity of someone sitting a couple feet away. Yet I had spent over twenty-five years lapping up a political culture that had erased everything that made him human, so maybe it was more startling it took only fifteen.

The rigs go up and down, up and down. The sun blasting the size of America. Blasting the wilderness, the wildness. Blasting the fields where the Cowboys and Indians once roamed, still roam. We called the

Navy SEALs of the Helmand the cowboys. When we were in Afghanistan we were in-country. Indian country.

By the time I rolled into Madison, protests against Governor Scott Walker were almost over. Walker had launched a full-throttled assault on public-sector unions by attempting to strip them of their bargaining rights while constraining their ability to collect dues and raise wages. I had listened to the latest on the drive in, and for the first time in my life, found myself on the side of the workers.

I ambled into a hole-in-the-wall near the state capitol and chatted up the bartender. She taught me about labor politics in Wisconsin and I taught her about the marines. By the end of it, a couple hours later, I was tipsy and ready to hit the rack, but also interested in continuing the conversation. We exchanged numbers, and I told her I'd take a quick nap and be ready to go back out when she called me after work. She handed me a RECALL SCOTT WALKER bumper sticker. By the time I woke up, it was the next morning and I'd missed her call.

The shitters of I-90 threw me back to the shitters of the Helmand. I'd gotten in the habit of documenting the shit-stall scrawls in-country, often the obscenest of them:

I hate TCNs
I HATE NIGGERS
Live for nothing or die for something—Aryan
my girlfriend told me she was pregnant. so I punched her in the gut

Some were available in pictorial form, like when swastikas with menorahs or other white power symbols were etched with a pen or pocketknife. Sometimes more cosmopolitan souls would respond in kind. One swastika was turned into a box with four quadrants, another into a crisscrossing of dicks labeled "Swasdicka."

In Chicago when I drove by an army of precincts, patrol cars, and security cameras, the skittish faces and anonymous forms maneuvering and surviving between the cracks, I knew I was taking in something familiar.

That déjà vu followed me throughout my Midwest run. The number of signs for military bases and prisons assaulted me. So did the hundreds of defense contractors puncturing the countryside, as if the whole nation had become Chevy Chase, Maryland, or Fairfax County, Virginia. Even the drilling and fracking had leaked into half the topography. With rest stops or backroad detours came rundown mugs and tumbledown backdrops, like timeworn stage sets but real—stripped siding, flickering lightbulbs, mustiness, loss.

Lines between destruction, extraction, and exploitation (or past, present, future) thinning, and everything taking on a polluted air of occupation.

Farah Stockman, a member of the editorial board at the *New York Times*, declared the US-occupied Afghanistan of the past two decades a "fantasy economy that operated more like a casino or a Ponzi scheme than a country." Her appraisal of the war's profiteering echoed writers from other formerly pro-war publications like the *Post* or the *New Republic*, as well as those like *The Guardian* or *Foreign Policy* that were critical from the start. Back in 1933, Major General Smedley Butler, one of the Corps' most decorated marines, came to a similar conclusion when describing his role in Asia, Central America, and the Caribbean as that of a "high-class muscle man for Big Business, for Wall Street and the bankers. In short, I was a racketeer, a gangster for capitalism."

In Butler's day the big businesses included US Steel or the American Sugar Refining Company and the financiers Brown Brothers or National City Bank. Today the racket has extended its reach and complexity, encompassing big tech firms, from Amazon to Facebook to Google, and big banks, from Santander to ING to Deutsche Bank. Indigenous warlords like Gul Agha Sherzai and international mercenaries like Erik Prince have also made fortunes. Most of all, trillions of dollars in worker-produced wealth have been redirected to the shareholders of the Big Five defense contractors: Lockheed Martin, Boeing, General Dynamics, Raytheon, and Northrop Grumman.

This has been accompanied by a boom in the US-led international arms trade and an explosion in the global homeland security industry. Schools and other public spaces have become more securitized just as police have become more militarized. Data companies have joined the highest ranks of the military-industrial architecture, with everything from immigration policy to the climate crisis to public health subsumed by a national security logic bent on profit above all else. The rise of financialization, privatization, and monopoly in the war economy (never mind our political economy altogether) has incentivized ever more sanguinary forms of moneymaking, and these developments have also made it easier for those involved to conceal the scale of their corruption while rendering accountability nearly impossible.

And yet, all this enrichment somehow represents the more agreeable side of the ledger. It is one thing to ponder the private jets or indoor basketball courts of defense contractors. It is quite another to consider the lifeless bodies or unpeopled villages left in their wake. In my wake. In *my* wake. Mine.

Next came the Mosaic fortresses: the Walmart Supercenter of Coal Township, Pennsylvania, morphing into the Walmart Supercenter of Yucca Valley, California, morphing into the Salaam Bazaar of Musa Qala, the marketplace of peace. As Thomas Friedman, one of capitalism's most enthusiastic boosters, put it in 1999: "The hidden hand of the market will never work without a hidden fist—McDonald's cannot flourish without McDonnell Douglas, the builder of the F-15. And the hidden fist that keeps the world safe for Silicon Valley's technologies is called the United States Army, Air Force, Navy and Marine Corps."

I thought of Genesis and Ecclesiastes and Micah and Jeremiah, how they all were warning about what happened when God's command was violated, which I was now in the habit of thinking meant God's command for a Shared World. And how I'd gaped at the murdered desert and murdered sky and murdered winds and murdered waters and thought: This is the world the prophets demanded we protect, that we make sacred. And this is the world the prophets saw desecrated.

And how it made me scream inside. And how everything outside was screaming with me, sometimes so loudly and constantly all I could hear and see and feel was the scream.

In the Book of Job, in the thunder of the King James Bible, it was written: "When then cometh wisdom? And where is the place of understanding? Seeing it is hid from the eyes of all living, and kept close from the fowls of the air. Destruction and death say, We have heard the fame thereof with our ears."

The fame of wisdom. The infamy of its absence.

Most of us had turned into something rotten back there. Before back there. Somewhere here. I thought of the letter from a care package that simply said,

> I think that you must miss your family I think you are brave I think you are strong I think you are giving
>
> Sebastian, eight years old, third grade

My parents were grateful to have me back and they let me stay with them in Bloomfield until grad school. In between, I delivered duct tape to occupiers at Zuccotti Park. They didn't seem to have much to say about war or empire, but I found their generic fear and trembling relatable. I attended panels with new friends in the city, some of whom were guests on the panels. I started writing for magazines I'd been reading for a couple years like *Dissent*. I published an edited version of my Afghanistan emails in an international journal on the culture of war called *CONSEQUENCE*.

Since I'd saved up officer pay during my yearlong deployment, I spent three months in Europe backpacking, hosteling, couch-surfing, and gallery-hopping. I cheered on trade unionists at a May Day march in Lyon and helped Palestine Solidarity activists put up flyers and spray-paint around Montmartre. I wore my USMC sweatshirt that night because I still wanted to feel close to the Corps even though my

USMC past felt like a cruel joke. The activists didn't seem to mind the sweatshirt. Or didn't say so. Or didn't know what USMC meant. I pretended to farm around a small chateau near Limoges, though all I really did was build part of a fence and paint part of an attic, and not too well either. I was terrible with the sledgehammer. I slept with my host, an older woman with silver hair like charcoaled icicles and gimlet eyes sharp as my knife. I'd brought the M16 CRKT knife with me from Connecticut and, before then, from the Helmand, and she seemed to like when I used it. She'd once served on the front lines of the international NGO racket and knew how it felt to suspect your profession was a joke. After the war I found so many so lovable, despite finding the world so cruel. Someone literary had once said she wanted to touch everything and be touched by everything. Maybe it was Anaïs Nin. I wanted to touch everything and be touched by everything. Even when it was melting. Maybe then I desired the touch even more.

I came back to America. I came back to save myself. I came back to America. Still coming back.

I became a graduate student in western New York.

I helped organize fast-food workers. I wrote short online pieces about police militarization in Ferguson and marched in the streets of Rochester after the murder of Freddie Gray in Baltimore. The more I wrote and the more I did, the more I felt like I was doing nothing.

I fell in love more times than I deserved, and hurt those I fell for. When people thanked me for my service, I felt like they were mocking me. When anyone complimented me, I felt like I was being duped. I overdid kindnesses and self-deprecations in person and overdid resentment online. I drank too much beer and ate too much cheese. I gained fifty pounds and didn't know it until my father pulled me aside and told me I had to lose weight. I took acid, molly, and whatever else my friends would hand me. At first, the healing worked. The trees became sagacious and avuncular, the mosquitoes confidants and comrades, everything precious. The minuscule corner of the sacred I wanted but had destroyed came back to life and told me I was all right. That everyone was all right and that we were all one. That I could go on living and be merry and maybe even love in a way that would last. Even though I knew that if I ever did find contentment, it would only be further proof of the universe's indifference.

In 2015, a grad school buddy invited me to a three-day Phish festival at Watkins Glen International, a historic Grand Prix racetrack turned occasional concert venue. I had been prepping to teach a course on the Vietnam War and made the mistake of wading into Michael Herr's *Dispatches* right before dropping whatever drug it was I dropped. In time, the tents took on the familiar dying mildew-green cast. I was fastened into the gyrating canteen of the Ferris wheel, where everyone below became vindictive termites, and my fellow trippers inquisitorial ants. By the time the ride stopped and we were flushed out onto the overrun grass, the landscape had assumed some variety of the demonic.

I implored the closest kiosk for water, but water didn't help. The nonperson who supplied me the cup was gangrened, pulsating with malice. I closed my eyes only to discover even grimmer revelations on the other side. I gripped the shoulder of one of my two companions, who was no longer human but who assured me everything would be all right if I held tight. I let go for fear of being deceived and wandered off into the crowded night. I straggled around the racetrack of my own mind, the sun ascending and descending like a malevolent rig. All that had survived was cruel dehumanized banter, threatening looks, a punishing repetition of external, inaccessible amusement.

I stepped on an IED and a compassionless throng gathered, scoffing at me. I became a curled fetus on a trafficked street. The lights arrived. A tussle with fiendish cops; they dragged me in my bare feet across the asphalt, and I was shipped from one holding site to the next. An M4-style semiautomatic rifle stood upright in the patrol car's rack, not far from my left knee. Eventually the handcuffs were replaced with ER bed restraints and IV tubing, as doctors, nurses, and imps that must have been medical students peered over me.

The emergency room of the Cayuga Medical Center treated me the full length of the morning, after being unmoored for something like eighteen hours. At some point, I'd removed the tubes and raced to the double doors before a fireteam of robed wraiths dragged me back.

Someone contacted my folks. They drove up from Connecticut, and after I was discharged, we went out for Chinese. I sat across from them, waiting for them to turn against me. But they stayed.

I don't know how to write about my guilt. It always feels like a trap. If you're sincere about examining society you're bound to incriminate yourself, since society is just the part of ourselves we share. And because you're a novice to the end, and because you're thoughtful, you'll become overburdened with humiliation and shame. It's forever your first time here, after all, a place already crowded with far too much hurt. And anyone who pretends they've navigated around the hurt, instead of absorbing and channeling it in graceless turns, is prone to hurt the most.

For my part, I had joined an institution that has delivered more hurt to more people than most of its historic competitors. I did so out of no economic duress, and after an education and upbringing that afforded me copious opportunities to know better. When I became doubtful, I tried to rein in the violence on the margins. But mostly I kept my mouth shut and went with the flow like everyone else (except those who didn't).

The other day I read an essay by historian and journalist Rachel Nolan about the CIA-backed coup in Guatemala in 1954. How its name, Operation Success, symbolizes a vanity that dwarfs my own, which maybe at some subconscious register I find comforting.

Philip Roettinger, a marine and one of the CIA case officers for the operation, remarked in 1986:

> "Operation Success" was a failure. The new regime burned books. It disenfranchised three-fourths of Guatemala's people. It dismantled social

> and economic reforms such as land redistribution, social security and trade-union rights. Our overthrow began 31 years of repressive military rule and the deaths of more than 100,000 Guatemalans.

And later:

> It is painful to look on as my government repeats the mistake in which it engaged me 32 years ago. I have grown up. I only wish my government would do the same.

I'd prefer to speak about that repetition, that eternal return, and maybe then and only then, speak about how that return makes me feel. How chilled I am by its stubbornness, and how even its subtlest recurrences chill me. Like when another National Defense Authorization Act gets passed with little to no comment. Or when someone lives and another dies.

In front of a mirror in a hotel room bathroom around midnight, in the nation's capital. Years after Afghanistan. Just attended the wedding of a college friend. Drunk and depressed. The Zoloft lessened the panic attacks, but the dysthymia remained. Ran into a woman I once dallied with, but now I'm fifty pounds heavier and depressed. We said hi and bye.

In front of the mirror, I punched as I was trained to punch, with my fists closed neither too tightly nor too loosely and the force of contact administered by the knuckles of my index and middle. By the time it was over, which couldn't have been more than a couple minutes, I was swollen on each cheek. I bawled and then conked out. The next morning, I slipped out of the hotel early so no one I knew might see the bruises.

I am drawn to the outside, to the impersonal aggregate, to the statistics. Most know veterans commit suicide at higher rates than civilians. Few, however, are familiar with the studies that show that the highest rate of suicides among servicemembers comes from those who were never deployed. One found the highest rate concerns those who were separated from the military irrespective of combat experience, especially those who were dishonorably discharged. Another, that the highest rate follows boot camp. Yet another concludes that though it is true men (uniformed or otherwise) commit suicide at higher rates than women, and even though women serve disproportionately in noncombat roles, the "difference in suicide rates" between those who have formerly served in the military and those who have never served "is greater among women than men."

None of this negates that those suffering traumatic brain injury or PTSD are at higher risk than those who aren't, or that combat veterans suffer these afflictions in notably high numbers. But it does suggest the need to place military and veteran suicide rates in greater conversation with civilian trends. This includes research that has determined that between 2007 and 2018, the suicide rate among Americans between the ages of ten and twenty-four increased by 60 percent; that between 1999 and 2018, the general suicide rate increased by 35 percent; during the same period, it increased 28 percent for males and 55 percent for females.

I will not pretend to know the cause of all this. I assume that the steep rate of military and veteran suicide can be explained in part by the exceptional wear and tear of a job that demands long hours, physical and mental strain, and extended periods of separation from family and loved ones. Military personnel and veterans also have easier access to guns. And the preponderance of suicides among those entering or exiting the service might have something to do with lifestyle gaps between military and nonmilitary worlds.

Yet I am inclined to push speculation a bit further. It seems to me that if the empire recycles trauma, which I believe it does, then it also recycles suicides. I once met a post-9/11 veteran in one of my classroom visits (this time in a college) who spoke of his father's suicide, which he was certain resulted from his military experience. And his grandfather's suicide, which he was certain resulted from his military service. And how he worried every day that he, too, would end it, and the only thing stopping him was his wife and his kids.

If the United States has become more militarized the past twenty years—and by any sensible metric it has—it stands to reason that it would become more suicidal. Women (never mind queer and trans people) bear a special burden in militarized societies. They are the ones most susceptible to rape, abuse, and exploitation. Given their lower propensity to commit violence, they commit fewer suicides. But, again, it makes sense such a propensity would increase at a faster rate when militarization and militarism return with a vengeance.

During the tail end of my Afghanistan deployment, right after Veterans Day, Martin, my on-and-off friend, emailed me. He told me he wasn't flag-waving and wasn't fond of most of America's wars. But he did respect those who transform themselves. He was especially fond of Malcolm X for this reason. After years of wandering the proverbial desert, he had decided he would become a doctor, and he would apply for the military's Health Professions Scholarship Program so he could attend medical school for free.

Before his medical turn, Martin had forged his own unorthodox path as an autodidact, handyman, and globetrotter. I wasn't elated about his imminent entry into the war machine, but as he set out on his belated professional course as a doctor and I set out on mine as an academic, we felt an added kinship.

A couple years back I reunited with him and Ian. Ian was making a life for himself as a real estate agent in New York, and we strolled up and down the High Line, reminiscing and debating the costs and benefits of the single life. Martin and Ian were committed to bachelorhood. I wanted a partner. I told them about my plans to write about manhood and empire.

We peered up at the 150-foot Hudson Yards Vessel, a monument to copper and steel. It had been marketed as the American answer to the

Eiffel Tower, a "jungle gym" to be climbed and explored by visitors, especially children. This, before it was shut down for the first time in January 2021 after its third suicide. It was opened again that May, but without additional fencing or barriers. In late July it was closed again after a fourteen-year-old boy leapt to his death.

PART SEVEN

AMERICAN HERO II

And in this house Christopher Columbus is a hero—end of story.

—*Tony Soprano*

Not long before my grandfather lost the ability to remember, I interviewed him on two separate occasions in December 2015 about his near century on this rotating earth. We sat at the same Victorian dining table that had served as a hallowed gathering spot for our extended clan since the eighties. For countless Thanksgivings and Passover seders I had watched our treasured patriarch, always at the head of the table, impart his wisdom on the primacy of family or how every Republican was an idiot and a crook. I had watched my grandmother, always beside him on the corner, caress his shoulder, elbow, or hand whenever he required calming, or whenever she required assurance he was still there.

During the first interview, which spanned late morning through early afternoon, Gramps's hands rested palms down on the age-old mahogany. I began with the basics.

"When were you born?"

"February twenty-fourth..."

Gramps did some inexplicable counting with his stout fingers.

"...1910...1928...1924..."

"Twenty-four?"

He nodded and I moved on. I could always confirm the date with Grandma.

"How old were your parents when they had you?"

More finger counting.

"My mother had me... I think at... seventeen or eighteen. My father was ten years older than her. Then three other brothers followed."

When I asked about his siblings, there was another long pause and it looked like he was about to cry.

"Gramps, if you want to cry, you can cry."

"No, I'm not gonna cry! It's just that I've gone through this, with myself, many many many moons, y'know."

He was just struggling with their birthdates, namely, the order of their births. But when he got to talking about his three brothers as people rather than as numbers, his face quickened with recognition. Gramps was the oldest, and he didn't get to know the youngest two—Bobby and Harvey—when he was growing up. But Jerry was just a year and half younger. Jerry couldn't hold a job. He worked at a hat and mink shop run by their uncles, but even that didn't go well.

After he came home from war, he went searching for his family in Manhattan but couldn't find them. Eventually he learned they'd moved near Sea Gate on Coney Island. When they reunited, he helped buy Jerry a used cab for $2,000 and Jerry became a career cabbie.

"He couldn't do anything else, but once he got in a cab he was good."

Jerry was still turning a profit off the leasing of his car and medallion. I wanted to ask follow-ups about the medallion system, Uber, and the death of taxiing as a middle-class livelihood, but Gramps had already jumped ahead, and I was trying to find a way to return us to my prepared questions. So I asked him about his parents.

"My father was a red, y'know. He couldn't hold a job. 'Cause he was union, kind of thing."

Gramps loved to finish his sentences with *kind of thing*.

"They would follow him...word went around you can't hire him. Even our relatives were afraid of hiring him."

His father had three brothers and at least three sisters.

"He brought them all over, okay, by working at a sweatshop or whatever it was."

"Where did they come from?"

"My father was born in Poland and my mother was born here."

It took him time to gather his thoughts into a legible account, and he tapped or brushed the mahogany as he did so. He wasn't so much frustrated or keyed up as anticipant. He knew it would all come rushing back, and it did.

"Everybody in that family lived in one building on the Lower East Side. I didn't even know who my parents were! They fed us, they took us to school."

I attempted some redirection to learn how Jack managed to bring everyone over. "Okay, so Jack brought his three sisters from Poland...."

"Maybe more than that. But he brought Grandma—his mother—"

"Yeah."

"But not the father—he was killed in the Holocaust...."

"Oh, so your grandfather—"

"Yeah, he wouldn't come. He died in a shtetl."

"Oh, wow."

I was shocked by my reply, like he'd just informed me that Jack had won a spelling bee. And though I knew ancestors of mine had been murdered by the Nazis, I had never bothered to learn exactly who. How had it taken me so long to realize my grandfather's grandfather was one of those exterminated? To comprehend that what Gramps was to me his gramps was to him?

Except he wasn't. He'd never had the opportunity. Because his gramps had been murdered in his shtetl. I imagined what the face of the goon might have looked like. I feared I knew his face.

"He wouldn't leave," Gramps reiterated, with a somberness that still eats away at me. I wish I'd asked if he knew why his grandfather decided to stay. But instead I sat in graceless silence.

Gramps went on to tell me his father brought his youngest sister with him to America. They were both very young. Then he orchestrated the trip for the rest of his sisters, along with his mother and at least one of the brothers. It was unclear how many brothers made it over.

Jack made money in the garment industry, and they all worked as supers in various buildings.

"We moved around. We shoveled the coal, made the repairs in the buildings. He was very handy, my father. My mother cleaned the halls and all that."

His pace accelerated when he spoke of his grandmother.

"And how did we survive—bread, eating, and so forth? Grandma had an apartment with her two sons. We had everything—she baked challies and—SHE HAD A STOVE BIGGER THAN THIS ROOM!"

I realized he had created his own plural form for *challah*, and that amused me.

Gramps was paradoxically fidgety and Zen. He sat motionless in his seat except for his hands, which rustled like aspen leaves in the breeze of each passing thought. There was still so much more he wanted to tell me. I was worried at least one of us had lost the thread, but still couldn't help being drawn into his reiterative beat.

Gramps went to PS 188. On top of getting good grades, he excelled in sports.

"I liked school. It had a good bathroom. Good teachers. I was a jock. I played basketball even though I was five foot two. Only problem was you weren't going anywhere. You couldn't finish school. You had to work. I joined the Marine Corps."

He started boxing on Avenue D when a coach took him under his wing when he was thirteen, making $10 every win. When he was fifteen, with 120 pounds to call his own, his trainer began taking him to Jersey for three-rounders, at $20 a win. He'd wear out his opponents—most in their mid-twenties—by gamboling and scampering like the fledgling he was. Peers and spectators took a liking to him. In honor of the late great, they had christened him "Dempsey."

Occasionally he'd go to the five- or ten-cent movies and spent a good amount of time at the library, too. He read the classics, including *Moby-Dick.*

"It was easy to have sex. The girls that were older than me were promiscuous."

"That was even better if it was someone older, right?"

"Oh, it was definitely better. I found it to be a learning process. When you turned fourteen or fifteen, you delivered, she delivered, it was a good thing. If you wanted to have sex, it was easy."

Our second interview took up most of an early evening. The goal was to spend much of the time going over his experience in the Pacific and Iwo Jima, but we talked about the details surrounding his enlistment first.

After Pearl Harbor, every street kid was signing up. Gramps joined the Marines at the Times Square recruiting station that's still there today. Although he'd let his folks know he was enlisting, he wasn't sure they'd understood, so he arranged for the recruiters to pick him up away from home. He imagined they knew he was going somewhere.

"It all happened so quick. I didn't even say goodbye."

"How did you feel signing up?"

"Gung-ho."

"Were you afraid?"

"No, I was a hero right away, sort of thing. I was a boxer. It was all fun. I was a little cocky for my size and what have you. I felt indestructible. And I was fearless. I never had any fears about dying or whatever. Just was never in my head."

When Gramps spoke of his cockiness, I blushed. I couldn't have defined my own entry into the Corps more differently. I couldn't have walked this earth more differently. For me, the culture of competitive violence marked something foreign and dangerous. For Gramps, it was life.

Then the war:

> First island was basically underwater. The enemy was already swimming to the next island.... We killed a lot of them. But they disappeared.... We were six months before Iwo Jima. There was a little island we had to take before then... Tinian! Sugarcane. We just burned them out. Flamethrowers. It was an ugly thing. We were horrible. They just went from one island to the next.... Survival was everything.... You know the ones who were dying, that's what was on our mind.... That wasn't what we had in mind when we joined.... It was chilling.

Toward the end of our time, I mentioned "the Good War" and asked him what he thought of that.

"Even though it was a good war, we were killing people. There were bad parts of that war, too. But you saw more of the bad parts than I did."

"Wait, you think *I* did?"

"What I saw in the groups coming back from Afghanistan—your war."

He was referring to his counseling sessions with post-9/11 vets at the VA now. He'd spent years leading therapy groups at the 23rd Street VA and was a local hero there. But he might have also had in mind Walker. Once my most able linguist got out of the Corps and moved to New York, he and his wife befriended my grandparents. Above all, they bonded not just as fellow Purple Heart recipients (which Walker would earn in a later deployment) but also as working-class kids of immigrants and as fathers who had hustled their way to comfort and opportunity for themselves and their children.

"The stories they tell," Gramps said. "Talking about Afghanistan and Iraq. It was worse than we saw. What they did to prisoners. What we did to prisoners. They couldn't stop it. And we were doing it. And they knew we were doing it."

His past and present, subject and object, were merging. I attempted some clarity.

"Did *you* take prisoners?"

"No, you had to kill them. They had twenty thousand. We had twenty thousand. We lost sixteen thousand guys in a month. It was crazy. Absolutely crazy. Everyone we knew was dying. Suribachi was already clean."

His numbers were off by the thousands, but he was right on the main point. Gramps made it to the seventeenth day. He was one of the few guys to make it that far.

"You had to kill them," he repeated. "They didn't go backwards, you follow?"

I got the gist. They couldn't afford to escort any Japanese prisoners to the rear, so they shot them dead on-site.

"They cleaned the airfields very quickly. The snipers were left at the hill. A thousand snipers keeping everyone back while their own guys could escape back to Japan."

"And that's when you got hit?"

"Right. I was lucky in every way. The Americans were shooting rockets and the Japanese were committing hara-kiri. Sixteen thousand of them were dead already. Someone at one of the meetings told me that."

That number was more accurate. I was wondering where he was getting his numbers.

"Four thousand left. That's who we had to worry about. But what saved everything was when the rockets came, they had to put their heads down and not us. And we were killing them. It's them—not us—who are keeping their heads down."

Then Grandma appeared in the dining room, murmuring about getting ready for sleep.

"I can't even put the jigsaw together," said Gramps.

"Hey, sweetie," said Grams, kissing her husband on his forehead.

Gramps had learned to say these things in ways that were accessible, or ways that summoned the preferred response. I'll never know what that preference was. Probably to inspire neither awe nor pity. Maybe he wanted to evoke a smidgen of the horror, or what Joan Didion called the "void at the center of experience," though Gramps, for all his late-life tough talk, for all his youthful violence, wasn't one to wish harm on others.

During the summer of 1982, five years after she'd delivered that mot juste, Didion visited El Salvador, where US-backed death squads were targeting suspected leftists and anyone else deemed bothersome. Just six months prior, the Atlacatl Battalion had raped hundreds and slaughtered 978 civilians (553 of them children) in El Mozote. The battalion was named after a mythical indigenous warrior who was supposed to have resisted sixteenth-century conquistadors, and Didion had this cruelest of ironies in mind when she wrote her two-part essay on the country's decade-long civil war. She also had in mind the *matanza* of 1932, when another right-wing government—a military government the United States would subsequently finance and train to the hilt—suppressed Nahuat Pipil peasants rebelling against the coffee plantocracy that had ruled them and their ancestors since the mid-nineteenth century. For their labor they were "tied by their thumbs and shot against church walls, shot on the road and left for the dogs, shot and bayoneted into the mass graves they themselves had dug."

At the fifty-year anniversary of the *matanza*, Didion attended a festival in Nahuizalco, where the Ministry of Education claimed it was supporting indigenous culture. "Since the public policy in El Salvador has veered unerringly toward the elimination of the indigenous population," she wrote, "this official celebration of its culture seemed an undertaking of some ambiguity." She described the "official imposition" of such culture, "the women, awkward and uncomfortable in an approximation of native custom"; the missing young men; the "little boys and old men," encouraged to dress "in 'warrior' costume: headdresses of crinkled foil, swords of cardboard and wood... unmanned not only by history but by a factor less abstract, unmanned by the real weapons in the schoolyard, by the G-3 assault rifles with which the *guardia* played while they drank beer with the Queen of the Fair—rendered this display deeply obscene." All to the soundtrack of "Roll Out the Barrel," "La Cucaracha," and "Everybody Salsa."

I like to think what my grandfather hoped to galvanize in his listeners wasn't so much a recognition of war's horror but of history's horror, and not just history's horror but also the specific history that had both scarred and, to some complicated and limited extent, spared him. How that history has been buried by the perpetual memorialization of victory and progress. How its burial has been accomplished by harrowing it into a thousand unrecognizable pieces, and then smoothing out those pieces into a never-ending ground for celebration, so that the fascism or imperialism Gramps had fought against in the Pacific came to seem entirely opposed to the wider and longer fascisms and imperialisms of Europe and the United States.

These are, of course, not my grandfather's hopes but mine. Though Gramps knew of the horror in ways I never will, he was never much for grand theories. Like many working-class kids who made it as immigrants or the children of immigrants, he had good reason to hold tight to the American dream. But one person's grand theory is another's common sense. Salvadoran campesinos, for their part, know of the history I speak.

When the journalist Mark Danner visited the erstwhile guerilla stronghold of Perquín years after the Atlacatl Battalion had seized and exploited the village as a staging area for the wholesale killing in El Mozote, he arrived at a church adorned with two giant murals. One featured the assassinated Archbishop Oscar Romero, who, on his popular radio program, had stood in solidarity with the tortured and the disappeared one too many times. With the cooperation and blessing of the state, Romero was gunned down after sermonizing at Mass. Dozens more were fatally ambushed at the archbishop's funeral.

The other mural faced north toward the Honduran border, San Pedro Sula, the Yucatán Peninsula, the Gulf of Mexico, and finally, in the far-off distance, the often menacing, sometimes promising coastlines of Mississippi, Alabama, and the Florida panhandle. The artwork was composed of a "brightly colored map of the Americas and Europe, in which a colorful stream of riches—cars, refrigerators, motorboats—flows from New World to Old above the caption 'Five Hundred Years of Pillage.'"

Like all histories, that of the *matanza* remains contested. One scholarly review describes the Salvadoran Right's remembrance of the event as "a victory over communist subversion" and the Left's as "an act of heroism by the Communist Party." And longtime foreign policy insider Elliott Abrams, who served as Reagan's assistant secretary of state for human rights and humanitarian affairs during the civil war, considers the US government's later role in holding continuous elections in El Salvador throughout the eighties a "fabulous achievement."

Abrams first affirmed this in 1993, after a UN truth commission attributed almost 85 percent of the war's more than 22,000 atrocities to the US-sponsored regime and its auxiliaries. From his perspective, such crimes against humanity were a worthwhile price to pay to prevent communist takeover and ensure democratic elections. The notion didn't occur to Abrams that these elections might have come sooner had the US government and its corporate clients resisted the temptation to replace FDR's Good Neighbor Policy of nonintervention and mutual commerce with a no-holds-barred enforcement of capital. Or that such savage enforcement might have even forestalled any substantive possibilities for not just political but also social and economic democracy, too, of the sort Roosevelt envisioned in his Second Bill of Rights. Although the leftist governments of Mauricio Funes and Salvador Sánchez Cerén made significant gains the last decade in reducing poverty and inequality (before voters rallied behind right-wing President Nayib Bukele and his party in 2019), the collective trauma of the war lives on in the form of state and gang violence. Tens of thousands have been rendered internal refugees while tens of thousands more have sought asylum abroad.

During a 2019 congressional hearing, Congresswoman Ilhan Omar would ask Abrams about this responsibility for the outcome, and he would defend his line on El Salvador's "fabulous achievement." By then, Secretary of State Mike Pompeo had appointed him special representative for Venezuela, where he would be tasked yet again with exporting putative freedom to a benighted land. Not long after his appointment, a regime change mission in Iran would be added to his office's portfolio.

Both assignments followed his stint as the special assistant to the president and senior director for democracy, human rights, and international operations at the National Security Council during the George W. Bush administration. It also followed his guilty plea in the early nineties for withholding information from Congress during its investigation of the Iran-Contra affair, when the Reagan administration illegally sold arms to the Khomeinist government in Iran to fund the anti-communist Contras in Nicaragua and their systematic rape, torture, and murder of civilians. That this man could be elevated, time and again, to high-level titles involving "humanitarian affairs," "human rights," and "democracy" only makes sense in a world that has been trained to yawn at even the deepest obscenities of a supposed liberal international order.

What happened in El Mozote in the eighties, and in Nahuizalco and western El Salvador in the thirties, happened again and again, to varying degrees, across those two decades. It happened before and after them. It happened and continues to happen. And by that, I mean both the illiberal violence and the liberal whitewashing that accompanies it.

As the historian Greg Grandin has pointed out, when Vice President Dick Cheney made the case for "democracy building" in Afghanistan and Iraq during his 2004 debate with vice presidential candidate John Edwards, he invoked El Salvador as the lodestar. Bill Kristol, editor of the *Weekly Standard*, the neoconservatives' flagship publication, agreed with Cheney and Abrams in seeing Reagan's policies in Central America as an "amazing success story" and one the Bush administration must aspire to in the Middle East. Rich Lowry, editor of the other great conservative periodical of the era, *National Review*, defended Bush's 2005 decision to tap John Negroponte for director of national intelligence despite (or because of) his role, as Reagan's ambassador to Honduras, in glossing over summary torture and assassinations at the hands of the country's security forces. Lowry hailed Reagan's Cold War in Latin America as a "spectacularly successful fight to introduce and sustain Western political norms in the region."

A month prior, in a piece titled "Been There, Done That: Iraq's Not Foreign Territory," Lowry included El Salvador alongside other alleged

Western triumphs in Greece, the Philippines, Peru, Ireland, and Palestine. The Pentagon, in short order, made the "El Salvador model" or "Salvador Option" a reality by investing in elite assassination units mapped off their Central American precursors. They even borrowed some of the same advisers. Defense Secretary Rumsfeld didn't hesitate, for example, to dispatch retired Army colonel James Steele to Iraq. A Vietnam veteran and facilitator of countless death squads in El Salvador and Nicaragua, Steele was tasked with training similar commandos, many of whom would promptly execute a spate of like-minded war crimes. US-backed paramilitaries of a similar cast were established in Afghanistan in the coming years, and they and their families were among those airlifted out of Kabul upon the US military withdrawal in 2021.

Greg Grandin has called Latin America the US empire's "workshop," and for reasons that go beyond tactical continuities running from the Cold War to the War on Terror. Before evangelical Christians, reactionary Catholics, and neoconservative Jews united in leading the charge against radical Islam, they had done the same across the Americas against similarly demonized versions of Christian humanism and liberation theology, enlisting religiose proxies from each war zone to their cause.

The globe-spanning alliance between multinational companies like Ford and Coca-Cola, religious zealots like Jerry Falwell and Pat Robertson, and militarists like Henry Kissinger and Jeane Kirkpatrick stretches back to nineteenth-century impositions across the New World. Between 1869 and 1897, the US government, often at the prodding of commercial interests, ordered warships to Central or South American ports 5,980 times. These policies, in turn, found their roots in the rise of Manifest Destiny during the antebellum period, when plantation owners spearheaded the military annexation of half of Mexico and the attempted acquisition—through private, mercenary filibusters—of as much slaver territory as possible in the Caribbean and Central and South America. These slave-owning filibusterers were supported by a hodgepodge of shipping merchants and traders, railroad and steamship concerns, miners, and Protestants who, on the heels of the Second Great Awakening, latched on to visions of an ever-expanding Christian birthright.

The millions directly killed in America's cold and hot wars, and the tens of millions more killed indirectly after the collapse of national or regional economies, governments, and infrastructures, are unfathomable. The hundreds of millions subjected to lives of severe injury, illness, or penury—homelessness, familylessness, and exile—this scale of suffering can only be intimated.

Then there is the greater number of the earth's population whose everyday regimen will remain one of crippling toil, for the sake of a world system built and maintained by the United States and its European forebears.

The intelligence services of the United States and Europe protected Japanese and Nazi war criminals well after the Second World War, sometimes employing Nazis like Klaus Barbie on the anti-communist front lines in the Middle East and Latin America. The US-backed Salvadoran military modeled itself off the Nazis, and the CIA dispatched white power militants—most of them Vietnam vets—to places like Nicaragua and El Salvador to join in the terrorism. Nazism itself, as Aimé Césaire insisted, marked a return to genocidal methods used in Windhuk and German South West Africa, methods not all that different from those used in Nahuizalco and El Mozote. And once the civil war among empires (what Americans antiseptically remember as "WWII") was won by the imperial victors, the United States reunited most of its sides—minus the conspicuous, convenient Soviets, their next Great Game contender—for the purposes of empire's renewal.

Elliott Abrams was born into a Jewish family in New York in 1948, two and a half years after the formal end of the war. His father was an immigration lawyer, and Abrams attended the Little Red School House, the first school in the nation modeled off the progressive educational ideals of the philosopher John Dewey. Many of the anti-capitalists, anti-imperialists, feminists, and other radicals who enrolled at the school would surpass Dewey and Elisabeth Irwin, the institution's founder, in their combativeness. They included Weather Underground militant Kathy Boudin and Communist Party USA and Black Panther leader Angela Davis. It also included, from the other end, Abrams.

Abrams, like so many Jews after the Shoah, came to love the foreign policy establishment that had granted his right to live and flourish, and therefore sought its defense. Davis, like so many blacks growing up in the Jim Crow South, came to love the brave communists in her hometown of Birmingham who had protected her right to live and flourish, and therefore sought their victory. I was raised not only to celebrate the achievements of those like Abrams and fear the motives of those like Davis but also to see them as existing in separate historical and moral universes altogether. No matter how much Jews like me or my parents—liberal or conservative—swore by the civil rights movement, we never afforded the same generosity to the most committed warriors of the black freedom movement as we did the most strident fighters for Jewish liberation. More tragically, we never acknowledged how our bipartisan embrace of the status quo had worked to ensure this incapacity, to blind us to our shared covenant of enslavement and emancipation, and to poison that bond. Or as James Baldwin wrote about Jewish landlords in Harlem in 1967, at the peak of the poisoning:

> Now, since the Jew is living here, like all the other white men living here, he wants the Negro to wait. . . . His major distinction is given him by that history of Christendom, which has so successfully victimized both Negroes and Jews. And he is playing in Harlem the role assigned him by Christians long ago: he is doing their dirty work. . . . The crisis taking place in the world, and in the minds and hearts of black men everywhere, is not produced by the star of David, but by the old, rugged

> Roman cross on which Christendom's most celebrated Jew was murdered. And not by Jews.

Raising the analysis to the global heights required in 1979, he wrote, "The state of Israel was not created for the salvation of the Jews; it was created for the salvation of the Western interests."

In 1967, just as Abrams was beginning to rise in the ranks at Harvard, Israel defeated its Arab neighbors in a war that would secure the Israeli occupation as a new religion and identity. Within the decade, Jewish officialdom, after a century of dissension, converged on establishing Zionism as a key—at times, seemingly *the* key—tenet of modern Judaism and Jewishness. During that period, Abrams earned a graduate degree in international relations from the London School of Economics and a law degree back at Harvard. He excelled at two consecutive white-shoe law firms and worked for Senator Henry "Scoop" Jackson's presidential campaign in 1976. Jackson was a New Dealer whose career tracked the arc of Cold War liberalism and, to a significant extent, the arc of postwar Jewry. Both sides of the Democratic senator's family came from hardy Norwegian stock, and Jackson was raised Lutheran. But his unqualified support for Israel, combined with his staunch anti-communism, would win him the adoration of numerous upwardly mobile Jews who had grown estranged from the working-class leftism of their parents and grandparents. No group encapsulated this transformation better than the neoconservative cadre to which Abrams belonged, many of whom would cut their teeth as staffers or aides under Jackson in the seventies before rallying behind Reagan.

The proto-Reaganite kernel in Jackson can be detected early in his career, when as a young congressman he not only cheerled for the internment of Japanese Americans but also demanded, as a matter of national security, that they never be allowed to return to the West Coast. He became an abiding proponent of the war in Vietnam and a vehement advocate of lavish military spending, and by '76 he was running on a tough-on-crime agenda and against school busing. None of this stopped the Irish Catholic Daniel Patrick Moynihan, another Democratic senator beloved by gentrifying Jews, from eulogizing upon Jackson's death in 1983 that the late politician was "proof of the old belief in the Judaic tradition that at any moment in history goodness in the world is preserved by the deeds of 36 just men who do not know that this is the role the Lord has given them. Henry Jackson was one of those men."

No surprise, then, that before joining the Reagan administration in 1981, Abrams worked as special counsel and then chief of staff for Moynihan. Like my grandfather, Moynihan had grown up in Manhattan (in his case, the Irish Hell's Kitchen) shining shoes and working other casual, thankless labor, and like Jackson, he never fully abandoned the social democratic promise of the New Deal. Also like Jackson, his egalitarianism had its limits. Ta-Nehisi Coates has argued that Moynihan's pathologizing of black people, specifically the purported criminality of the black underclass, contributed to the rise of the carceral state. This tendency culminated with the passage of the 1994 crime bill, the legislation most responsible for setting the national tone of mass incarceration and one Moynihan and the Democratic majority supported.

But the reactionary side of Moynihan went beyond this. Despite his democratic proclivities, he was an ardent antagonist of those leaders in the Global South demanding a new international economic order, and he claimed these demands added up to a call for what Gerald Ford termed the "tyranny of the majority." His Cold Warrior politics were animated by a disdain for any attempts to scale up the welfare state ethos across borders, and although he would come to regret—as US ambassador to the UN—his role in enabling the Indonesian government's genocide in East Timor, as well as oppose Reagan's interventions in Central America, he never stopped pathologizing the darker-skinned nations of the world in much the way he had black Americans.

In his report "The Negro Family," moreover, he disclosed the reinforcing fraternity between the racial and gender politics of the United States and the maintenance of its empire. When recommending black men for uniformed service because of the military's "utterly masculine world," Moynihan wrote:

> Given the strains of the disorganized and matrifocal family life in which so many Negro youth come of age, the Armed Forces are a dramatic and desperately needed change: a world away from women, a world run by strong men of unquestioned authority, where discipline, if harsh, is nonetheless orderly and predictable, and where rewards, if limited, are granted on the basis of performance. The theme of a current Army recruiting message states it as clearly as can be: "In the U.S. Army you get to know what it means to feel like a man."

Critics of America's wars mock the fact that most of the wars' architects haven't experienced combat or even enlisted or commissioned. But it isn't these idiosyncrasies I find most appalling, but rather their ordinariness: how their paths speak for entire generations of those who had heroically fought their way into once exclusive, Waspy corridors, and how they fast came to adopt the wasp's sting.

Booker T. Washington had good reason to counsel gradual change in the Jim Crow South, and white capitalists and planters had good reason to elevate him above more threatening figures like W. E. B. Du Bois. That it was ultimately not Washington's complacence but the righteous indignation of organizations like the National Association for the Advancement of Colored People that turned back lynching taught many black Americans the benefits of breaking off accommodationist friendships for the sake of more meaningful solidarities. And it was this lesson that motivated more ambitious demands in the ensuing century, from the civil rights movement to anti-apartheid activism to the Congressional Black Caucus's pushback on the empire in the seventies and eighties.

Self-proclaimed proponent of socialism Martin Luther King Jr. believed the "white moderate" was the greatest obstacle to racial progress and the United States government "the greatest purveyor of violence in the world today." He insisted that "a nation that continues year after year to spend more money on military defense than on programs of social uplift is approaching spiritual death." While helping to organize striking sanitation workers in Memphis, right before he was murdered in 1968, he warned Americans that if their nation spurned radical social and economic reforms, it was "going to hell."

Although King was a supporter of nonviolent protest, it was a qualified support. His goal, at times, was to spur his enemies' brutality, "dramatizing" injustice. This was the thinking behind the Birmingham campaign in 1963, where the civil rights leader and others deliberately provoked Bull Connor and his men into violent confrontation, an event that played a significant role in bringing about the Civil Rights Act of 1964 and the Voting Rights Acts of 1965.

Although King was a true believer in a certain species of nonviolence, he was sympathetic to more militant voices, including Malcolm X. Understanding riots as "the language of the unheard," he was more concerned about overturning the material conditions in which riots festered than in condemning rioters. About 75 percent of the public disapproved of King upon his death, a larger number, for the record, than those who disapproved of Donald Trump throughout his presidency.

Helen Keller was a proud member of the "Wobblies," the anarcho-communist Industrial Workers of the World labor union. Albert Einstein was a socialist. Harry Belafonte is still a socialist. The author of the Pledge of Allegiance, Francis Bellamy, and the author of "America, the Beautiful," Katharine Lee Bates, were Christian socialists.

Abraham Lincoln wasn't a socialist, but he surrounded himself with them. One of his confidants was Charles Dana, managing editor of Horace Greeley's *New York Tribune*, whom Lincoln tapped to be his "eyes and ears" in the War Department, and Lincoln corresponded happily with Marx through the mediation of the US ambassador to the UK, Charles Francis Adams (grandson of John and son of John Quincy, that Boston sap).

Founders like Jefferson and Madison hosted and promoted the

socialists of their day, from Cornelius Blatchley to Robert Owen. The entire Congress, in 1824, honored Owen by inviting him to give multiple addresses in their chambers. Jefferson was a dear friend of Fanny Wright, one of the great socialists of the era.

One of the dominant notions of nineteenth-century workers and social thinkers, that of "wage slavery," anticipated much of what is now called socialism. When Frederick Douglass declared that "experience demonstrates that there may be a slavery of wages only a little less galling and crushing in its effects than chattel slavery, and that this slavery of wages must go down with the other," he was calling for the end of capitalism.

For many, these evolutions and devolutions must amount to curious twists and turns on history's road. For me, it's something more. From the communism of my grandfather's parents to the neoconservatism of Abrams, from Du Bois to Moynihan, King to Steele—these stories do not only live in the history books. Nor are they only relived in the halls of power. It is the past we all belong to and, on my darkest nights, the past I fear we can never escape. Even history's most righteous interludes seem to be refreshing intermissions in the main show. A show whose cast numbers the worst of heroes.

All I've wanted to do since coming home was stop the war. And short of that, commiserate with those who, at the very least, could see it. Maybe that desire had something to do with my string of fated romances. That through touch alone others could see me, *really see me*, and then, in so doing, see the war that embodies me. That this could bring some hint of peace.

I didn't see much of Leah in the decade that followed my war. She was still finding crevices around the earth's hard surface where she could hide. But occasionally we'd pass emails. Or she'd call me out of the blue, from the skies, like a sonic heaven.

Eventually I learned to stop sending her my sick thoughts. And in time she came to trust me, enough to call me more often. And then we were back to talking every day and night and then back together, from opposite ends of the globe.

I have neither the will nor energy to tell that story. But there is a conversation we had that still holds me, that I'll never shake. I had just published the essay that would inspire this book, and Leah called me up in tears.

"I read it."

"And?" I could already hear her sniffling. "Are you okay?"

"I'm so mad at you!"

I had always wanted someone to say this to me. No one ever had. And now the person I had always loved, the one I had always imagined myself spending the rest of my life with, had said it.

"How could you do that! Any of that! I'm so fucking disappointed in you! The way you described just watching them destroy that village. You were . . . you were . . . *gawking*, Lyle! Fucking gawking!"

"I know! That's exactly what I did. I gawked. That's the point. I fucked up. I was feckless . . ."

I expected her to interrupt me again, but she just sobbed louder.

"And you have to realize I'd spent months traveling from outpost to outpost. And I got used to . . . used to . . ." At this point I was hoping she'd intervene, for my sake. But she seemed to have switched modes to something that, in its wordlessness, felt more generous.

"I got used to—I don't know—deferring. Because these guys had been in the shit and I hadn't. And it had been drilled into me—even as an officer—to support them. To give them the intel they said they needed. And that's what I—or really, my guys—got used to doing. And these guys were getting hit. They were dying, too, you know?"

"Not as much—"

"Of course! We were killing them way more than they were killing us! But when you're there, with *your* guys, with *your* team—and especially when you're just a visitor, a rover—it's incredibly hard to suddenly interrupt an exchange of fire or whatever and say STOP! You know?"

"I mean, to begin with, no, I don't know. Because I would have never put myself in that position in the first place. And you knew better, Lyle!

You knew better and you still joined! So you could be some kind of hero!"

"But that's it, isn't it? I'm not a hero. I'm pathetic. I'm a pathetic piece of shit like any other pathetic piece of shit."

"No! Because now you're being treated as another kind of hero. A writer hero. What you always wanted to be."

"I know, Ley, it's completely fucked."

"It is fucked! I mean, they didn't publish one of the villagers from the village you destroyed. They didn't publish a reporter there in the aftermath. They published *you*."

"If I don't write, then others still write. And everyone around me keeps thanking me. And the world keeps dying. And they keep dying. But if I write, then I'm profiting from the death. Even if I were to give away every dollar, I'm still profiting. I'm still building a reputation, making connections, finding new opportunities. I know all that. And it drives me insane."

"I know. I just love you and I'm so mad at you and I fucking hate you and every other guy like you. You all get to make careers from your mistakes—and that's the nice way of putting it—while the rest of us..."

"I know."

No matter what I write, I'm commodifying what I did. It's precisely because I did the evil—even if in a support role, even if by omission—that I'm allowed to be heard in this Godforsaken country. There is no way I can speak about my past or my politics without risking the encouragement and benefits of America's cheap yet profitable obsession with war. Yet the only way I can unmask the war that obsession is concealing is by leveraging my authority as someone who served. To unveil the treachery of my service, I must first capitalize on it. Jose Vasquez, a conscientious objector, veteran activist, and anthropologist, has dubbed this problem "the veteran mystique." I wish I could capitalize on that mystique without satiating the mass desire to be enchanted by it. I wish I could rail against the war that is America without dwelling on the war proper.

Heroism can be dangerous, in part because it disappoints. Martin

Luther King's behavior toward women, both as leader and liaison, bore the marks of the patriarchy that had raised him. Francis Bellamy issued racist screeds against immigrants. Echoing the sentiments of another friend, Andrew Jackson, Fanny Wright wrote early in her career, about a decade before Jackson engineered the ethnic cleansing of the Cherokee, Creek, Seminole, Chickasaw, Choctaw, and Ponca in the Trail of Tears, that the "savage, with all his virtues, and he has some virtues, is still a savage [and] the increase and spread of the white population at the expense of the red, is, as it were, the triumph of peace over violence." When Lincoln approved the hanging of thirty-eight Dakota men in Minnesota in 1862, all accused of participating in the US-Dakota War, he presided over the largest one-day execution in US history. The hanged were fighting against those settlers who had coerced them into ceding their land and thrust them into destitution by accelerating the exhaustion of wild game.

Heroism can be dangerous for other reasons, too. Like everything else, it tends to flatter power and insult the powerless. But sometimes it does the opposite. And it's moments like that when those living under the boot are granted some reprieve. Those delivering the boot are granted some pardon, too, since true contentment seldom comes from either the taking or dealing of needless, desireless pain.

I am suspicious of heroes. I prefer humans. But I am practical enough to admit that a world without heroes is not a human world. And to the degree we must have them, I would prefer they serve to heal.

As for me, I keep watching. Everyone I know watching.

Gawk. Gawk. Gawk.

The cruelest, truest word I've ever heard.

EPILOGUE

Preparing the French press and oatmeal, Herman Melville pays another visit. I can always count on Melville to tell me what I feel. This time his voice returns as I'm scanning Twitter. Twitter often instigates the feelings most prone to summoning Melville. "Having a wild western waste," my literary hero says to me, "overrun at last it will be; and then, the recoil must come."

A reporter has shared a fundraising text from the National Republican Congressional Committee. It reads "ALERT," with a photograph of Trump at a lectern:

> You're a traitor.... You abandoned Trump. We were told you were a tried & true, lifelong patriot.... This is your final chance to prove your loyalty or be branded a deserter. We're giving you one final chance to stand with Trump. You only have 17 min

A commenter adds: "17 minutes. Q is the 17th letter. It is a cult."

Of my college squad, the only one I still see every few years is my friend Phil. He's a Q guy now. An anti-vaxxer, too. The whole package. I feel a nostalgic pull toward our undergrad days when we'd talked of David Hume, before his right-wing libertarianism curdled. Before he spoke of "patriots" and "traitors" with the venom of any two-bit demagogue.

I wonder if he'll ever want me behind bars or exiled or dead. Judging from the far-right media he now traffics in, venues that cheer on vigilantes like Kyle Rittenhouse or push legislatures across the nation to grant civil and criminal immunity to those who drive over progressive protesters, maybe he already does.

Last I checked, our buddy Luntz had run for office on an anti-immigrant platform, only to lose the primary after it was revealed he'd posted comments critical of Trump early in the 2016 presidential campaign. At least Luntz appeared to have experienced a moment of doubt about the kind of nationalist vitriol that had once killed or threatened to kill his own ancestors, unlike other Jewish Republicans such as Stephen Miller or Josh Mandel, the latter making a bid for an Ohio Senate seat while slobbering all over social media about the "Judeo-Christian way of life" or how Palestinians "hate everything we stand for as Christians, Jews, and Americans" or that a modest plan to maximize vaccinations in a historic pandemic is like "the gestapo [showing up] at your front door."

Mandel's stretch in high school student government and rise from a well-to-do Jewish suburb are enough to make me queasy. But it's his experience as a marine, and an intelligence specialist, no less, that bothers me the most. Lately he's used his veteran cachet to rail against Afghan refugees fleeing their country after the formal withdrawal of the US military, demanding not a single one make it to the States. "It's un-American," this grandson of refugees wrote, "to use taxpayer dollars to resettle foreigners into the country when we have almost 40,000 homeless veterans in the US on any night." He said they will bring nothing but "covid" and "child brides" and wrote: "You can keep feeding the alligators, but eventually you will be eaten as well."

As I sit down at our wobbly table with my oatmeal bowl and cup of coffee, my fiancée emerges from the bedroom to pour some coffee of her own. I think about ranting about Mandel's rants, but she's already heard me go off too many times this week, so instead I say, "Good morning, love." We kiss and hug, and I return to the device that drives me up the wall.

I'm well aware of how defenders (or aggravators) of the status quo pit groups against one another to further the desolation. But Mandel—the person I could have been had I never stopped redoubling on the histories that had shaped and advantaged me—has taken the strategy to a new level. He's also become a master of the historical inversion, in which rulers become the ruled and vice versa; the entirety of the past becomes a plaything for cynical powerbrokers and those in awe of them.

As thinking people have become used to saying, nothing matters anymore. It doesn't matter that the Afghan people have spent the last forty years living under US-led occupation or surviving US-fueled wars. Nor does it matter that by opposing elementary anti-contagion policies, policies the US government (and most governments) has instituted for centuries, it's men like Mandel who have proved themselves the greatest threat to public health and safety. Or that among the many distinctions of the Nazis—first and foremost the unprecedented scale of their slaughter, torture, and enslavement—compulsory vaccination cannot be included. (The Nazis, in fact, loosened the compulsory vaccination measures of their Weimar predecessors.)

The sense of decay and anomie that has engulfed me throughout my years-long homecoming and the melting that escorted me across Europe seem to be spreading beyond heads like mine. I suppose, just like truth becomes the first casualty of colonial wars, a wider feeling—and reality—of dissolution becomes empire's final fate. The unshackled id that has been terrorizing the periphery takes center stage. For empires in their terminal phase, everything becomes permissible.

If men like Luntz are too far gone, at least men like Josephs, Rosen, and Walker might still listen and engage other ideas with a compassionate ear and say things that I can make sense of, that could even begin to change my mind. I'd love for them to join me in glimpsing a world beyond the carceral state and the warfare state and the capitalist state, of course, but I know that's improbable.

I clasp my fiancée one last time and make my way down the stairwell of our Baltimore apartment building, to my car on the other side of the alleyway. I've just learned to set up the phone GPS and Audible so they function simultaneously and without interruption. I've already memorized the route to my workplace in Columbia, but I like having something to guide me in case of unexpected traffic, accidents, or detours.

This time it's Heather Ann Thompson's *Blood in the Water: The Attica Prison Uprising of 1971 and Its Legacy*, but for the last couple weeks I'd been listening to Toni Morrison read *Beloved*. After being sent to a prison camp in Georgia, the enslaved Paul D listened to the doves,

> having neither the right nor the permission to enjoy it because in that place mist, doves, sunlight, copper, dirt, moon—everything belonged to the men who had the guns. Little men, some of them, big men too, each one of whom he could snap like a twig if he wanted to. Men who knew their manhood lay in their guns and were not even embarrassed by the knowledge that without gunshot fox would laugh at them. And these "men" who made even vixen laugh could, if you let them, stop you from hearing doves or loving moonlight.

I was one of those "men," and I knew those "men." Even though I personally abhorred the thought of anyone ever being enslaved, I came from the same lineage. If only Americans could see Morrison's story as a global story, one that hasn't died and still lives and kills like a ghost, and the empire they can't see as the ghost incarnate. Paul D's dove wasn't even his dove, but it was more his than theirs, because he hadn't fully lost the ability to listen to the world instead of owning it.

I had never really listened to the birds until I came home and saw home for what it was, and what it had made me and what I had allowed it to make and unmake. Now I listen to the birds everywhere I go, and by listening to them, I see them. I hope to see a red-tailed or red-shouldered hawk on I-95. Before the eight-hour cubicle. Before I turn off the part of myself (before the boss turns it off for me) that could still hear and see.

As I pass Maiwand Kabob, I'm brought back to the Special Forces ops that were underway in Maywand District when I was in the neighboring Helmand, which my unit would assist with intel. The restaurant's competition, the Helmand, is owned and run by Qayum Karzai, former Afghanistan president Hamid Karzai's older brother. My fiancée and I had stumbled over there a couple months back, only to be greeted by a sign saying they'd be closed for a while (the Talibs had just taken Kabul).

I pass Camden Yards, the unadorned brick of the Baltimore and Ohio Railroad warehouse that was nearby the site of the Great Railroad Strike of 1877—when President Rutherford B. Hayes called in the marines to quell the workers—and the Pratt Street Riot of 1861, when opponents of the Unionist war effort assaulted Northern troops en route to Washington in the "first blood" of the Civil War. Rutherford B. Hayes—one of America's great enigmas, a man who progressed from abolitionist to Union Army general to the Republican president pressured into ending Reconstruction in the South to strike breaker to late-life admirer of Henry George—wrote in his diary a decade after the railroad strike, "It is time for the public to hear that the giant evil and danger in this country, the danger which transcends all others, is the vast wealth owned or controlled by a few persons."

On Martin Luther King Jr. Boulevard, a street that can be found in most cities yet found by most only in the least meaningful sense: the landmark those of us rich enough to have cars tend to pass through on the way to work. The third Monday of every January, our inboxes are overrun by insipid emails from CEOs about a defanged Martin Luther King, re-created as a fiction in the CEO's image: diversity, inclusion, forward together, nonviolence. (But come Veterans Day, the emails preach something other than peace.)

Interstate 95, the Interstate Highway System, the Dwight D. Eisenhower National System of Interstate and Defense Highways. Built for military expansion. Built for destruction. Eisenhower in his 1961 farewell address said:

> This conjunction of an immense military establishment and a large arms industry is new in the American experience. The total influence—economic, political, even spiritual—is felt in every city,

> every state house, every office of the Federal government. We recognize the imperative need for this development. Yet we must not fail to comprehend its grave implications. . . . We must guard against the acquisition of unwarranted influence, whether sought or unsought, by the military-industrial complex. The potential for the disastrous rise of misplaced power exists and will persist.

If only Ike had listened to Ike.

Columbia, Maryland. Home of Woodlawn Plantation, then Bendix Field Engineering. Home of Integral Systems. Home of thousands of workers for the Applied Physics Laboratory and close to my own fleeting, festering home, the NSA headquarters at Fort Meade. Conceived as a New Deal–inspired planned city and a proof of concept for a desegregated USA. One of its villages: "Harper's Choice." Named for Baltimore native Robert Goodloe Harper, member of the American Colonization Society and influential in the founding of Liberia: Place of Freedom.

One of its neighborhoods: "The Longfellow Community." For Henry Wadsworth Longfellow. The curse of Cain.

I've arrived.

Every morning I pass through an interminable industrial park, like any other office park in its austerity, headiest dreamland of the besuited American psychopath. A phantasmagoria of disciplined hedges and sterile glass. Even the empty space, the emptinesses hovering above the pavement and grass like drones, has been sterilized. Even the interstices have left zero trace of spirit, eccentricity, or thought. The bleached landscape again enters my veins.

Perhaps that's too harsh. Columbia has left the street names to ponder, all testaments to progress. Alexander Bell Drive. Bell, Scottish polymath, phone inventor. *Inventor*—a peculiar word. As if the straw that breaks the camel's back ought to assume full responsibility for the breaking. Or the last blade of grass that feeds the camel ought to assume the same for the feeding. A warped rendering of history's shape and weight. A word and a world built for winners.

As a West Hartford kid, I was always driving by the American School for the Deaf, a red-brick structure as prodigious as the iconic B&O Warehouse, where Bell had taught the Visible Speech system. He also tutored Hellen Keller in Boston, before she made a name for herself as a radical and before Bell secured a second life as a prominent eugenicist.

On my right, Eli Whitney Drive. The man who invented the cotton gin in part to weaken slavery as an economic institution, only to later witness his invention embolden it. He had counted on the machine's efficiency making enslavement obsolete, failing to recognize the hierarchies and humiliations that had born it. Having failed to turn a sustainable profit, Whitney retreated to Connecticut to find his fortune in the contrivance and manufacture of interchangeable rifle parts.

Then a right from Columbia Gateway Drive to Columbia Gateway Drive (were I to have remained on the first Columbia Gateway Drive, I would have, somehow, still remained on Columbia Gateway Drive), past Thomas Edison Drive on my left. As legend has it, someone asked the famous innovator during World War I if he could make a weapon more deadly than poison gas. He replied, "Yes, I could, but I don't want to destroy life; I want to make the world a better place in which to live. The dove is my emblem."

Less apocryphal was his leftward turn toward his twilight years: "You see, getting down to the bottom of things, this is a pretty raw, crude civilization of ours—pretty wasteful, pretty cruel, which often comes to the same thing, doesn't it?...Our production, our factory laws, our charities, our relations between capital and labor, our distributions—all wrong, all out of gear. We've stumbled along for a while, trying to run a new civilization in old ways, and we've got to start to make the world over." Upon a visit to the Arc de Triomphe, he remarked, "I always see beside it another and greater arch, thousands of feet high, made of the phosphate of the bones of victims sacrificed for Napoleon's personal glory."

Edison first read Tom Paine as a boy and never stopped reading him after that. In his final decade he contributed an introduction to a collection of Paine's writings. He became a progressive monetary reformer, a sometimes conservationist, self-avowed pacificist. At the same time, he flirted with a social Darwinist defense of oligarchy. He was a suffragist, but by no means a feminist. At thirty-eight he wrote, "I haven't heard a bird sing since I was twelve years old" and sometimes suggested it was his deafness that encouraged his genius, yet he never joined Keller or others in advocating for disability rights.

Edison's lurch toward progressive causes didn't stop him from supporting the arch imperialist Teddy Roosevelt. Or from marshalling his talents, and much of the scientific enterprise he represented, on behalf of the American warfare state. During the Great War, he prophesied a future where machines would fight machines rather than humans fighting humans, and where his central involvement in military research and development would be used solely for the purposes of defense. Like Whitney, he hoped wrong, and his Faustian bargain only helped to fuel the charnel house—and sometimes his profits, as with the mercenary sale of phenol to all interested buyers, including the Germans. When Edison died in 1931, many of the forces he had once spoken up against made quick use of him. In 1940 the Navy named a destroyer in his honor, and in 1962 they did the same for a nuclear-powered ballistic missile submarine.

Another right onto Robert Fulton Drive, in honor of the man who developed submarines, torpedoes, and steamboats. He attempted to help Napoleon equip his navy with a suite of weaponry and then, when that relationship soured, did the same for William Pitt's Royal Navy. The US Navy has christened four USS *Fulton*s, and dozens of America's towns, cities, and counties—along with the empire's neighborhoods, freeways, and streets—go by the name. In the main reading room of the Thomas Jefferson Building at the Library of Congress, Fulton and Columbus make up two of the sixteen statues. They are coupled under a ten-foot womanly form called Commerce—one of the eight pillars of civilization surrounding the balustrade and its reading room below—her plaster figure wreathed with olive leaves of peace, and her hands clutching a schooner on one side and a train on the other.

Despite his martial legacy, Fulton occupied the cutting edge of the enlightenment pantheon. He befriended Robert Owen and followed Paine and others in adopting the most egalitarian teachings of Adam Smith. As a republican, he appreciated labor as the source of wealth and opposed myriad privileges. Like Edison, he convinced himself that his participation in the arms race would guarantee the end of war and colonial oppressions. For a time, he figured revolutionary France could forge the peaceful and reciprocal commerce he sought. Then it was England. And, by the War of 1812, the United States.

Park my car in the open corner spot, badge at the ready. I reach my cubicle in Columbia but find I've returned to my regimental desk in Delaram. Somewhere on the internet someone said *Delaram* meant "tranquil" or "peaceful" in Pashto. Maybe "heart-bearing" in Persian.

Once, on a conference call, I overheard my gunnies going back and forth in the background about one of our sergeants.

He was patrolling when a bunch of LNs approached with blankets.
And?
And he says I don't want the blanket.
Okay.
There's a dead child in the blanket.
Fuck.
He thinks it might have been a victim of one of Recon's triggered airstrikes in the USV.

USV was short for Upper Sangin Valley. Now I knew why Petraeus wanted details on the compound bombings up there.

Hope he has someone to talk to.

Whenever I open a new tab in my cube, it sends me to the homepage for MSN. I wade though the propaganda for a minute. The Fox News hysterics, the CNBC hysterics, the CNN hysterics, the MSNBC hysterics. The empire is hysterical.

The CEO told us last year that he was proud to give back to those in uniform by caring for veterans across the country. Today MSN is crowded with more native advertising attempting to scam vets with fake mortgage loans and other refinancing baits. Sometimes they abut graphic stories about marines going on shooting sprees. I think of one I came by not too long ago, about a marine who murdered a family thinking they were part of a child-sex-trafficking ring. For a split second I feared I knew this marine. The sheriff called the marine a coward.

My heart drops to a dangerous low, so I get to work trying to figure out how to get United Healthcare to pay *X* claim and Blue Cross Blue Shield to pay *Y* claim. And how to get away with having my small handful of private-pay families pay the slimmest fraction of what they owe. Melville's Bartleby the Scrivener keeps ringing: *I would prefer not to I would prefer not to.* I happen upon a state Medicaid page featuring the mugshot of a black woman, a mother brought up on nineteen counts of fraud because she allegedly attested to living in one state when actually living in another. If convicted, she could be slammed with a 243-year prison sentence. The press release goes on to talk about over three thousand other poor people they've managed to imprison for similar reasons. It concludes with the Cash for Tips phone number.

Anand Gopal has written about how the war in Afghanistan was lost the moment the United States decided to start paying off warlords and other opportunists to bring them names of suspected terrorists. Most Afghans, including most Talibs, wanted to work with the US-led government after it set up shop in Kabul. This created a problem for the Bush administration and the cavalcade of militarists and contractors behind him. They were counting on more war and had to find new ways to reproduce it. Paying off mercenaries to manufacture terrorist suspects offered the way. When Special Forces started encaging and murdering these suspects—most of them local rivals, bystanders, or passersby—they started inspiring real acts of terror. By 2006, the majority of those living in the countryside, which constituted most of the Afghan population, had lost faith in the Americans, their allies, and their client state. The engine of war was restarted.

I think of this when I think of that mom facing 243 years for doing what she thought she had to do to keep herself and her kids alive, and how easy it is to keep the gears turning. United Healthcare and BCBS will keep getting richer in peacetime, just like their counterparts will at war. For me, it's hard to tell the difference anymore.

We call hedge funds that prey on poor people vultures. And uniformed thugs that prey on the downtrodden pigs. There are sharks and rats and weasels and chickens and snakes and wolves and sheep. Of course, we also have the hawks and the doves. The doves are the exception. It's morning or night in a cube or somewhere out there, and the lamps are going out all over. I worry the empire will transcend its convenient divisions and conquests once and for all, not by resolving them but by throwing them into a pressure cooker of cross-class, cross-racial, cross-gender ressentiment and watching it all blow through the earth.

Maybe then money and power will have no value and the architectures built to accumulate them will lose their function of survival by way of expansion. Freud wrote about the phobia being thrown before the anxiety like a fortress on the frontier. But if everything is blown to bits, then there is no longer any cause for such phobias and their fortresses. The frontier itself loses its context. Anyone can be anything. Then and only then will we find the freedom and solidarity we could never find in life.

I say this not because I believe it or want it but because I know what I really want is hope. And I'm having a harder and harder time finding it. All I have are the good souls all around me. The kind and gentle, but not too gentle, souls that knew the death drive but rejected it before me and will reject it after me. Are rejecting it this second. James Baldwin, speaking of his unspeakably remote father, imagined that "one of the reasons people cling to their hates so stubbornly is because they sense, once hate is gone, they will be forced to deal with pain."

A different pain. A different strength.

A gaggle of geese blocks my way on the drive home. I am crying and loving every single feather.

ACKNOWLEDGMENTS

To sufficiently thank those who have made this work possible would require another tome. Everyone already mentioned would have to be included. People who didn't make it on the page would, too, ranging from teachers to mentors to family members to friends to enemies to all those in between. Since I haven't the space, and since I suspect others haven't the desire to be associated with a book of this kind, I will settle for an inadequate brevity. I am grateful to the counter-recruitment organization We Are Not Your Soldiers for enabling rare conversations with high school and college students about what would become the themes of this book. I am indebted to my agent, Alice Whitwham, who worked without respite to find this unorthodox memoir a home (Alice also played a major role in crafting each part's title and structure), and to Claire Gillespie for additional support during those early months. To enthusiastic readers of the proposal like Dan Gerstle, and to Katy O'Donnell for taking the risk in acquiring it. To Remy Cawley for guiding me with editorial wisdom and acumen at the initial stage of the writing—a time when I was no doubt unraveling. To Ashley Patrick for shepherding me and my (our) project at its most crucial moment. To Hillary Brenhouse for her patience and passion and for giving *Pain Is Weakness Leaving the Body* its perfect name, and to Claire Zuo for their ongoing wholehearted assistance. I am also appreciative of art director Pete Garceau for the equally perfect cover, Sara Krolewski for the scrupulous fact-checking, Elisa Rivlin for the thorough legal review, Christina Palaia for the seasoned copyediting and kind encouragement, and Emily Andrukaitis and Mike McConnell for the last line of defense proofreading. Thanks to Melissa Raymond, Katie Carruthers-Busser, and Olivia Loperfido for their always ready and expert management and production, Amy Quinn for the elegant interior design, and Brooke Parsons and Miguel Cervantes for the top-notch publicity and marketing.

I would be remiss without expressing my gratitude for superb editors the past decade, from Catherine Parnell and the late George Kovach at *CONSEQUENCE* to Brigid Hains and Ross Andersen at *Aeon* to Nick Serpe and Sarah Leonard at *Dissent* to more recent collaborators like Marco Roth at *n+1* (Marco served as a valuable mentor well after my *n+1* debut) and Jackson Lears and Stephanie Vollmer at *Raritan*. When it comes to my editors, the list is long, and I owe them all. I must also issue my utmost appreciation to the producer and director Eric Felipe-Barkin and the writer Patrick Blanchfield for championing me through the years. To George Scialabba for changing my mind when I was still a marine, and then convincing me I had the power to change the minds of others. And to all the journalists, essayists, artists, filmmakers, scholars, activists, organizers, and thinkers whose work infuses every page of this account, and whose labors I've attempted to catalog at www.lylejeremyrubin.com/pain.

As I write this the US government continues to terrorize the people of Afghanistan, this time by redirecting half of the nation's currency reserves to the families of 9/11 victims and the lawyers and lobbyists representing them. Were victims of US-led terrorism granted the same justice, American coffers would be emptied within minutes. But justice of that variety is not forthcoming, and most Afghans now risk destitution or starvation. I am reminded of the words of the lay theologian William Stringfellow, who once counseled his compatriots to stop reading the Bible "Americanly" and start reading America biblically. To my parents, my grandmother, my brothers and cousins and aunts and uncles and nephews and niece and beloved therapists and all my loved ones—including my ballast, Colette—thank you for reminding me, every step of the way, of the goodness.